BEYOND THE BANALITY OF EVIL

CLARENDON STUDIES IN CRIMINOLOGY

Published under the auspices of the Institute of Criminology, University of Cambridge; the Mannheim Centre, London School of Economics; and the Centre for Criminological Research, University of Oxford.

General Editor: Robert Reiner
(London School of Economics)

Editors: Manuel Eisner, Alison Liebling, and Per-Olof Wikström
(University of Cambridge)

Jill Peay and Tim Newburn
(London School of Economics)

Ian Loader, Julian Roberts, and Lucia Zedner
(University of Oxford)

RECENT TITLES IN THIS SERIES:

Lush Life: Constructing Organized Crime in the UK
Hobbs

'Grooming' and the Sexual Abuse of Children: Institutional, Internet, and Familial Dimensions
McAlinden

The Multicultural Prison: Ethnicity, Masculinity, and Social Relations among Prisoners
Phillips

Breaking Rules: The Social and Situational Dynamics of Young People's Urban Crime
Wikström, Oberwittler, Treiber & Hardie

Tough Choices: Risk, Security and the Criminalization of Drug Policy
Seddon, Williams & Ralphs

Beyond the Banality of Evil

Criminology and Genocide

AUGUSTINE BRANNIGAN

OXFORD
UNIVERSITY PRESS

Great Clarendon Street, Oxford, OX2 6DP,
United Kingdom

Oxford University Press is a department of the University of Oxford.
It furthers the University's objective of excellence in research, scholarship,
and education by publishing worldwide. Oxford is a registered trade mark of
Oxford University Press in the UK and in certain other countries

First Edition published in 2013
Impression: 1

Published in the United States of America by Oxford University Press
198 Madison Avenue, New York, NY 10016, United States of America

British Library Cataloguing in Publication Data
Data available

Library of Congress Control Number: 2013937829

ISBN 978–0–19–967462–6

Printed in Great Britain by
CPI Group (UK) Ltd, Croydon, CR0 4YY

*The book is dedicated to Terry Wilcox Brannigan,
my life-long companion.*

General Editor's Introduction

Clarendon Studies in Criminology aims to provide a forum for outstanding empirical and theoretical work in all aspects of criminology and criminal justice, broadly understood. The Editors welcome submissions from established scholars, as well as excellent PhD work. The *Series* was inaugurated in 1994, with Roger Hood as its first General Editor, following discussions between Oxford University Press and three criminology centres. It is edited under the auspices of these three centres: the Cambridge Institute of Criminology, the Mannheim Centre for Criminology at the London School of Economics, and the Centre for Criminology at the University of Oxford. Each supplies members of the Editorial Board and, in turn, the Series Editor.

Augustine Brannigan's book is a thorough critical review of how criminology as a discipline can shed light upon what many would consider the crime of crimes, genocide. It has frequently been observed that the almost complete absence of the paradigmatic case of the Holocaust during the Second World War (and the sadly all too many smaller-scale genocidal atrocities before and since that dark period) from the repertoire of criminological study damages the credibility of criminology as an intellectual project.

Professor Brannigan brings a wealth of expertise to this challenging task, reflecting his distinguished career in academic criminology in which he has written on a wide range of sociological, social psychological, philosophical, and historical topics in addition to crime and criminal justice. His book combines a rigorous and scholarly analysis of past work in several disciplines that has sought to explain the Holocaust and other genocidal projects. It also reports on fieldwork on the 1990s Rwandan genocide. There is extensive review of other recent cases, in particular during the break-up of the former Yugoslavia. The book concludes with a sober critical assessment of the various responses seeking to achieve justice and redress by legal and other means.

Brannigan begins with a fascinating and challenging critique of the prevailing understandings of the Holocaust and genocide generally. These stem from the seminal notion of the 'banality of evil' formulated in Hannah Arendt's book on the Eichmann trial, and Milgram's celebrated experiments on compliance to authority. The joint intellectual inheritance of these interpretations is the depiction of the Nazi and other perpetrators of genocide as 'desk murderers', compelled to follow the authority figures that demanded their compliance in atrocity. Brannigan draws on recent historical work by Cesarani, Browning, Goldhagen, and others on Eichmann as well as the face-to-face killers in Nazi police units to show that they operated with a considerably greater degree of autonomy than the standard account suggests. He also synthesizes recent social psychological critiques of Milgram that show that his legendary experiments fall short of establishing that people can be made to inflict suffering because of unquestioning obedience to authority.

This opens the way for the application of criminological theories explaining violence in everyday contexts, notably Jack Katz's influential account of 'righteous slaughter'. Brannigan notes that three paradoxical consequences follow. First, perpetrators of genocide 'typically act without evidence of psychopathology, evil, provocation, or a guilty conscience'. Second, the acts that constitute genocide have frequently been 'conventionalised' as legitimate deeds on behalf of the sovereign. Third, the 'dark figure' of unmeasured genocide is 'breathtaking' compared with its notoriously extensive counterpart in unrecorded everyday crime, because its perpetrators so often see it as just and conventional 'retaliation' to imagined evil.

The following two chapters raise further standard criminological questions about genocide. How do events get labelled as genocide? The construction of genocide as a category and its application in specific cases is analysed, and a typology of forms of claims-making is developed. The politicization of genocide renders its labelling continuously fraught with controversy.

The chapter on aetiology draws primarily on 'control theories'. The inspiration is partly criminological control theory as developed by Hirschi, Gottfredson, and others. However, the main guiding perspectives are the analysis of 'the civilizing process' in the work of Norbert Elias with an admixture of Bauman's attribution of the Holocaust to modernity, and the notion of 'altruistic' suicide in Durkheim. The perpetrator of genocide is so captured by the sovereign's inspiration that her autonomy is relinquished 'altruistically' in pursuit of a 'barbarous' ideological deviation from the civilizing process, and the horrific scale of resulting atrocities is facilitated by the bureaucratic and technological efficiency of modernity.

The fruits of these sophisticated and challenging (but always lucid and compelling) theoretical chapters are then applied to a case study of the 1990s genocidal massacres in Rwanda. This is based on extensive interviews and analysis of documents, in particular the proceedings of UN courts and truth and reconciliation commissions. The theoretical framework is deployed to understand not only the perpetrators but also various types of bystanders—individuals but even more significantly formal organizations such as the UN and France.

The final chapters are a highly informative critique of alternative forms of reaction to genocide that seek to rectify the harms as much as possible as well as prevent future atrocities: formal legal processes, criminal and civil; innovative quasi-legal processes such as restorative justice; and truth and reconciliation commissions, of which the best known is the South African model chaired by Bishop Desmond Tutu. Each is valuable at least in terms of symbolizing that there is no impunity for genocide and allowing victims' voices to be heard. But they have limited practical impact in punishing or preventing crimes (a feature shared with criminal justice more generally in relation to everyday offences), or in providing redress. The conclusions call for the monumental but necessary task of a fundamental reconstruction of global civil society, to provide the necessary 'checks on the otherwise unbridled exercise of power of the sovereign. These checks—a free press, a culture of political negotiation, autonomous civil and religious sectors, a responsive international community, and the embrace of cosmopolitan norms in respect of human rights—are among the keys to a future free of genocide.'

The Editors are delighted to welcome this inspiring and challenging contribution to the *Series*.

Robert Reiner
London School of Economics
April 2013

Preface

The point of departure for the contemporary social science understanding of genocide is outlined in Chapter 1. Following the Eichmann trial, Hannah Arendt concluded that the Holocaust arose from *the banality of evil*. This perspective was reinforced by the famous experimental studies of obedience conducted by Stanley Milgram at Yale University. Milgram suggested that the Holocaust was made possible by submission to authority of countless 'desk murderers' who simply obeyed orders without reflection, and with little appreciation of the consequences for victims of 're-settlement' in the East. Arendt attributed the widespread compliance to Nazi rule to totalitarianism, to the repression of the very people who carried out mass murder. Recently, there has been a reassessment of this view. In his biography of Eichmann, David Cesarani (2006) suggested that a generation of scholars was hijacked in its analysis of the genocide by the joint intellectual impact of Arendt and Milgram. On the fiftieth anniversary of the Eichmann trial, Deborah Lipstadt (2011) similarly challenged Arendt's perspective, and offered a new interpretation of the significance of the Eichmann trial. In 2010 and 2011 Jerry Burger's replication of Milgram's work suggested that students of genocide had to reconsider radically the relevance of the obedience paradigm. These developments are the background to the current study.

I have reflected as a criminologist about how to interpret the Holocaust as a crime. I have endeavoured to understand how our theories of criminal motivation might shed light on these stunning events. I have also examined other genocidal events that have occurred in my lifetime to determine what my profession provides by way of ideas that can make these events comprehensible. I have travelled to Rwanda and Tanzania to confer with people who witnessed and experienced the mass murders that occurred in that part of Africa in 1994. This book summarizes my conclusions. It may be useful to outline the narratives contained in the following chapters. In the first chapter I provide a thorough re-analysis of Milgram's account of aggression in the social psychology lab. I explain why it cannot support the idea that compliance during the Holocaust

arose from fear of consequences administered by 'authority figures'. Milgram's own evidence suggests that not all the subjects
were taken in by his design. Many subjects were sceptical about the
harm experienced by the 'Learner'. In fact, defiance in the experiment was correlated with the perception that the Learner was being
hurt. According to his own evidence, if subjects thought that someone was being injured, this increased their defiance dramatically—an
observation that leads to a conclusion starkly inconsistent with the
obedience paradigm. In addition, in Burger's recent replication of
Milgram, direct orders from the authority figure were singularly
ineffective in producing compliance to authority. This chapter com-
pels us to reopen our whole approach to the understanding of genocide. If we view genocide only in terms of the alleged banality of
the 'desk murderers', we entirely miss its social significance, and its
enormity as crime.

Chapter 2 argues that much violent behaviour is actually
grounded in existential experiences of righteousness, and is aptly
described by Jack Katz as 'righteous slaughter', where the actor
behaves violently to redress what he or she feels are challenges to
The Good, and rebukes humiliation in acts of rage. However, there
are three ironic consequences. The dictator's followers typically act
without evidence of psychopathology, evil, provocation, or a guilty
conscience. They are 'ordinary men' motivated by positive factors
(the first paradox)—which later makes it difficult to hold them
accountable with a guilty conscience, the *mens rea*. The second
paradox: the activities which create the genocide have often been
'conventionalized' in the past, and treated as rights of the sovereign, and hence not answerable to a criminal indictment. And
accordingly, they produce a 'dark figure' of crime that is breathtaking in its scale (the third paradox). Criminology has been slow to
put the topic of genocide as a political crime on its agenda (Hagan
and Kaiser 2011).

The next two chapters tackle different but related questions.
First, how does something become labelled as genocide? Second,
what social events bring it about? Chapter 3 discusses the constitutive question, the genealogy of genocide. The following chapter
tackles the causal or explanatory question. Regarding genealogy,
I contrast the liberal versus realist conception of the origins of the
genocide law, and how it is invoked (or not) in practice. I outline the
competing explanations of international law found in Gary Bass
and Hedley Bull. I discuss how competing narratives over social

conflicts can lead to genocide affirmation, genocide denial, false genocides, and missed genocides—and I depict these in a typology created by juxtaposing whether events are accepted or rejected as genocide, versus whether they contain or fail to contain the elements required of genocide. I canvas the recent debates over the politicization of genocide allegations and denial to illustrate the precariousness of claims-making in respect of such crimes.

My explanatory chapter—4—is informed broadly by the control perspective. I allude to the common mechanism found in the contemporary work of Travis Hirschi and the historical work of Norbert Elias—impulse control. Elias provides competing accounts in *The Civilizing Process* (1939) and *The Germans* (1989). I compare the analysis of civilizing in the first contribution with the analysis of de-civilizing processes in the second. I question Elias's characterization of de-civilizing during the Nazi period as a reversion to 'barbarism'. In my view, the feudal period and the Nazi regime did not share the same emotional economies. On the contrary, Elias's views suggest that in political matters, the Germans were *over*-controlled, or were externally controlled—consistent with his analysis of the link between a nation's history and the typical political outlook of its citizens. I revise the Eliasian perspective following Durkheim's analysis of 'altruistic' pathologies where ego's autonomy is absorbed by authoritarian rule, and crime arises when the individual's authority for action is governed by the sovereign's grip over the public imagination, and the apparatus of state. I also contrast Elias's focus on primitivism at the heart of genocide with Zygmunt Bauman's emphasis on modernity; the former reflects the barbarous ideation at the core of the Nazi movement; the latter reflects the utilization of bureaucracy, science, and technology to achieve the goals of the latter.

I apply the model to Rwanda, and draw from personal observations in 2004 and 2005. I travelled to Rwanda initially in 2004 to determine whether it was possible to conduct research there. I found that respondents were extremely supportive of our efforts and facilitated access to key documents and scores of persons of interest. I returned in 2005, and I have kept in touch with contacts since then. I also visited the International Criminal Tribunal for Rwanda in Arusha, and was able to compare the proceedings of the Gacaca courts that I attended in Rwanda and the UN courts in Arusha, Tanzania. In the analysis of the Rwandan genocide, I employ Elias's distinction between sociogenic processes and their psychogenic consequences. The pre-colonial and colonial political arrangements created tight hierarchical interdependencies that permitted post-colonial elites to marshal widespread activation of the populace. I provide evidence that the Rwandan genocide in some areas was all but completed after two weeks—not three months, as most authorities argue. However, there is good evidence that the spread of the genocide was uneven across the country (Straus 2006). Also, I point out that the events occurred without any widespread evidence of moral anguish, contrition, or regret—and that this is a feature commonly observed at Nuremberg, Arusha, and The Hague. I translate the amnesty law, created near the start of the republic in 1963, that absolved Hutus for political crimes against Tutsi chiefs and their supporters. I also describe the numerous massacres against Tutsis that occurred repeatedly throughout the history of both republics (1961 and 1975), and whose frequency suggests that such inter-lineage murders had been effectively decriminalized, and were undertaken with little apprehension of guilt by their perpetrators.

We tend to minimize the role of bystanders, allies, and third parties in the escalation or de-escalation of violent events. In Chapter 6, I examine how parties who are peripheral to the planning and execution of genocide can become catalysts that enlarge the scale of the massacres. In this context, I review the failure of the UN to effectively limit atrocities in both Bosnia and Rwanda, as well as the role of Rwanda's European allies, particularly France, in providing logistic and diplomatic support that expedited the genocide, and made it far graver than it would have been in the absence of that support.

In the next three chapters, I deal with the legal responses to genocide, with particular attention to the ad hoc tribunals for Rwanda and the former Yugoslavia, and the recent hybrid courts for Cambodia, Sierra Leone, and East Timor, and the advent of the permanent International Criminal Court at the Hague. The criminal prosecution approach (Chapter 7) has been unimaginably costly, has been isolated from the communities where survivors and victims live, and has not effectively created peace in such societies. In addition, I describe research that suggests that the quality of evidence presented at the courts raises serious questions about their credibility and future utility. I also question whether an institution that evolved to prosecute individual criminals provides a suitable platform for crimes undertaken collectively and righteously.

Subsequently, I investigate the possibility of remedies for genocide in civil law through reparations and compensation in Chapter 8. Although I advocate for a remedy that is an alternative to the criminal process, the civil remedies that I review are by and large additional to the criminal remedy, and typically different in targeting and compensating corporate or collective stakeholders.

In Chapter 9 I review the evidence that healing after enormous human rights violations can be achieved by truth commissions designed to re-establish social cohesion through a transparent airing of the previous atrocities, and by heralding the value of collective justice over individual criminal liability. Frequently, these commissions occur in periods of social transitions from tyranny to democracy, where the emerging political powers are able to expose past atrocities without indicting those responsible. Hence, the TRCs are frequently premised on the idea that amnesty for crime can be exchanged for public acknowledgement of responsibility, and the expression of remorse. The strengths and limitations of this approach are explored in a review of the most memorable expression of the genre: the South African Truth and Reconciliation Commission. In retrospect, it appears to have been flawed as a fact-finding forum, and marked by uneven community support, and frequent evidence of misrepresentation and denial. However, the stewardship of the commission under Bishop Desmond Tutu gave the challenge of forgiveness a deeply religious basis that added to the commission's international credibility. Despite its shortcomings, the commission was better than the alternative—low-level, ongoing civil war. Other TRCs suggest that the detailed exposition of previous atrocities may reopen old wounds, intensify existing animosities, and challenge the assumption that healing follows automatically from truth telling. Potent memories of atrocities are volatile and can cleanse or sear, depending on how they are negotiated. Nonetheless, the truth commissions represent the third option for restoring security and the pursuit of happiness in the aftermath of atrocity.

Finally, I argue that there is no one simple legal solution to genocide, nor any reliable legal arrangement that can prevent it. I call for a civil society solution to genocide management. In an anarchical international order mediated by the current UN, the world does not have a reliable capacity to prevent genocide, in spite of evolving norms regarding the international responsibility to protect vulnerable communities worldwide. Nonetheless, the clues to genocide management are obvious: they consist of checks on the otherwise unbridled exercise of power of the sovereign. These checks—a free press, a culture of political negotiation, autonomous civil and religious sectors, a responsive international community, and the embrace of cosmopolitan norms in respect of human rights—are among the keys to a future free of genocide.

Acknowledgements

Personal

This work was supported by the Social Sciences and Humanities Research Council of Canada basic research grants. It also attracted the support of the Killam Research Fellowship Fund at the University of Calgary in 2009, and a Visiting Research Fellowship at the East-West Center in Manoa, Hawaii in winter 2011. Preliminary findings were reported at the Big Rock University Lecture Series in March 2010. The author enjoyed feedback from the Postcolonial Study Group at the University of Calgary, as well as helpful comments from Nick Jones, Paul Millar, Clara Joseph, Travis Hirschi, Kit Carson, Tullio Caputo, George Pavlich, Zhiqiu Lin, Leslie Miller, Art Frank, Amal Madibbo, John Ellard, Rebecca Carter, Lucie Pratte, Sharon Williams, David Pevalin, Kelly Hardwick, Erin Van Brunschot, Hank Stam, John Winterdyk, Karla Poewe, Tamara Karagic, and Siegfried Ramler. The writing also benefited enormously from the detailed and thoughtful comments and suggestions provided by three anonymous reviewers from Oxford University Press.

Acknowledgement of Field Contacts

In Rwanda I am indebted to the following people for sharing time and ideas, sometimes over several meets, to help educate me about the events of 1994 and thereafter: Seraphine Bizimungu, Former First Lady, the then Director of the Tumerere Foundation; Jacques Lépine, then Canadian Consul in Kigali; Christian Pouyez, Head of CIDA; Edda Mukabaweza, then Minister of Justice; Professor Laurent Nkusi, Minister of Information and Linguist at NUR; Professor Anastase Shyaka, Political Scientist at NUR, Butare; Professor Charles Kayitana, journalist and business school instructor; Domitilla Mukantaganzwa, National Director of the Gacaca Jurisdiction; Innocent Musafili, Public Relations and Communications at Gacaca; Emmanuel Bayingana, criminologist, former RPF Commander and Deputy Director of National Judicial

Police; Fiacre Birasa, Court Reform Project, Rwanda Department of Justice; Martin Ngoga, then Deputy Chief Prosecutor; Jean-Dieu Mucyo, then Chief Prosecutor; Jean-Boscoe Mutangana, Senior Prosecutor; Samuel Rugege, Deputy Director of the Supreme Court of Rwanda; Elizabeth Onkango, Research and Programs at African Rights; Tom Ndahiro and Filbert Kigabo at the Rwanda Human Rights Commission; Richard Renault, Director of Investigations at ICTR; Amahora Hotel; Mohammed Ayat Investigator with ICTR; Theo Nkembe ICTR Archivist at Amahora Hotel; Philip Gafishi, Senior Statistician and Damien Mugabo, Director of Census; Fatuma Ndangiza, National Reconciliation Commission; Ildephonse Kerengera and Joseph Nkuranga at the Department of Monuments; Immaculé Ingabire, journalist; Pére Jacob Irinée, African Missions and Kinyarwanda Linguist; Klaas de Jonge and Jean-Charles Paras at PRI; Dieter Magsam, Director of German Aid; Cpl. Christophe Bizimungu, Military Prosecutions; and numerous others. In Arusha, I had the benefit of contact and conversation with the following: Moustaphe Hassouna with the ICTR Protocol; Stephen Rapp, Senior Prosecutor with OTP; Drew White, Prosecutor; James Stewart, Prosecutor; J. Bastarache, Investigator with ICTR; Jacques Baillargeon, Investigator with ICTR; Chris Black, Defence Counsel ICTR; Andre Tremblay, Defence Counsel ICTR; Zuhdi Janbek, Investigator ICTR; Thomas Moran, Defence Counsel ICTR; Ian Morley, Prosecutor ICTR; Ronnie Macdonald, Defense Counsel ICTR; Alloys Mutabingwa, Rwanda Envoy to ICTR; Dr Alex Obote Odora, Special Assistant to the Chief Prosecutor; and Tom Adami, Chief Archivist at ICTR; and several others. I thank them all for helping me understand the events of 1994, the subsequent processes, and the realistic options for the future.

Contents

List of Figures and Tables

Figures

Tables

List of Abbreviations

ANC	African National Congress
AR	African Rights
ASP	Assembly of States Parties
CDR	Coalition for the Defence of the Republic (Rwanda)
DPKO	Department of Peacekeeping Operations (UN)
DRC	Democratic Republic of Congo
ECCC	Extraordinary Chambers in the Courts of Cambodia
ECOWAS	Economic Community of West Africa
FAR	armed forces of Rwanda
FMLN	Farabundi Marti National Liberation Front
IAC	International Auschwitz Committee
ICC	International Criminal Court
ICISS	International Commission on Intervention and State Sovereignty
ICJ	International Court of Justice
ICTR	International Criminal Tribunal for Rwanda
ICTY	International Criminal Tribunal for the Former Yugoslavia
IFP	Inkata Freedom Party
IMTFE	International Military Tribunal for the Far East
R2P	Responsibility to Protect
RPF	Rwandan Patriotic Front
RUF	Revolutionary United Front (Sierra Leone)
SATRC	South African Truth and Reconciliation Commission
SCSL	Special Court for Sierra Leone
SPSC	Special Panels for Serious Crimes (East Timor)
TFV	Trust Fund for Victims
TRC	Truth and Reconciliation Commission
UNHCR	UN High Commission for Refugees
UNPROFOR	United Nations Protection Force
UNSC	United Nations Security Council

URNG   Revolutionary National Unity of Guatemala
VPRS   Victims' Participation and Reparation Section
VRS   the army of the Republika Srpska
VWU   Victims and Witnesses Unit

1

Genocide and the Obedience Paradigm

Introduction: From the Holocaust to Genocide

My inquiry into genocide began in the 1990s with the appearance of new scholarship on the Holocaust. Two books in particular caught my attention. Christopher Browning's *Ordinary Men: Reserve Police Battalion 101 and the Final Solution in Poland* (1992) and Daniel Goldhagen's *Hitler's Willing Executioners: Ordinary Germans and the Holocaust* (1996) were based on research into the role of police battalions in genocide in Eastern Europe beginning in 1941. Browning begins his account with a story about the first mass shooting of civilians assigned to Police Battalion 101 in Józefów, Poland. The men were told that they had received orders from the highest authorities to enter the village and to remove the Jews completely. All the old men, the infirm, all the women and children were to be shot dead. The able-bodied men were to be arrested for slave labour and shipped to a concentration camp in Lublin. But Major Trapp tempered his orders with this consideration: if the men did not feel they were up for the assignment, they could step out without recrimination. Some 10–20 per cent did so. What that implied to Browning was that the men who *did* participate were not coerced, or forced, to do so. Goldhagen, who recounts the same incident, goes so far as to say that they participated because they thought it was the right thing to do—that the Jews deserved to die. These two studies reopened the issue of agency in the ordinary soldier's cooperation in mass murder.

The ensuing 'Goldhagen debates' generated an enormous outpouring of historical reconsideration (Shandley 1998). While this academic conversation was underway, two new genocides occurred. In 1994 in Rwanda, over 550 000 civilians were massacred by the national army, political militias, and peasants recruited to genocide by elements of the Rwandan government. It occurred with lightning speed, and received indifferent media coverage in Europe and America. A year later, in Srebrenica, Bosnian Serbs reportedly murdered an estimated 7 000 to 8 000 Bosniac men and boys. News stories circulated of young Serb soldiers making digital films on their cell phones of these executions, and posting them on websites as mementos,[1] just as an earlier generation of German policemen took photographs of ghetto clearings in Jósefów, Łomazy, and Warsaw to circulate at home some fifty-odd years earlier (Klee, Dressen and Riess 1996; Browning 2000: 154). At the time, few criminologists grasped the enormity of these events.

In criminology, mass murder, atrocities, and genocide appear to attract little attention. Instead, there is a preoccupation with individual-level predatory behaviour. In North American criminology, there is a consensus around the utility of what have come to be known as 'control' theories of criminal behaviours (Ellis and Walsh, 1999). These are basically Benthamite theories of human nature that assume that the pursuit of pleasure is driven by natural appetites checked only by internal and external sources of pain. Hence, control theories suggest that crimes arise when the individual's attachment to the community becomes undermined, and antisocial impulses go unchecked. In the late 19th century, Durkheim (1893) diagnosed the condition of 'anomie' brought about by rapid industrialization, and the demise of institutions that effectively bonded individuals and families to the economic structure through craft guilds and traditional modes of production. For Durkheim, criminal impulses were suppressed because villainy evoked the deepest condemnations of society and integrated the population around common moral feelings.

The success of this line of thinking suggests that the direction of criminology over the past few decades has led to a mindset in which we have become almost incapable of grasping the phenomenon of state-initiated crimes, such as those associated with inter-ethnic conflict. This is ironic inasmuch as individuals were far more likely to be killed in the past century as a result of collective crimes such as aggressive war, genocide, and state-initiated mass slaughter than to die at the hands of an individual perpetrator. We keep official statistics on the latter, but not the former. We develop theories on

---

[1] Associated Press, 3 June 2005 on MSNBC <www.msnbc.com/id/8085091/> retrieved 19 January 2009. The video was broadcast on Serbian television in June 2005.

crime causation, and develop policies to ameliorate garden-variety crimes, while oblivious to crimes associated with political violence. Because criminology has focused on the crimes of individual perpetrators, we have few intellectual leads in explaining the most prevalent forms of killing in modern times, crimes which appear to be more, not less prevalent. Genocide and analogous behaviours are largely uncharted water for criminology. They have become orphaned in the field devoted to the study of crime. Criminology has already tackled what makes individual murder, rape, and robbery possible. Can we capture the structural and agentic processes that operate in genocide?

The social science literature on genocide has its roots in the study of the Holocaust. Polish jurist, Raphael Lemkin, coined the term 'genocide' in 1944 in his analysis of the Nazi domination of Europe. As a result of his lobbying, the United Nations adopted the 'Convention for the Prevention and Punishment of Genocide' in December of 1948 (Chalk and Jonassohn 1990). It defined genocide as:

Any of the following acts committed with intent to destroy, in whole or in part, a national, ethnical, racial, or religious group as such:
  A. Killing members of the group;
  B. Causing serious bodily or mental harm to members of the group;
  C. Deliberately inflicting on the group conditions of life calculated to bring about its physical destruction in whole or in part;
  D. Imposing measures intended to prevent births within the group;
  E. Forcibly transferring children of the group to another group

Several specific crimes were named: genocide, conspiracy to commit genocide, incitement to commit genocide, attempt to commit genocide, and complicity in genocide. Such crimes could be committed whether they occurred in times of war or peace. All perpetrators became liable whether they were constitutionally responsible rulers, public officials, or private individuals. Trials could be held in the jurisdiction in which the crimes occurred, or in a specifically designed international tribunal. And the contracting parties could call on the UN to initiate the prevention and suppression of genocide when they thought it was occurring.

In the years after the Second World War, the motives and the methods of the Nazis and their allies were documented in many sources, most notably in the work of Raul Hilberg (1985) and William Shirer (1960). There also arose a comparative literature seeking to evaluate the distinctiveness of the Holocaust as well as some parallels to other 20th-century massacres, most notably the murder of 1.7 million Armenians in Turkey and theft of their wealth, a process that started in the 1890s and continued during the First World War (Hovannisian 1986; Staub 1989). This 'barbarity and vandalism,' as he called it, had preoccupied Lemkin during the 1930s. How could the Turkish state annihilate the constituent Christian community that pre-dated Islam in Anatolia with impunity? After the UN adopted Lemkin's concept of genocide, the definition was broadened substantially by academics to cover the mass killing of civilians by governments—'democide' (Rummel 1991)—and the mass slaughter of political enemies—'politicide' (Harff and Gurr 1988). In addition, there has developed a body of theoretical sociology describing the role of genocide as a function of political struggle (Kuper 1981; Fein 1984, 1993). Attempts have been made to develop typologies of the leading types of genocide, and how they differ in motives and outcomes (e.g. Chalk and Jonassohn 1990). However, in acknowledging the burgeoning field of genocide studies, it would be premature to claim that significant consensus has emerged about the 'hard facts' of genocide in this literature, and how they might figure in a coherent theory of it.

In terms of explaining genocide and democide, the most promising line of thinking is the suggestion that the liability of engaging in genocide is a function of state political development, and particularly that autocratic or authoritarian states (whether fascist or communist) have a far greater proclivity to engage in the systematic murder of unarmed civilians than more democratic states (Rummel 1994; Horowitz 2002). This is not to say that democratic states are blameless, but they are both more restrained in their ability to mobilize mass murder, and may be better able to ensure that their aggression escapes such criminal labelling. Nonetheless, this political tendency is a hard fact of the kind largely absent in the individualistic turn of modern criminology, and reinforces the need to integrate the explanations of crime with the social science literature on genocide. Ironically, the most significant contribution to social science thinking about genocide is associated with the experimental studies of Stanley Milgram in social psychology. As a social psychologist, Milgram did not focus on the state as such, but on the role of bureaucracy and its restraints on individual freedoms. He developed the 'obedience paradigm'—the notion that the Holocaust occurred as a result of the subservience of individuals to hierarchical and bureaucratic social structures. Milgram's work has grown to mythic proportions in today's social science (Blass 2004). I review this work since it has generated more comment and speculation than any comparable contribution in the social sciences. I also outline why I think this work has become outmoded in advancing our understanding of genocide.

The Holocaust, Obedience, and the Banality of Evil

Stanley Milgram was the son of immigrant Jews, born in New York, and raised in a social environment starkly cognizant of the Holocaust. Like many of his generation, he was deeply troubled by German anti-Semitism. In his research as a doctoral student in psychology, he researched national differences in conformity since this promised to shed light on German mistreatment of the Jewish minority. When Adolph Eichmann was seized by Israeli agents in Argentina, Milgram was already exploring ways to investigate obedience in a psychological setting. The evolution of Milgram's design of the obedience study has been researched through archival materials by N.J.C. Russell (2009, 2011) and Gina Perry (2012).

Milgram closely followed the five *New Yorker* reports filed by Hannah Arendt who covered the trial of Adolph Eichmann in Jerusalem in 1961, and which were the basis of her 1963 book. Adolph Eichmann was captured in Argentina on 11 May 1960, and returned secretly to Jerusalem by the Israeli secret police for trial as a war criminal several days later. He was given the option of being assassinated in Argentina, or standing trial in Jerusalem, and chose the latter. Before capture, he had already recorded dozens of hours of audio tapes with Willem Sassen, a low-ranking SS officer on the run, and produced thousands of unpublished pages of transcripts describing the 'German side' of the story. Eichmann was the Nazi 'bureaucrat' who helped orchestrate the mass murder of European Jewry by concentrating the victims in Poland after the Nazi conquest of Poland, France, and most of Western Europe. He advanced to a senior position in the Department of Jewish Affairs, and played a pivotal role in deporting entire Jewish communities to the factories designed for their large-scale extermination at Auschwitz, Belzec, Chelmo, Majdanek, Sobibor, and Treblinka. Over five million innocent people, men, women, and children, were murdered at these death camps with the assistance of ordinary German administrators, policemen, soldiers, and camp guards. In respect of Auschwitz alone, Rudolph Höss signed a confession that acknowledged that 'at least 2.5 million victims were executed and exterminated there by gassing and burning, and at least another half million succumbed to starvation and disease making a total dead of about 3 million' (quoted in Ramler 2008: 68–71). In Arendt's view, Eichmann was not a psychopathic killer, nor had he exhibited deep animosity towards the Jews. He followed orders with zeal and without any evidence of inhibitions of conscience. Milgram appears to have accepted Arendt's diagnosis of 'the banality of evil'—the idea that Eichmann participated in mass murder simply as an obedient cog in a state bureaucracy.

Milgram developed a laboratory protocol that attempted to capture the essence of behaviour at the core of genocide: individual obedience to malevolent authority. This is the subject of the current chapter. Subjects were recruited for a study of learning. They were informed that the experimenter was testing the effects of punishment on learning. The subjects saw 'The Learner' strapped into a device in which he received electrical shocks as a punishment for failure to learn a series of specific word pairs. All this was simulated, and no one was actually shocked. Milgram's question: at what point would the subject refuse to comply with demands to administer the shocks? The issue of social conformity had been suggested by Solomon Asch's study of 'the line judgment task' in which subjects were pressured by a group to accept a conclusion they knew to be untrue. Subjects were asked to match a stimulus line to one of three choices where two out of three were clearly erroneous, but were chosen nonetheless by the majority. Asch's subjects were more likely to capitulate based on the size of the group, and less likely to capitulate when one other subject resisted group pressure. As a graduate student, Milgram had been assigned to Asch as a research assistant, and became intimate with his famous work. Indeed, Milgram used Asch's protocol to examine national differences in social pressure. Milgram's obedience protocol differed inasmuch as the pressure to comply with such injurious demands came from the orders of an authority figure, a lab-coated 'Scientist'. The experiments attracted enormous attention in the academy and in society at large (Miller 1986; Miller et al. 1999). They were extremely controversial for both empirical and ethical reasons (Orne and Holland 1968; Mixon 1971, 1989; Baumrind 1964; Patten 1977a, 1977b).

In Milgram's experiment, ordinary subjects were made to play the role of aggressive teachers, of people who acted violently against innocent victims. In what Stam, Radtke, and Lubek (1998) refer to as the 'received view' of this work, Milgram took people from all walks of life and revealed their incipient capacity for evil. Following the Eichmann trial, Milgram suggested that the capacity for evil was fostered in individuals by bureaucratic authorities. The study was advertised as an experiment designed to test the effectiveness of punishment on human learning. The 'Teachers' were paid to teach the 'Learner' to memorize a long series of word pairs. The experimenter explained the rationale for the study: to determine the effectiveness of *negative* reinforcements on learning. The Learner's errors were to result in an electric shock. Each successive error resulted in a small increase in the level of shock. The shocks began at 15 volts and escalated up to 450 volts. The experiment advertised for both teachers and learners, but all the subjects were assigned the role of 'Teachers'. The Teachers were given a sample shock to demonstrate the discomfort that resulted from the device used to discourage errors. The machine was an impressive electrical appliance with switches, lights, and verbal designations describing the severity of the shock (i.e. mild, moderate, high, extremely high, XXX). Over 700 subjects were drawn from a wide range of occupations and professions to participate.

Milgram hired John Williams to play the role of the Scientist, and James McDonough to play the role of Learner. Williams's task was to encourage the Teachers to comply with demands to administer increasingly severe levels of shock. The assignment was designed so that the Learner's performance always failed, and attracted increasingly severe (but simulated) levels of punishment. Many subjects experienced tremendous anxiety. Unlike the classical experimental approach, Milgram did not specify specific hypotheses a priori. He did not begin by testing the validity of any particular theory of behaviour or hypothesis. There are no references to earlier studies of group influence (i.e. Asch and Sherif) in his articles. Milgram proceeds as though his work was generated without influence from the earlier studies. Milgram consulted many groups to determine how they thought normal individuals would react to the situation, and how many would refuse to take part. Everyone predicted that all of the subjects would defy the authority figure and refuse to administer severe shocks.

The Blackwell Reader in Social Psychology summarized the study as follows: 'there is no experimental design as such; no factors are manipulated. No statistics are reported on the data nor are they needed since no experimental variations were compared' (Hewstone, Manstead, and Stroebe 1997: 54). This does not give Milgram his due. Milgram studied various conditions of aggression, the best known of which was proximity. He argued that the closer the victim to the context of aggression, the lower the levels of compliance. Some argue that this was his most salient discovery (Russell and Gregory 2005). He also tested other effects. In fact, in his 1974 book, he reports eighteen different conditions of obedience, although he had completed twenty-three (Perry 2012). In his baseline study, Milgram found that the majority of subjects *did* administer the maximum level of shock (65 per cent), and that this did not decline even when the Learner reportedly suffered from a cardiac irregularity. He concluded that compliance of individuals in these conditions resulted from the force of authorities over their subordinates. His experiment extracted this general human tendency from the reports of the Holocaust killers who reported, initially at Nuremberg and later in Jerusalem, that their role in mass murder was a result of 'following orders'. That has been the paradigmatic view of the obedience studies over the last five decades.

Criticisms were raised both in terms of internal and external validity. Internal validity depends on whether the protocol employed by the experimenter actually succeeds in defining the situation for the subject as intended; external validity depends on whether the protocol corresponds credibly to features of everyday life to which the experiment might be generalized. As for internal validity, contrary to the paradigmatic view, Orne and Holland (1968), Mixon (1971), Darley (1995) and other critics argued that, in psychology experiments, subjects presume that no one will actually get injured. In this study, Milgram assumed that subjects would define the administration of shocks as tantamount to assault or cruelty. However, in the pretests of the study, Milgram reported 'in the absence of protests from the learner, every subject in the pilot study went blithely to the end of the board' (1974: 22). Every subject in the pretest administered the maximum shock level without pressure from anyone. Presumably, subjects did not assume the worst about administering electrical shocks. It was only at this point that Milgram introduced the various feedback conditions, initially a knock on the wall, to indicate that the Learner receiving the shocks was actually experiencing discomfort. In the *Obedience* film, it is evident that when the Learner-actor exhibits pain by actually calling out loud, the real subjects *initially* laugh, and appear to be *startled* that anyone is actually being hurt. In the later designs, when the subjects hear similar complaints from the Learner testifying to the painfulness of the shocks, they also have in their presence the 'authority figure', the Scientist, who contradicts their perceptions that something is going wrong, and who reacts passively as people are audibly suffering. The experimental design is ambiguous. The subject is drawn between what is heard—a suffering victim—and what is seen—a non-plussed authority figure subject to the same information, but not alarmed by it. This causes enormous conflict for the subjects. Subjects frequently sweated, stuttered, and trembled. They may have started with an assumption that nothing-can-go-wrong only to have this contradicted by what they could hear from the Learner, but not by what they could see from the scientific authority. The design of internal validity is questionable since the subjects are exposed to *conflicting* information. As Orne and Holland (1968: 287) noted, the most incongruous aspect of the experiment was the behaviour of the experimenter who sat by indifferently when the Learner called out in agony, and demanded to be released. Orne and Holland concluded that subjects must have inferred that the harm being experienced through the shock administration was not what it appeared to be, just as the audience at a magic performance knows that the magician's assistant is not being cut in half with a saw, and cannot be suspended in thin air without support.

The credibility of the experiment in terms of external validity may have been further eroded by the fact that the role of the Teacher was actually superfluous in the experiment since the teaching could obviously be carried out without volunteers. In the same vein, it could not have escaped notice by all the subjects that the learning task was simply impossible. Mantel's analysis of the external validity of the experiment was highly critical:

Every experiment was basically preposterous...the entire experimental procedure from beginning to end could make no sense at all, even to the laymen. A person is strapped to a chair and immobilized and is explicitly told he is going to be exposed to extremely painful electric shocks...The task the student is to learn is evidently impossible. He can't learn it in such a short space of time...No one could learn it...This experiment becomes more incredulous and senseless the further it is carried (Mantel 1971:110–11).

In a similar vein, Baumrind (1985: 171) noted that 'far from illuminating real life, as he claimed, Milgram in fact appeared to have constructed a set of conditions so internally inconsistent that they could not occur in real life. His application of his results to destructive obedience in military settings or Nazi Germany...is metaphoric rather than scientific.'

Don Mixon suggests that every experimental manipulation that Milgram developed which introduced less ambiguous evidence that a subject was being hurt reduced the aggression of the Teacher. When the Learner's pain was signalled through knocking on the wall, compliance dropped from 100 per cent to 65 per cent. The slightest evidence that harm was occurring produced the largest measure of defiance that Milgram measured. All the elaborate verbal feedback of the Learner's suffering, which formed the 'baseline' measurement, reduced the compliance by only a further 2.5 per cent over the knock on the wall; only one less person in forty resisted going to the highest shock level.

Russell (2011: 153) writes that 'where I have probably added most to the literature was, first, in revealing Milgram's yet, in his publications, unmentioned goal to maximize the first official experiment's completion rate, and second how he set about achieving this goal'. The completion rate refers to the percentage complying with the highest level of aggression described in the first publication. It was achieved by the ad hoc introduction of tweaks designed to bind the subjects to the assignment, and to reduce their stress in complying during the trial runs. The 'binding factors' included the presentation of the task as a legitimate university pursuit, represented by a mature Scientist, in a task that created foot-in-the-door 'momentum' through numerous incremental steps in shock administration. Several 'stress reduction mechanisms' were introduced to offset the subjects' instinctual resistance: the subjects were advised that the procedure produced no permanent damage, it was presented as a legitimate learning experiment, the 'lethal' label on the ultimate switch was replaced with 'extreme', and the experimenter assumed responsibility for any adverse effects. Under these protocols, Milgram produced his best-known result (Russell 2011: 160). The received view focuses only on the authority figure, and ignores the framing that generated the provocative 65 per cent outcome.

Reicher and Haslam (2011: 166) reject the received view and suggest that the levels of compliance 'depend upon participant's exposure to the voices of different constituents'. When the victim's suffering was brought into the room and portrayed dramatically by an actor in a real subject's presence, although the authority figure's comportment suggested no harm, the aggression declined. When the authority figure was totally removed from the lab and apparently out of earshot, the pain feedback information from the Learner reduced the shocks from 65 per cent to about 20 per cent. The more evident the painfulness of the procedure to the Learner, the lower the levels of obedience (Brannigan 2004).

Milgram investigated this issue in a post hoc questionnaire completed by 658 former subjects a year after the study. He asked subjects whether they thought anyone was actually harmed—a good check on internal validity (1974: 172). Fifty-six per cent suggested that they fully believed the Learner was receiving painful shocks; 24 per cent thought the Learner was *probably* getting the shocks. So far, so good. However, this belief was *not* spread evenly across the obedient and defiant groups. Those who were convinced that the shocks were real were more likely to be *defiant* of authority. I have re-analysed Milgram's table to highlight the link between the perceptions of harm and the resulting defiance of authority. For the sake of simplicity, in Table 1.1, I omit the category in which subjects reported 'I just wasn't sure whether the learner was getting the shocks or not'. This permits us to dichotomize the subject responses. The omitted category comprised 6.1 per cent (n = 40) of the total pool of respondents. The following table reports the numbers of persons falling into each of the other categories. For the sake of simplicity, I analyse the view of the *believers* versus the *sceptics* by summing the first and second rows and contrasting them to the third and fourth rows.

Table 1.1 Defiance gauged by perception of harm

Subjects' reported perception during the experiment measured afterwards	Subject was defiant	Subject was obedient
1. 'I fully believed the learner was getting painful shocks.'	230	139
2. 'Although I had some doubts, I believed the learner was *probably* getting the shocks.'	83	75
3. 'Although I had some doubts, I thought the learner was probably not getting the shocks.'	28	47
4. 'I was certain the learner was not getting the shocks.'	5	11

The benefit of this procedure is that it permits us to calculate the *odds* of being defiant of authority based on the perception that the shocks were believed to be real (n=230) or were *probably* real (83), versus were believed to be unreal (n=5) or were *probably* unreal (n=28). The odds are calculated as $a*c/b*d$.[2] If a subject thought the shocks were real or were probably real, this increased their likelihood of defiance 2.57 times. This conclusion is consistent with an internal report written by Taketo Murata for Milgram in 1962. Murata hypothesized that those who reported 'fully believing that the Learner was being shocked would not reach as high shock levels as those not fully believing. This is found to be so' (Murata 1962; Perry 2012). In eighteen out of twenty-three conditions, the believers had lower shock means than sceptics. On this basis, it is quite clear that the experimental protocol was far from being internally valid. Not only did a significant portion of the subjects fail to accept the experimenter's definition of the situation, but also when the subjects *did* accept the harm definition, they tended to be *defiant* of authority.

Milgram and the agentic shift

How did Milgram explain the behaviours he observed in the lab? As noted earlier, he did not begin with a theory and design an experiment to test it. He tested various levels of Learner feedback (distal, proximal), the role of group mediation of response, the role of gender, location, and Teacher-choice of shock levels, and discovered enormous variation in compliance. However, when he summarizes his work, Milgram largely ignores all these conditions in the variability of obedience. He focuses exclusively on the power ascribed to the authority figure and his ability to extract obedience from the subjects. In his explanatory chapters, Milgram proposes that obedience appears to have a biological basis, that it probably confers fitness during evolutionary competition by making coordinated action more effective than the sum of individual actions. Echoing

---

[2] a=230 + 83 (313), b=139 + 75 (214), c=28 + 5 (33), d= 47 + 11 (58). a x c/b x d = 313*58/214*33 = 18,154/7,062 or 2.57. Fisher test p = .000. If we calculate the OR for the 2 extreme groups that accepted the harm or denied it completely, we arrive at the following estimate: a x c/b x d = 230*11/139*5 = 3.64. Hence, among those with the most certain views, the perception of harm increased the likelihood of defiance by 3.64 times.

Hobbes, Milgram writes: 'a curb must be placed on the unregulated appetites, for unless this is done, mutual destruction... will result' (1974: 127). In the first instance 'the presence of conscience in men' inhibits destructive competition among those who 'occupy a common territory'. Conscience makes individuals self-regulating, and inhibits mutual exploitation. However, in hierarchical social organizations, the individual conscience is not sufficient and may be anarchical. Here another process comes into play at a higher level: 'the psychology of the ultimate leader demands a different set of explanatory principles' (1974: 130). For this different set of principles, Milgram turns to Freud. Freud (1922: 78) had analysed the psychodynamics of authority in the army, the Church, and the family, and the common patterns of submission to leadership. Freud explained it this way: 'the individual gives up his ego ideal and substitutes for it the group ideal embodied in the leader'. For Freud, subordinates in social hierarchies comply with the demands of leadership because of anxiety associated with the Oedipal desire to challenge the leader. Anxiety is based on *Thanatos*, the destructive instinct, which is directed against the self. It fosters a deep sense of moral obligation to comply, and a sense of dread in defiance, and substitutes the group's ideals for the individual's. Milgram's mechanism is quite different. How is it that otherwise decent and conscientious individuals act so horribly against the Learner in the lab? They do so, writes Milgram, 'because conscience, which regulates impulsive aggressive action, is per force diminished at the point of entering a hierarchical structure' (1974: 132). The individual's moral compass changes when he or she enters a group, and conscience appears to take a holiday when it joins a hierarchy.

By what mechanism does this happen? Conscience appears to undergo 'an agentic shift'. Milgram notes that 'the state of agency is the keystone of our analysis' (p. 133). Something magical or transformative happens when ego enters into a pattern of hierarchical social action—ego moves from an autonomous mode of self-direction to an agentic mode unencumbered by individual conscience. Milgram indicates that this is probably associated with changes in patterns of neural functioning. And while it was then difficult to identify neurochemical changes with certainty, Milgram nonetheless asserted that the 'chemical inhibitors and disinhibitors alter the probability of certain neural pathways and sequences being used'. In addition, he said there is compelling phenomenological evidence of such a shift reflected in 'an alteration of attitude'. When one joins a hierarchy, one sees one's self as 'an agent for executing the wishes of another person' as opposed to acting on one's own agenda. Given the presence of 'certain critical releasers...the shift is not freely reversible' (p. 134). While this capacity for the agentic shift may have biological origins, it is reinforced throughout the life cycle as individuals move from families, to schools, to employment. Family socialization is premised on child obedience to parents. Education is premised on discipline and compliance to teachers. Jobs come with expectations defined by employers. While social theory applauds the effective bonds between children, their families, schools, and communities, Milgram sees this as a liability. 'The very genesis of our moral ideals is inseparable from the inculcation of an obedient attitude' (1974: 136). If the family, school, and work inculcate an obedient mindset throughout the life cycle, one might ask at what point does the autonomous conscience appear? Despite entering a relationship with an authority figure, many of Milgram's subjects did not experience an agentic shift. Neither Milgram's nor Freud's analysis reflects the findings in the lab: in the received view, subjects appear to be mortified because they fear that someone innocent may have suffered at their hands.

Milgram's theory of the agentic shift emerged years after the conclusion of his experimental work, and it was never itself tested experimentally. Nonetheless, his work still appears to retain relevance in contemporary studies of genocide. In his chapter on 'Ordinary Men', Christopher Browning refers to Milgram at some length (1998: 171–5). While generally sympathetic to Milgram's approach, Browning suggested that, in contrast to the experiment, the 'authority figure' in his analysis, Major Trapp, was actually a rather weak leader, though much loved by his men, and that their participation in mass executions appears to have arisen more from duty and interpersonal loyalty than blind obedience.

There is also significant 'gerrymandering' in the moral assessments associated with Milgram's account. I raise this because it points to a major problem of external validity. If Milgram knew during the course of his experiment that subjects were being hurt, that is to say, were being emotionally traumatized, why did he not terminate the experiments immediately? Milgram (1963: 375) noted:

many subjects showed signs of nervousness in the experimental situation, and especially upon administering the more powerful shocks. In a large number of cases the degree of tension reached extremes that are rarely seen in sociopsychological laboratory studies. Subjects were observed to sweat, tremble, stutter, bite their lips, groan and dig their fingernails into their flesh. These were characteristic rather than exceptional responses to the experiment...One observer related: 'I observed a mature and initially poised businessman enter the laboratory smiling and confident. Within 20 minutes he was reduced to a twitching, stuttering wreck, who was rapidly approaching a point of nervous collapse'.

If accurate, why did Milgram not terminate the study once he had observed such trauma? It appears he thought science and society might benefit from it in the long run. However, in characterizing the conduct of his teachers as acting in what he described as a 'shockingly immoral way', Milgram overlooks the fact that the subjects might be entitled to the same excuse since they were encouraged to administer electric shocks to advance human knowledge about the effectiveness of punishment. They were also assured that the shocks would not result in any lasting harm. If acting to advance science, would the subjects characterize their conduct as 'immoral aggression' (bad) or 'reinforcement' (good)? Milgram seems to be keeping two sets of books. In one set, he describes the task to subjects as a legitimate exercise, then, in a second, characterizes it as immoral. Abse suggests that if one wants to view the subjects as so many Eichmanns, then 'the experimenter had to act the part, to some extent, of a Himmler' (1973: 29).

There is a further moral ambiguity in respect of Milgram's depictions of authority. We see this in his concluding paragraph to the 1974 monograph where his language mystifies the moral standing of authorities associated with collective violence. He refers to 'the character' of the kind created in modern societies (mentioning America in particular) and its inability to 'insulate its citizens from brutality and inhumane treatment at the direction of *malevolent* authority' (1974: 199, emphasis added). Then he says that a substantial part of the population will act badly 'without limitations of conscience, so long as they perceive that the command comes from a *legitimate* authority' (emphasis added). Within the same paragraph, Milgram conflates malevolence and legitimacy at the highest level of the state. But surely it makes a difference whether the leadership is legitimate or criminal, since political defiance may turn on this perception. Did Eichmann view the rule of the Third Reich as illegal, or did he act with a 'clear conscience', as Erber (2002) suggests?

Duress, duty, and the obedience paradigm

Hannah Arendt focuses on a point that Milgram, as a psychologist, appears to miss. The orders for aggressive war and the special treatment of subject populations were undertaken within the rule of law in Nazi Germany and its conquered territories. Eichmann, as well as the defendants at Nuremberg, invoked obedience to orders. Their behaviour was lawful within the state structure inasmuch as the orders for deportation and extermination came from the head of state or the sovereign, and the sovereign historically has been immune from prosecution by other states for politically sanctioned activities within the sovereign's jurisdiction, save for crimes covered by international conventions. That impunity would have extended to persons acting under delegated authority, such as Eichmann. The 1948 UN Convention on the Prevention and Punishment of Genocide altered this doctrine fundamentally, but it was *ex post facto* law, and did not apply to Eichmann.

This raises a question about the entire way in which Milgram approached the Eichmann case. When Eichmann and other Nazis offered the defence of 'following orders', the obedience paradigm confused *duress* and *duty*. Milgram appears to have associated the concept of 'orders' with the idea that officers and enlisted men who followed them were acting under duress. Where Milgram creates a situation of enormous emotional conflict, and where the authority figure attempts to coerce the subjects, Eichmann's case attracted interest for the opposite reason—because he followed orders with zeal, not because of fear of a superordinate power, or because of coercion. In addition, there was never any evidence of self-doubt, contrition, shame, embarrassment, remorse, or mortification on Eichmann's part. He does not denounce his past, prostrate himself, apologize profusely, and seek forgiveness. He was not a 'desk murderer' distantly removed from the mass killings and disinterested in the fate of the Jewish victims. He was the project's most enthusiastic supporter. Information released in 2011 from tapes recorded in Argentina prior to his arrest corroborates this: 'I was no ordinary recipient of orders. If I had been, I would have been a fool. Instead, I was part of the thought process. I was an idealist' (quoted in both Aderet 2011and Spiegel 2011).

I noted briefly Browning's references to Milgram. In his analysis of the Order Police, Daniel Goldhagen also dealt at some length with this work. He reports a series of misconceptions about the

Holocaust that have influenced our understanding of how it occurred—again associated with the idea of duress and coercion. First, there was 'a widespread conviction' that any German soldier who refused to participate in the killings would have been killed himself or severely punished (1997:10); and second, that the perpetrators were merely 'blind followers of orders'. According to Goldhagen, the evidence suggested otherwise. Goldhagen also challenged the idea that the Germans were subject to 'tremendous social psychological pressure' arising from 'the institutional roles that individuals occupy' (1997: 12); and that 'the callous disregard for the victims' was a result of the large, impersonal bureaucracy that undermined any personal responsibilities for the killings. These factors appear to suggest that the perpetrators were 'beings moved solely by external forces or by trans-historical and invariant propensities' (1997: 13), a characterization at the root of Arendt's *banality of evil*. For Goldhagen, it is important that the students of the Holocaust appreciate the motives and self-understandings of the perpetrators, the fact that they were Germans, and that the object of their fury was the Jewish community. Milgram takes an historical observation and reduces it to a species-trait. Arendt similarly glosses Eichmann's development as an enthusiastic Nazi and reduces it to totalitarianism (Cesarani 2006). Lipstadt (2011: 163ff) shares Cesarani's suspicions about how Arendt's political ideology led her to overlook the agency of those who endorsed the Nazi philosophy with zeal.

If we follow Goldhagen, Milgram's perspective turns things on their head. Milgram's depiction of the Holocaust transfers our focus away from the real victims by dwelling on the murderers, as though they were the victims of *their* bureaucracies, and reifying their alibi of 'following orders' as though this entailed coercion. Milgram's conceptualization seems to depict the Germans as unwilling executioners, as victims of totalitarianism. In transporting these issues to the laboratory, Milgram's design is based on the supposition that the Teacher's aggression is not only illegitimate, but is *seen* to be illegitimate by the subjects, by implication, suggesting that ordinary Germans participated in genocide involuntarily. This makes our adherence to the Milgram paradigm impossible. When accused Nazis invoked the defence of state orders, they were raising the positive *duty* that empowered them through the command structure to do what they did, that the orders did not originate from them, nor were they in a position to openly subvert them (Osiel 1999). They had an opportunity to be reassigned, as in Police Battalion 101. Likewise, Himmler told his senior generals on the Eastern Front that if they were unable to follow orders, they could resign and collect their pensions (Browning 1992: 74–5). Goering's statement at Nuremberg was similarly telling. 'We had orders to obey the head of state. We weren't a bunch of criminals meeting in the woods in the dead of night to plan mass murders' (quoted in Ramler 2008: 60). The Final Solution to the Jewish Problem was proposed by Hitler's most senior advisors, Heydrich and Himmler, probably following his private suggestions, and instituted at the Wannsee Conference in Berlin in the early winter of 1942 by the most senior bureaucrats of the German state. After their defeat, the defence of 'following orders' may have been heard as duress, but this conceals the positive agency that came from duty, and the zeal with which the officers and soldiers furthered the political goals of the Reich. To the extent that Milgram and Arendt filtered our understanding of the Holocaust, we require a new approach that is more faithful to the original events.

Replicating Milgram

J.M. Burger (2009) replicated Milgram's work, at least partially. His work was based on a revised protocol in which the Learner reports medical problems with his heart, and the Teacher receives remote voice feedback from shocks appearing to originate in a separate room. Given the grave worries over the potential traumatization of subjects caused in part by Milgram's original work, Burger limited the maximum shock level to 150 volts. In Milgram's original study, 79 per cent of persons who went *beyond* this level of shock showed total obedience. This was also the point at which the Learner first expressed serious complaints, and loudly demanded to be released from the study. Burger measured whether the subjects *tried* to continue after the 150-shock level; all subjects who had not desisted at this point were prevented from continuing. Hence, the experimenter avoided the prolonged pressure on the subjects to comply at higher shock levels, while getting a measure of aggression that correlated with the original conditions and findings. There were 70 subjects (29 men and 41 women) aged from 20 to 81 years (median = 41). Burger eliminated subjects who had prior knowledge of the Milgram paradigm and/or who seemed prone to unpleasant reactions. Subjects were paid $50 for attending two forty-five-minute sessions at the university, and were debriefed immediately following the completion of their individual tests.

Burger also administered a series of psychometric tests before the experiment. These picked up such tendencies as empathetic concern for the plight of unfortunates; prior levels of anxiety; desires of respondents to master control of their lives; and subclinical symptoms of depression. Burger also explored a protocol in which a second Teacher (a confederate) refused to continue after hearing Learner complaints following the 90-volt switch level. Thirty of the subjects were tested in this variation, each with a 'rebel' of the same gender. The real subjects were asked to replace the first Teacher. Unlike the original experiment in which the real subjects had already administered multiple shocks before two rebels broke off, in this design there was no practice effect before the real subject began to administer shocks. Burger hypothesized that the modelled refusal condition would reduce obedience in the real subjects.

What were the results? Burger reports that 28 out of 40 (70 per cent) attempted to continue after 150 volts. Milgram had found that 32 out of 40 (82.5 per cent) did likewise but, due to differences in sample sizes, these results are not statistically different. Secondly, he failed to find defiance in the model refusal group, contrary to Milgram. Third, there were no gender effects and no effects associated with individual differences based on the psychometric tests. As for whether the Teachers were convinced that the Learners were getting the shocks, Burger did not conduct the same sort of post hoc survey used by Milgram. He reported (personal communication, March 2011) that after personally debriefing every subject, he was of the opinion that not a single person was in doubt about the veracity of the shocks. This was a much higher level of conviction than Milgram reported. His subjects were told explicitly that at any time they could withdraw from the study, as could the Learner. 'Several of the participants who stopped the procedure after hearing the learner's protests pointed out that the confederate had been promised he could stop when he wanted to' (2009: 9). Since the Learner did not, this could be taken as an indication that the shocks were not as bad as they seemed.

The most interesting finding from Burger's replication was reported in a second paper in which he and colleagues analysed subject responses to the prods from the Scientist. Burger argues that Milgram was not really studying obedience to orders at all. In the original study, if a Teacher hesitated after resistance from the Learner, the

Scientist used four escalating prods to get him or her to continue: 'please continue', 'the experiment requires that you continue', 'it is absolutely essential that you continue', and 'you have no other choice, you must go on'. Only the last prod looks anything like an order. 'When participants heard the only prod that we might reasonably consider an order, not one individual "obeyed"' (Burger, Girgis, and Manning 2011). Indeed, the evidence shows that compliance declined with each level of escalation. Burger et al. concluded by noting that alternative interpretations to Milgram's work should be explored and 'the way the research is portrayed to students, scholars, and the public may need to be reassessed' (2011: 6). Burger et al.'s results about the ineffectiveness of direct orders are corroborated by Stephen Gibson's analysis of the audiotapes from two of Milgram's original experimental sets. He examined the exchange between subjects and John Williams in each case when prod 4 was employed. 'The first, and perhaps most striking, observation to make is just how ineffective prod 4 appears to have been' (Gibson 2011: 301). It was used on twenty-three occasions but in only one case was it followed by full obedience. Typically, it resulted in the experimenter acknowledging that the subject indeed had a choice!

Why Milgram fails on the question of genocide: beyond the banality of evil

I believe Milgram will always enjoy an important place in social science simply for bringing the issue of genocide and mass murder so vividly to the attention of scientists and society. His use of the electrical shock device, his casting of the innocent, middle-aged Learner, Mr Wallace, and the grim-faced lab-coated Scientist, Mr Williams, have etched themselves into the memories of successive generations of professors and their students. His work has become something of a touchstone for anyone researching genocide. However, major problems have been identified in his work, and ironically there has been no development of the ideas that he advanced in the 1960s, particularly at the theoretical level in the area of the agentic state. Agency remains a core issue in social sciences, and the constraints on agency leading to compliance in mass murder still haunt the study of genocide as noted in the recent histories of the police battalions in Poland.

   In this chapter I have raised methodological issues pertaining to the continuing utility of Milgram's ideas based on issues of internal and external validity. I have argued that there exists strong evidence that in the original study, a substantial number of subjects did not actually believe that the Learner was being hurt, making it difficult to attach any significance to their behaviour, and making it difficult to generalize to conditions in real life. This view is shared by many, including Daniel Goldhagen (1997: 592) who wrote that Milgram 'discovered that the more the people who administered the shocks confronted the apparent pain of the person being shocked, the more frequently they were willing to defy the authority of the Yale University experimenter'. Even in his replication of the basic Milgram observations, Burger makes a different but equally worrisome observation: however you characterize their behaviour, the subjects in the Milgram protocol were not following orders at all. Prods that most closely approximated orders were singularly unsuccessful in achieving compliance.

This raises another issue in terms of the application of the research to everyday life. The original case that provoked Milgram (Eichmann) did not have the character of an individual bullied into submission by a bureaucracy or by an authority figure. Nor did the later attempts to fit such atrocities as the My Lai massacre in Vietnam follow the Milgram paradigm of 'just following orders'. Lieutenant Calley did not get orders from 'the highest authorities' to carry out the shooting of civilians; nor did Charlie Company's massacre resemble the routine executions carried out on the Eastern Front by the *Einsatzgruppen*. In his biography of Eichmann, Cesarani (2006: 15) says the following:

Ironically, her book, *Eichmann in Jerusalem*, more than the trial itself shaped Eichmann's legacy. Anyone writing on the subject today works in the shadow of Hannah Arendt. Her notion of 'the banality of evil', combined with Milgram's thesis on the predilection for obedience to authority, straight-jacketed research into Nazi Germany and the persecution of the Jews for two decades.

In the following chapters I sketch an alternative account of genocide, starting with some paradoxes about the nature of genocide from the perspective of criminology, followed by a genealogical account of genocide and an alternative explanation of genocidal behaviour. When we think about genocide, we have been conditioned to think of 'the banality' of evil. Were we to take the perspective of its advocates, there is nothing banal about it. Genocide is a political crime whose architects seek a complete transcendence of their historical circumstances, and pursue their version of The Good through mass atrocities.

2

Three Paradoxes of Genocide in Criminology

Introduction

Although the world has experienced atrocities throughout history, we have only recently adopted the term genocide to describe these events. There are problems of definition that anyone studying crime must confront in the context of these events. As a criminologist, I prefer to start with a *broad conception* of the events meant to be captured by this term. Generally speaking, we mean to capture the vernacular sense of such terms as 'mass killings', 'massacres', and 'atrocities', committed sometimes in war time, sometimes in peace time, against non-combatants by politically controlled agents with exterminationist intentions, or overwhelming aggression against combatants who are essentially defenceless. These phenomena have been common throughout history prior to Lemkin's coining of the term 'genocide'. They are distinct from 'mere murder' inasmuch as the victims are killed *en masse* in collective patterns of violence that transcend individual conflicts, and personal animosities and revenge. Legally, these events *may* fit the 1948 UN Convention's criteria, although it is hardly necessary for our purposes that the events of interest to us do so. Sometimes the events of interest to the criminologist may amount to war crimes, or sometimes they may refer to that more broadly defined offence known as 'crimes against humanity' (Bassiouni 2011). Historically, some of the events of interest *pre-date* the 1948 Genocide Convention, and can only be described as 'genocidal' retroactively. Some events may be described as crimes in one or another of the Hague *Conventions* on war crimes, and others can only be viewed as contrary to the *customs* of war.

The reason the student of crime need not confine attention to what has been formally admitted to the canon of law is because, as we shall see, the social processes that influence what is within the reach of the law, and what lies beyond it, are of tremendous interest in our understanding of force and fraud and how they are constituted politically as crimes. In addition, for our purposes it is not always critical which crime is which, since we would not a priori expect to advance an explanation for crimes against humanity that was essentially different from, for example, genocide. Because the elements of the offence differ legally does not require a separate explanation any more than the explanation of murder differs necessarily from an explanation of robbery. Persons who murder wholesale do not *specialize* in war crimes anymore than they specialize in crimes against humanity or genocide. Generally speaking, crime is the use of force or fraud in the pursuit of self-interest. Sometimes this is illegal, sometimes immoral, and sometimes imprudent.

Rummel offers an explanation of 'democide' in his preface to *China's Bloody Century*.

Many explanations have been offered for such killing, but I contend that most fundamentally the root cause is arbitrary, undisciplined power in the hands of tyrants; that wherever such power has been centralized and unchecked, the possibility exists that it will be used at the whim of dictators to kill for their own ends (1991: ix–x).

Hirschi and Gottfredson (2008: 227) report similarly:

if there are no apparent negative consequences, the unrestrained offender, as Hobbes told us long ago, is free to do as he pleases. The crime lurking behind such large terms as *genocide* and *massacre* is homicide. If it pleases a dictator to…shoot, bomb, gas, hack or starve to death weak and unarmed people, he is free to do so…

Or at least he was in the past.

Without disposing of the problem of definition, we can initiate our inquiry *nominally* by identifying some commonly accepted cases. The paramount instance for students of modern world history would arguably be the Holocaust of European Jewry during the Second World War—the 'shoah' or the historical calamity of the European Jewish communities. Some five to six million people from across Western and Eastern Europe and Russia, men, women and children, all non-combatants, and constituting the plurality of their communities, were systematically murdered according to a political policy designed to erase their presence from Europe (Hilberg 1985: 1048). This was the 'crime of crimes' virtually unparalleled in historical memory. More recently, readers will recall the murder of Tutsis and moderate Hutus in Rwanda; some 550 000 to over a million people are estimated to have been killed in less than 100 days in the spring of 1994 (Prunier 1997). A year later, Bosnian men and boys were isolated and executed *en masse* by Bosnian Serbs in Srebrenica in July 1995 (Honig and Both 1996). Although the full details of these events appeared only afterwards, the 'killing fields' of Cambodia led to the torture, starvation, execution, and killing through exhaustive labour of 1.7 million Cambodians under the revolutionary policies of Pol Pot in the four years after the seizure of the Cambodian state by the Khmer Rouge in 1975 (Marchak 2008). Other cases of interest earlier in the 20th century would include first, the murder of 1.7 million Armenians by leaders of the Committee of Union and Progress in the government of Turkey in 1915–16 (Bloxham 2005; Melson 1990), and, second, the destruction of the Hereros at the hands of the German colonial army in German South West Africa 1904–07 in which over 75 000 natives were driven off their lands to starve in the Omaheke desert (Drechsler 1980). All but the last instance resulted in legal proceedings against the perpetrators, usually with only halting success. It should also be mentioned that this list is neither definitive nor exhaustive. On the first point, it is not clear that every case mentioned would fit (even retroactively) the definition of the 1948 UN Convention. On the second point, it is clear that the list does not include *all* massacres since 1900 that might be defined as genocide (Darfur, Bangladesh, East Timor, Guatemala, Burundi, etc.). Nonetheless, these illustrations will suffice as a working list to outline a number of paradoxes of interest to students of politically motivated mass murder. These paradoxes are identified to indicate that the sort of events we wish to consider appear to resist the ken and reach of contemporary criminology. They appear inexplicable, and challenge long-standing suppositions about the nature of crimes, the persons who commit them, and their accountability for the most serious breaches of laws, morals, and conventions. There is another reason to explore the scope of the subject matter at the start of the study: this is a live issue in legal circles.

Genocide sensu stricto *versus atrocity and the consequences*

There are two schools of thought that have emerged in the international criminal law literature regarding the merits of a strict focus on genocide per se, along with its distinctive mental requirements and elements of the offence, as opposed to pursuing a broader term. The former approach argues that there are benefits to conceptualizing international crimes as forming a distinctive hierarchy of evil, and that their suppression is required to end complicity primarily in the case of genocide, 'the crime of crimes'. Indeed, Kantians argue that justice entails a *duty* to prosecute such offences. Speaking from the other side in *Reducing Genocide to Law*, Payan Akhavan, an experienced observer and advisor to the ad hoc tribunals at The Hague and Arusha, challenges the supposition that we should treat genocide as the ultimate crime, and that it should be placed at the apex of the pyramid of international crimes above crimes against humanity and war crime. 'The weight of judicial opinion does not deem genocide to be categorically more serious than either war crimes or crimes against humanity' (2012: 59). This is because the gravity of the crime can vary so dramatically within instances of the same legal offence, and also because there is often great overlap in the offences themselves. Jean-Paul Akayesu, mayor of Taba in Rwanda, was the first person convicted at trial under the 1948 Genocide Convention. However, Akhavan argues that he was found guilty of all three principle crimes '*on the same set of facts*' (2012: 54). Not only that, Akhavan argues that the application of the genocide charge to *Akayesu* was highly controversial since the Tutsis were not, strictly speaking, an ethnic group, and hence not protected by the convention. 'By any standard, the Trial Chamber's legal methodology in *Akayesu* was highly problematic' (2012: 151). By contrast in the *Jelisić* case, the International Criminal Tribunal for the Former Yugoslavia (ICTY) dismissed the charge of genocide to avoid applying the label of genocide to a low-level thug, and convicted on crimes against humanity and war crimes, even though a strict reading of the convention would create a liability for 'private individuals', and even though the maximum penalties available to the court are the same for all such crimes. Akhavan's point is that the term genocide has taken on a mystique that creates the impression that the word can adequately capture the pinnacle of evil that frequently defies rational comprehension, and, in the words of Hannah Arendt (1992: 51) 'explodes the limits of the law…and shatters any and all legal systems'. As a result the trial courts felt compelled to seek a conviction for genocide in *Akayesu*, but not *Jelisić*, and followed the letter of the law in neither case.

Mark Drumbl in *Atrocity, Punishment and International Law* advocates a broader approach to remedies than those confined to individual prosecution based on personal guilt for genocide. For Drumbl, the main problem is the huge disconnect between 'extraordinary evil' associated with atrocities, and the design of the legal responses based on models of crime imported from national courts. 'Whereas ordinary crime tends to be deviant in the times and places it is committed, the extraordinary acts of individual criminality that collectively lead to mass atrocity are not so deviant in the times and places where they are committed... In such cases, participation in atrocity becomes a product of conformity' (2007: 8; Alvarez 1999). The application of punishment models in international courts based on individual models of deviance is, in Drumbl's words, 'ill-fitting'. One important consequence of this broader conception of the nature of the problem is that it promotes the search for a wider range of remedies than those criminal indictments currently pursued at the ad hoc tribunals and the International Criminal Court (ICC), which in turn justifies an approach to genocide that is not defined *sensu stricto*, and which does not presume that one remedy fits all cases.

First Paradox: The Ordinary Agents of Extraordinary Murder

Conventional wisdom suggests the Holocaust and other crimes of mass murder must be the work of extraordinarily evil people. In criminology, profiles of 'life-course persistent' offenders or 'heavies' (Moffitt 1993; Katz 1988) suggest that they start early in the life cycle, are versatile in areas of offence, show little evidence of criminal specialization, are overwhelmingly male, engage in hedonistic offences that tend to provide short-term pleasures, are urban, and are over-represented among marginal racial, ethnic, and/or class communities. They frequently exhibit developmental deficiencies and exhibit psychopathological symptoms (Robins 1966; Hare 1970). In the case of the Holocaust, there was a tendency to attribute mass murder to a vanguard of psychopathic Nazis and their sadistic counterparts in the SS, and other military and quasi-military organizations. Reflecting on 'the excommunication of Hannah Arendt' by her contemporaries, Amos Elon (2006) notes that when Arendt (1963) reported on the trial of Eichmann 'most people still assumed that murder was committed by monsters or demons'. Recently, Oakley (2008) has suggested that the 20th century's leading tyrants exhibited 'Machiavellianism', a trait reminiscent of psychopathy or personality disorder. This resonates with Adorno et al's (1950) post-war assessment of the role played by 'authoritarian personalities' in the Nazi movement, and Walter Langer's 1943 psychiatric assessment of Hitler for the US Office of Strategic Services (Langer 1972).

However, there is another line of thinking suggested in criminology by Jack Katz in *Seductions of Crime* (1988). Katz describes a range of homicides that are undertaken in a frame of mind he describes as 'righteous slaughter'. These cases may help us think about the mentality of perpetrators of political crimes like genocide, without making assumptions about their sanity. For example, a husband confronts his unfaithful wife and her lover in the act of fornication, and shoots them dead. The wife of a long-time abusive husband douses him with gasoline while he lies unconscious in an alcoholic delirium, and sets him on fire, then drives to the police station to make a confession. A young man shoots his wife after she repeatedly shouts the name of her previous boyfriend while coming to a sexual climax making love. A woman deserts her husband, and is stabbed to death when she later returns to try to remove their children from his care. Katz describes these homicides as 'righteous slaughter' because they are undertaken in a sense of righteousness, and reflect the defence of a communal good, or a value that the victim is seen to transgress. In the cases he reviews, the perpetrators are not motivated to 'get away'. They may be enormously emotional when confronted by police, but they rarely exhibit signs of guilt or remorse. The legal system typically minimizes their culpability. In cases where a spouse is caught *in flagrante delicto*, many courts have recognized the defence of provocation. Where the spouse has endured years of abuse, murder as self-defence is recognized through the doctrine of temporary insanity. What these cases have in common is humiliation. The perpetrators face a challenge that threatens to degrade or humiliate them. They lose all self-restraint, and respond in a rage, and strike out against the provocateur. They transcend the humiliation, and seek satisfaction in violence by making a last stand in defence of The Good. Katz does not condone these crimes. His point is that frequently people let themselves be seduced by the moral attractions of crime. They 'go ballistic,' lose self-control, and perpetrate violence without remorse, thereby transcending a challenge to their status or identity.

Political crimes also may have this transcendent logic. Alan Bullock (1962) makes this point in his biography of Adolf Hitler. Bullock says that one of Hitler's most habitual devices was 'to place himself on the defensive, to accuse those who opposed or obstructed him of aggression and malice, and to pass rapidly from a tone of outraged innocence to the full thunders of moral indignation' (1962: 376). Bullock reports that time after time Hitler, once he had decided on a course of action, 'would whip himself into a passion which enabled him to bear down all opposition' (ibid). Again: 'Hitler in a rage appeared to lose all control of himself. His face became mottled and sullen with fury, he screamed at the top of his voice, spitting out a stream of abuse, waving his arms wildly and drumming on the table or the wall with his fists.' Then he would stop and re-compose himself, suggesting that the transitory loss of control was operatic.

Whatever case can be made for the mentality of the top leaders in cases of politically motivated violence, as Drumbl noted earlier, the case made for the rank and file is a different story. The recent historiography suggests that tens of thousands of followers who implemented the policies of genocide were not delusional, evil, temporarily insane, or acting out of a sense of provocation. Browning's research on the police battalions in Poland mentioned in the last chapter (1992; 2000) stresses that it was 'ordinary men,' not psychopaths, who paved the way to the Holocaust. Browning points out that in the spring of 1942, some 75 to 80 per cent of all the victims of the Holocaust were still alive, but eleven months later, most had been killed. 'At the core of the Holocaust was a short, intensive wave of mass murder' (1992: xv). Aside from Warsaw, most Polish Jews lived in small villages and scattered communities. At the time of the active military campaign on the Eastern front, the Germans had to invest tremendous resources in personnel and material to uproot, 're-settle', concentrate, and transport millions of people to sites to be gassed, shot, worked, or marched to death. In the process, 'the grass-roots perpetrators became "professional killers"' (p. xvii). 'Particularly for the Nazi occupiers stationed in the conquered lands of Eastern Europe—literally tens of thousands of men from all walks of life—the mass murder policies of the regime were not aberrational . . . mass murder and routine had become one' (p. xix). Police Battalion 101 was composed of middle-aged policemen too old for normal military service, but they and other battalions were responsible for the shootings of hundreds of thousands of civilian because they were Jews.

Daniel Goldhagen's examination of the same records was reported in *Hitler's Willing Executioners*. He stresses more the particular animosity of the Germans toward the Jews. Goldhagen argues that the elimination of European Jewry was only possible because hundreds of thousands of ordinary Germans were complicit in the slaughter, and participated because they thought that it was an appropriate thing to do. Indeed, without their participation, it would never have happened. Also, had the Nazis not been defeated, the toll would probably have been the complete annihilation of the 11 million Jews from every corner of Europe. By contrast, the euthanasia programme was stopped because ordinary Germans objected to it. But regarding the Jews, the Germans neither viewed their actions as criminal, nor did they shrink from opportunities to inflict suffering, humiliation, and death, openly, knowingly, and zealously on their victims. As Goldhagen comments on some recent cases:

Who doubts that the Tutsis who slaughtered Hutus in Burundi or the Hutus who slaughtered Tutsis in Rwanda … that the Serbs who have killed Croats or Bosnian Muslims, did so out of conviction in the justice of their actions? Why do we not believe the same for the German perpetrators (1997: 14)?

The first paradox of genocide is that of agency—the voluntary nature of murderous behaviour by otherwise virtuous individuals. The issue of agency was well known to the first generation of Holocaust scholars in the 1960s. The police battalion records contained the accounts of individual policemen interviewed twenty years after the events, and after the men had returned to normal civilian life in Germany. What did they reveal about the mentality of the policemen? Goldhagen begins his account with a telling illustration. Captain Wolfgang Hoffmann, commander of Police Battalion 101, received an order from his superiors in 1943 requiring that all the policemen under his command sign a declaration that they would not steal from the local Polish population. He simply refused to comply because the order injured his 'sense of honour' and impugned the decency of the men under his command (Goldhagen 1997: 1). So much for rigid obedience to authority. Hoffmann's actions reflected his sense of moral autonomy.

The debate between Browning and Goldhagen focused on the extent to which the perpetrators were seized by unique mental pressures ('eliminationist antisemitism' for Goldhagen) or in-group loyalty and peer influence (for Browning), by moral righteousness (Goldhagen) or moral indifference (Browning), and by national solidarity (Goldhagen) versus individual accommodations (Browning).

In a study of other court records, Browning (2000: 166) found evidence that a small number of the policemen consistently desisted from murdering civilian Jews without reprisal, and that an equally small number were Nazi party members who were flagrantly anti-Semitic, and who became enthusiastic murderers. Whether one favours Browning's perspective or Goldhagen's, the evidence suggested that the perpetration of the murder of entire communities was undertaken by individuals who had freedom to refuse, who acted, often reluctantly, sometimes enthusiastically, but who acted for the most part effectively, without undue pressure or compunction, to take the lives of unarmed civilians—time after time, until the Jewish communities were cleared, and their inhabitants eradicated. Once the hostilities were ended, the perpetrators returned to peacetime reconstruction and, for the most part, laid the memories of mass murder to rest. As for the resisters, 'unfortunately, the presence of a minority of men who sought not to participate in the regime's racial killing had no measureable effect whatsoever' (Browning 2000: 169).

Then and now

Certain events in the 1990s were a wake-up call for many students of political crime. At the same time that Browning and Goldhagen were revisiting the phenomenon of voluntary compliance in mass murder in the historical records, the news accounts of contemporary atrocities in Rwanda and in the former Yugoslavia pointed to something quite comparable: the mass mobilization of ordinary people in unofficial militias to engage in 'ethnic cleansing'. History was repeating itself. The 'Eastern front' had reappeared in history, first in Central Africa, then in Bosnia, and the agents of death were not professional, hard-core assault troops, but broadly mobilized young men, sometimes with makeshift uniforms, sometimes without, sometimes with professional weapons, sometimes with machetes and hoes. In 1994 the world was appalled by a torrent of bloody massacres in Rwanda carried out in large part by youthful militias and peasants targeting the country's minority Tutsis. In 1995, following years of the shelling of civilians in Bosnian cities during the Balkan conflicts, Nazi-type concentration camps had appeared as Trnopolje, Kereterm, and Omarsk in Bosnia (Power 2002: 269–76). 'No one in the post-World War II generation could have anticipated the re-appearance of such camps in Europe' (Vulliamy 2007: 102). The term 'ethnic cleansing' arose from the common practice of Serbs,

Bosnians, and Croats of constructing ethnically autonomous political units in the former heterogeneous Yugoslavia through the forceful removal of their former neighbours. It also occurred in Rwanda throughout the history of the republic when waves of Tutsis were forced into exile by violence. Recently, the international world observed a new genocide in Darfur that it appeared unable to stop (Hagan and Rymond-Richmond 2009). Here the agents of murder and rape were Janjawiid, tribal horsemen destroying thousands of agricultural villages in southern and western Sudan, and displacing the population into Chad.

How can we reconcile offences that we normally associate with morally deficient individuals and the most horrific crimes of the 20th century with the normality of their perpetrators? Ironically, the top echelons of the Nazi party were not mediocrities or reprobates. Eric Zillmer (2006: 269) writes that 'the Nazi elite were overconfident, entitled, arrogant and egocentric. They were well-educated and bright, and in fact had average to superior intelligence...The Nazi data suggested that the Nazis [were] ordinary, well-educated, middle class, family-type people...and did not demonstrate any particular inclination toward violence.' According to Raul Hilberg (1985: 288–9) in his discussion of the mobile execution squads unleashed against the Jews and commissars in Russia, 'the great majority of the officers of the Einsatzgruppen were professional men. They included a physician (Weinmann), a professional opera singer (Klinglehoffer), and a large number of lawyers. These men were in no sense hoodlums, delinquents, common criminals, or sex maniacs. Most were intellectuals.' This suggests that the history of earlier investigations of the pathological origins of the initiation of the Holocaust were misplaced (Browning 2000: 165). This type of crime is more likely to be born of national defiance, in-group loyalty, self-sacrifice, and disillusionment with the group's mistreatment by others, as opposed to individual pathologies. Rather than viewing them as peripheral to the social order, they appear to be closely attached to it, perhaps too much so.

Second Paradox: The Conventionalization of Mass Murder

A case can be made that throughout history, genocide and war crimes have been conventionalized, and that their perpetrators have largely escaped the illegalities of murder. This is the second major paradox. What does conventionalization mean? In *Discipline and Punish*, Foucault identified a restructuring of 'the economy of illegalities' as the bourgeoisie's stamp came to mark the legal order of 18th-century Europe. Economy is used here in the sense of the actor's responsiveness to incentives: rewards and punishments replaced by profits and costs. 'For illegalities of properties—for theft—there were the ordinary courts and punishments; for the illegalities of rights—fraud, tax evasion, irregular commercial operations—special legal institutions applied with transactions, accommodations, reduced fines etc.' (Foucault 1977: 87). Similarly, in *Whigs and Hunters*, E.P. Thompson (1975) outlined how the new class of manufacturers and merchants were able to expropriate forestry land in rural England for the creation of bourgeois country estates, and to displace occupants who had rights therein under ancestral forestry laws. The rural population were excluded from their rights, and through the Black Act of 1723 faced liability to over fifty new capital offences for actions taken in opposition to the expropriation of their entitlements; these offences covered such things as 'blackening the face' and wandering at night, hunting deer, and breaking the dams of trout ponds. Their access to subsistence in forest properties was redefined in terms of theft. W.G. Carson (1979) extended this analysis to the way in which 19th-century English manufacturers were able to escape the criminalization of their activities under factory regulation designed to create safe work environments. His analysis identified

the processes whereby, despite a succession of criminal laws purporting to restrict the hours of labour to be performed by children and young persons in cotton and other textile mills, their early nineteenth century employers successfully retained a 'right'...to substantial immunity from the penal and other adverse substantial implications of their criminal conduct (Carson 1979: 37–8).

Following Becker, he called the process 'the conventionalization' of crime. Such crimes escape stigmatization. 'A wide range of criminal activities...although banned, are freely resorted to, and while proscribed, are only infrequently punished' (1979: 38). Attached to these crimes are a series of justifications or rationalizations which tend to undermine the moralizations of the offence, and minimize the spontaneous emotional rejection of crime that Durkheim associated with retributive justice.

Exactly what crimes were conventionalized? In the context of 19th-century manufacture, Carson reports the public discovery of brutalizing working conditions in which employees were fettered, flogged, starved and tormented to the point of suicide. Children as young as nine years of age were forced to work fifteen-hour days, and sometimes relegated to night shifts for a period of up to a year. In a similar vein, Engels (1892) described the widespread starvation of impoverished workers as 'social murder' that went unacknowledged by the bourgeoisie. Karl Marx had similarly reported on the privations associated with work in London and Manchester including the occupational diseases such as lockjaw associated with the manufacture of Lucifer matches; and children as young as nine or ten dragged out of their squalid beds at two or three o'clock in the morning to work in the lace trade. In addition to the interminable hours required of bakers and their assistants, he reported on the wholesale adulteration of bread which contained 'human perspiration mixed with the discharge of abscesses, cobwebs, dead black beetles, and putrid German yeast, without counting alum, sand, and other agreeable mineral ingredients' (Tucker 1978: 367–9). This caused enormous public alarm, but attempts to bring such activities under the control of the law proved difficult for the factory inspectors. Fines were opposed because they would put a burden only on those businesses 'caught,' and would artificially undermine their competitiveness. The motives of the employers were not criminal, but consistent with the creation of national wealth and domination of international trade. The factory regime also contained the promise of educating the great underclass of society, and advancing the industrial success of capitalism as a whole. In this context, prosecutions were infrequent, penalties were minor, and the modal form of control consisted of a cease and desist order, effectively transferring the role of legal control to industrial diplomacy. This situation persisted in spite of the abysmal human carnage it created. The process of conventionalizing occupational health and safety crimes has persisted in certain industries largely unchanged to the present day. Carson's work (1982) on the epidemic levels of preventable deaths in the offshore petroleum industry has been corroborated in the more recent work of Johnstone (2007) and Woolfson (2007). The explosion in April 2010 on the BP oilrig in the Gulf of Mexico took the lives of eleven workers and polluted hundreds of miles of coastal waters, but resulted in no criminal charges until 2012. Likewise, the 2008 worldwide trafficking of worthless financial instruments that precipitated the worst financial collapse since the Depression resulted in not a single criminal prosecution. The fact that entire economies were swindled with worthless and dubiously rated financial investments was not crime, but business (Lewis 2011).

One of the implications of Carson's theory, and Becker's earlier labelling theory (1963), is that the harmfulness of the crime does not always dictate the form of law under which it is regulated, or the extent to which it is regulated as crime at all. The 'societal reaction' to crime is negotiated by actors with differential access to power, ideology, and legitimizing institutions. If this is true of what have come to be known as 'white-collar crimes', it is even more so for political crimes, state crimes and crimes against international humanitarian law. By way of illustration, in her analysis of the US political actions towards genocide and war crimes in the 20th century, Samantha Power argues that successive US administrations were reluctant to recognize the reality of mass murder. 'Policy makers, journalists, and citizens are extremely slow to muster the imagination needed to reckon with evil…they assume rational actors will not inflict seemingly gratuitous violence' (2002: xvii). The US has repeatedly delayed interventions to end international violence. Her cases include the destruction of the Armenians by the Turks during the Great War; the Cambodian civil war, the rise of Pol Pot and the subsequent 'killing fields' created by the Khmer Rouge; the Bosnian war atrocities and the Srebrenica massacres; the Rwanda genocide; and the destruction of the Kurds by Saddam Hussein. Her conclusion is that, in spite of repeated early warnings about mass murder, US political figures repeatedly ignored evidence of atrocities, and/or were hesitant in their response. Genocide occurred under the watch of successive presidents because it was not in their strategic interests to act, and because, in terms of domestic politics, there were no political costs for inaction. It was treated as an unfortunate fact of international society best resolved through diplomacy. In Carson's lexicon, it was conventionalized.

There is a wider context for understanding the conventionalization of genocide. Historically, European sovereigns have enjoyed immunity from criminal prosecution. In the common law tradition, when Norman law supplanted Anglo-Saxon law in England, the sovereign was identified as the primary victim of crime, and his power over his subjects, particularly the serfs or commoners, was absolute. Norman criminal law replaced the system of compensation between victims and offenders that was typical of Anglo-Saxon law. The power of the king was only gradually reduced by such agreements as the Magna Carta of 1215. After the early formation of the first European states and the termination of the Thirty Years War, the Peace of Westphalia (1648) led to the recognition of the autonomy of states within their own territories free from external interference (Bull 2012). The reluctance of states such as the US or Britain to interfere in the internal affairs of other sovereign states to prevent atrocities is well founded on the norm of reciprocity, i.e. if one state assumed the right to invade another to rescue its citizens from their sovereign, was it likewise not liable to invite reciprocal invasion on the same basis? Or in the case of the ICC, would US adoption of the treaty to protect itself from international criminals not expose its own citizens to prosecution in an international forum for *their* war crimes? This has been a live issue in the cases of Kissinger (Hitchens 2002) and Rumsfeld (Ratner 2008), both of whom are potentially at risk of apprehension overseas on warrants for international crimes from zealous prosecutors. The conventionalization of genocide has arisen in part from political interests in protecting national sovereignty.

There is *always* a link between justice and politics, in the sense that crimes and their prosecution cannot operate in a political vacuum. However, the pursuit of 'universal justice' in the context of political self-interest, particularly where the offences are those defined by international agreements between parties of uneven power, frequently makes arbitrary the definition of what *count* as crimes, and who *count* as criminals. Frequently, this is not so much by what is included (deportation, enslavement, and murder of Jews), but as to what is left out (the fire-bombing of civilian populations in Dresden, Hamburg, Berlin, and Tokyo). In this view, it is not that garden-variety criminals are innocent of their misconduct, but more a question of those whose harmful and aggressive actions escape the reach of the law (Reiman 2007). The way in which certain horrendous behaviours are conventionalized is connected to the first paradox discussed earlier—the mass mobilization of ordinary people to do the killing. This suggests that the perpetrators who carry out the crimes adopt the same 'conventionalized' frame of mind when it comes to the murder of civilians as the sovereigns who devised the policies. The next paradox in this story is the magnitude of the crimes.

Third Paradox: The Dark Figure of Politically Motivated Mass Murder

Criminologists have long worried about the difference between the official rate of crime and the actual rate. The gap between the two numbers has been referred to as 'the dark figure' of crime. Interest in this was intensified in the 1970s when feminists' evidence that violence against women, domestic assault, and rape were significantly underreported (Polk 1985). Crime surveys were employed to fill the gap between official statistics and actual criminal victimization. More recently, a similar question has been raised about the under-reporting of white-collar crimes (Friedrichs and Schwartz 2008). Given the problems of crime recognition created by the conventionalization of genocide, it is prudent to ask how much we actually know about the levels of victimization arising from genocide and analogous behaviours. This question dominated the life of one scholar: R.J. Rummel. For three decades Rummel investigated 'the murder of any person or people by a government, including genocide, politicide and mass murder' (Rummel 1994: 31). He wrote about the Nazi period in *Democide* (1992), and described not only the genocide of the European Jews, but the wider policies of repression that led to the murder of the insane and infirm in the euthanasia programme, the wholesale murder of Poles, Ukrainian, and Russian citizens in reprisal killings, slave labour camps, forced deportations, and starvation. He described the mass killing of civilians in China throughout the 20th century, and reported the brutal effects of suppression of peasants by war lords in the early part of the century, the privations of the civil war between Mao Zedong and Chang Kai-shek, the wholesale destruction of civilians during the Japanese occupation, the forced collectivization of agriculture after 1949, the starvation of millions during the Great Leap Forward, and other programmes during the consolidation of communist rule (Rummel 1991). In *Lethal Politics* (1990) Rummel documented the massacres of civilians in the struggle of the Bolsheviks to establish power in Russia, the creation of the enormous gulag archipelago which killed millions through slave labour, cruel policies to force collectivization in agriculture, and the physical liquidation of the regime's class and ideological enemies by arbitrary execution quotas. He spelled out his theory in two books, *Death by Government* (1994) and *Power Kills* (1997), and has reported his summary estimates of the entire range of politically motivated mass murder in *Statistics of Democide: Genocide and Mass Murder since 1900* (1998).

At the capstone of the hierarchy of killers, Rummel (1994) identifies the atrocities committed by regimes he describes as 'megamurderers', regimes responsible for over 10 000 000 deaths (including the Soviet Union, the Peoples Republic of China, Nazi-occupied Europe, and the domination of third-world countries by the Western colonial powers). Next, he identifies 'the lesser megamurderers', regimes guilty of causing over 1 000 000 deaths (i.e. Japanese atrocities against civilians in occupied Asia, the Khmer Rouge in Cambodia, the Ottoman Turks and their successors, the North and South Vietnamese, the Polish 'cleansing' of the ethnic Germans, Pakistani mass murder in Bangladesh, and Tito's pacification of political opposition in Yugoslavia). In a chapter on 'The Crowd of Lesser Murderers' (1998: 268ff) he details the activities of 156 regimes including rebel movements and non-state groups responsible for the deaths of 'no more than 99 999 people' (e.g. suppression of political opposition in Columbia, Brazil, Chile, Algeria, Argentina etc.). For the 20th century he reports on a total of 141 state regimes responsible for democide in one form or another.

What is the total figure given by Rummel for democide in the 20th century? His initial figures in *Statistics of Genocide* (1998) have been revised. The main changes come from revision of the estimates for the PRC based on Chang and Halliday's biography of Mao. The 'Great Leap Forward' is thought to have led to the starvation of 38 000 000 peasants in 1959–61 as food was hoarded to be sold to the East Bloc to raise hard currency for the purchase of weapons and technology (Chang and Halliday 2005: 426–39). Also, Rummel raised his estimates of indigenous people killed in Western colonial adventures in Africa and Asia to 50 000 000. The total deaths reported for the century were 262 000 000. This figure is net of the death of actual combatants, but includes estimates of deaths caused by indiscriminate Allied bombing of civilian targets in Japan and Europe. Table 2.1 is based on Rummel (1998).

The exact figures must necessarily be treated with caution. Rummel's method is to canvas the leading authorities in the area, and identify their estimates of deaths. His books are distended with tables that often run to scores of pages or more. He identifies the country, the regimes, the years and months, and the various estimates by different authors. He also identifies the categories of death—genocide, assassinations, starvation, rebellion, political

Table 2.1 Rummel's estimates of 20th-century democides

Levels of democide 1–5	Years	Estimates (millions)	Totals (millions)
Level 1	1900–87		219634
China (PRC)	1949–87	76 702	
USSR	1917–87	61 911	
Colonialism		50 000	
Germany	1933–45	20 946	
China (KMT)	1928–49	10 075	
Level 2	1900–87		19 180
Japan	1936–45	5 964	
China (Mao Soviets)	1923–48	3 468	
Cambodia	1975–79	2 035	
Turkey	1909–18	1 883	
Vietnam	1945–87	1 670	
Poland	1945–48	1 585	
Pakistan	1958–87	1 503	
Yugoslavia (Tito)	1944–87	1 072	
Level 3	1900–87		4 145
North Korea	1948–87	1 663	
Mexico	1900–20	1 417	
Russia	1900–17	1 065	
Level 4	1900–87		14 918
Top 5	1900–87	4 074	
China (Warlords)	1917–49	910	
Turkey (Ataturk)	1919–23	878	
United Kingdom	1900–87	816	
Portugal (Dictatorship)	1926–82	741	
Indonesia	1965–87	729	
Other	1900–99	10 844	
Level 5	1900–87		2 792
WORLD TOTAL	1900–87		260669
WORLD TOTAL	1987–99		1 331
WORLD TOTAL	1900–99		262 000

massacre, disappearance, etc., and typically calculates an estimate based on the average report. There are numerous limitations with this methodology. It only captures relatively large-scale events that attract news coverage, government inquiries, and/or NGO estimates. For the most part, the cases were not adjudicated in any formal judicial process so that *mens rea, actus reus*, absence of lawful defences, and other legal niceties are all gainsaid. Also, the bases of the estimates vary dramatically from actual body counts to journalistic impressions. The records also omit grey areas such as 'ethnocides', i.e. the erasure of traditional language, knowledge, and social structures of aboriginal peoples through residential schools and religious proselytizing. Nonetheless, Rummel's cataloguing of such large-scale atrocities is unparalleled in contemporary scholarship. It is paradoxical that such a large record of atrocities, however much over- or underestimated, has tended to escape the attention of mainstream criminology.

Two further observations should be made in this context. The perpetrators of the vast majority of these crimes are political elites, governments, politicians, dictators, and other heads of state, or persons acting under their powers. Normally, the politicality of crime is understood to be confined by and large to the transgressions of interests *contrary* to the state, and that the state itself is the repository of, in the words of Max Weber (1918), 'the legitimate use of force'. When sovereigns make war on other sovereigns, this is understood as statecraft. When the sovereigns capriciously extirpate the lives of their own subjects, they act as though the latter are criminals. And when they do act, they obviously have an ability to mobilize gallows and gas chambers virtually without limits. This explains the magnitude of the crimes.

The second observation is that the vast majority of sovereigns also appear to act with legal impunity. Following the First World War, Britain attempted to bring members of the Young Turks to trial for their role in the extermination of the Armenians. When Britain forced the post-war government to initiate proceedings, there were several convictions, but the Turkish government halted the trials. Britain responded by moving the remaining accused to the island of Malta; the Turkish army seized members of the British occupying army in Turkey as hostages. All the Turkish prisoners were released in a 'prisoner swap' (Power 2002: 16). Perhaps, the only justice for the Armenians occurred when Soghomon Tehlirian was acquitted in Germany for the assassination of Talaat Pasha, former Turkish Minister of the Interior. This was one of seven assassinations of former members of the genocidal government by members of the Armenian Revolutionary Federation. The Allies pressured Germany to prosecute former military officers and their superiors for war crimes against civilians during the Great War. From a list of several thousand candidates, forty-five names were called to trial at the German Supreme Court at Leipzig in May 1921. Many 'escaped custody' and, of those convicted, the sentences were more appropriate to misdemeanours that made a charade of the prosecution, and amounted to an exoneration of the accused (Bass 2000: 80). Although Nuremberg is identified as the apex of truth in terms of war crimes accountability, it must be remembered that of the 5 000 names originally advanced for the core trial, only twenty-four were indicted. The individual American, British, and French courts had more success. Between 1947 and 1953 they obtained about 5 000 convictions in some 10 000 prosecutions. When the files reverted to the German courts in 1957 they obtained 6 000 convictions among 200 000 names (Zillmer et al 1995: 27). What about the megakillers? Lenin, Stalin, Mao Zedong, and Pol Pot all died in their beds. And what about the other Khmer leaders? Thirty years after the end of the regime five frail old men were returned to face justice in a hybrid Cambodian-UN court in 2005. Sukarno, Pinochet, and the other generals? Virtually never charged or convicted. But there were strong men who did not escape the reach of the law: Hussein, Milošević and Taylor, each of whom found themselves in the defence box, not so much for legal reasons, as for reasons of geopolitical convenience, and their loss of political power (Moghalu 2008; Mandel 2004). Bosnian Serb leader, President Radovan Karadžić and General Ratko Mladić have been added to the docket. Then there is the case of Omar Bashir, president of Sudan, indicted for genocide in Darfur by the ICC. Is it a coincidence that the ICC has limited its indictments to African leaders of marginal states? The point here is that the magnitude of the crimes as tallied by Rummel are nearly incomprehensible. They arise from sovereign powers, and the prosecution of the sovereigns for their atrocities is a rare event indeed (Ball 1999).

Conclusion

In the last chapter we raised the thesis of the banality of evil—the idea that people who embodied wickedness were constrained to participate in it because of their social role and the compunctions associated with their hierarchical social placement. We rejected the banality of evil thesis because it suggested that people become automatons in bureaucracies, and pointed to fixed elements of nature (biology for Milgram) or the state (totalitarianism for Arendt) to explain genocide through the concept of obedience or submission to authority. The paradoxes of genocide suggest a different picture. In criminology, we would expect that serious offenders are quite different from the average citizen, that the acts which comprise their crimes are widely condemned and suppressed, and that, as a result of these two conditions, its occurrence would be rare. The paradoxes of genocide suggest just the opposite. The perpetrators are not outcasts or dysfunctional villains with histories of developmental problems and sociopathic relationships that made them outsiders to their communities. If the SS is any guide, its members were recruited from the ranks of the best and the brightest elements of society, and were intelligent, competent, and reliable. When confronted with evidence of their crimes, they displayed little evidence of subjective guilt. Siegfried Ramler was a translator at the Nuremberg trials from 1945 to 1949. He reports on this element of 'the guilty mind' as presented by the Nazi defendants. The prosecution at Nuremberg presented films of concentration camps liberated by the Allies depicting piles of corpses, thousands of emaciated inmates, and evidence of gas chambers and large crematoria. The films horrified most of the defendants. Some turned their backs to the screen to dissociate themselves from the evidence. Hans Frank, who had been the governor of occupied Poland where the largest camps were located, said 'when such atrocities are committed in the name of Germany and the German people, we all bear the guilt of these crimes' (Ramler 2008: 63). Ramler notes, however, that 'while he accepted Germany's guilt, he refused to accept his own personal involvement and specific guilt, despite evidence that Auschwitz and other concentration camps were under his jurisdiction'. This was a recurrent pattern: acceptance of guilt in a general sense but no sense of individual culpability. Similarly Eichmann, who cooperated with Israeli police interrogators in describing his role in the Final Solution 'refused to acknowledge personal guilt' (quoted in Lipstadt 2011: 43). 'He was not guilty, he insisted, because his superiors ordered him to do terrible things ... If he was guilty of anything, it was of being too loyal.'

This is related to the second paradox: the crimes tried at Nuremberg were not viewed as crimes when they were planned and executed. They were state orders adopted at Wannsee in 1942. The 'Final Solution' was adopted as government policy. Mass murder was conventionalized. The concentration camps were built to expedite the elimination of European Jewry with industrial efficiency, and the European railways were commandeered to deliver the victims to their fate 'on time'. No moral objections were aired among those charged with the responsibility of carrying out the policy, and the public was largely ignorant of the process since it was sold as a 'resettlement' of Jews to the East. It is known on other matters that persons with expertise that contradicted Hitler's policies were unable to muster the courage to contradict him publicly. Ramler, as translator, participated in the pretrial interrogation of leading military defendants at Nuremberg, including Generals Keitel and Jodl and Admirals Raeder and Dönitz. 'Their testimony revealed the spell Hitler exercised on them, even when they disagreed with his policies. Keitel mentioned the occasions when he resolved to present objection to Hitler's plans, such as waging a two-front war, but in Hitler's presence was unable to articulate any point of view which differed from that of the Führer' (2008: 62). Hence, there was no moral challenge to policies that were known to be contrary to the customs of war, or even inconsistent with the ultimate interests of the German nation. These orders may have struck individuals as unpleasant and regrettable but unavoidable. And so in the absence of strong moral compunctions and embedded in the rule of law, the magnitude of the violence unleashed on the Jews was totally without restraint, linking the third paradox of genocide—the dark unreported figure of crime—to the first two. In his Afterword to the revised edition of *Ordinary Men*, Browning (1998: 216) suggests that in his earlier edition 'I should have emphasized more explicitly the legitimizing effects of government.' This appears to offset the individual perpetrator's sense of moral compass.

In the next two chapters, I confront two different but related problems: how do events get defined as criminal, versus what circumstances or forces induce people to commit them. The former is sometimes posed as 'the constitutive problem', the latter as 'the causal problem'. Sociologists sometimes treat these as alternative and mutually exclusive issues. In my view, both questions are essential. The constitutive problem asks—what makes this or that activity a case of genocide? The causal problem asks—what events or circumstances brought about that event? Both are valid questions. In the next chapter, I examine the constitutive question as a problem of labelling or genealogy, and in the following chapter, I examine the causal question.

3

Labelling Genocide: The Constitutive Problem

Introduction

In the 20th century a new theory arose in the context of international conflict among some Anglo-American defence analysts. A nation's foes were not merely enemies in war, but their actions became increasingly redefined as those of criminals. A proper response required not only self-defence and military victory, but legal convictions as well. The aggressors were to be dealt with through prosecution for war crimes and other breaches of international law. This 'judicial turn' was foreshadowed by the defeat of Napoleon in 1814, and Europe's impotence to neutralize him. Napoleon had vastly extended French territorial influence as Emperor, and had plunged Europe into a series of wars. After his disastrous invasion of Russia, Napoleon retreated to France and faced several new enemy armies in the 'Battle of Nations' at Leipzig. He was defeated. The triumphant European Allies transferred the defeated ruler to the island of Elba off the coast of Italy with several hundred of his followers where he was made ruler. To the chagrin of the Europeans, he returned surreptitiously to Paris in 1815, and again captured the enormous popular support of the French people. He subsequently invaded Belgium with a new army. After his (second) defeat at Waterloo near Brussels, he was ordered by the British to an extrajudicial penal confinement on the tiny island of St Helena in the remote South Atlantic where he died in 1821. At the time of Napoleon's defeat in 1815, there had never been any contemplation of prosecuting a head of state for 'war crimes,' i.e. violating the sovereignty of neighbouring states through war. It was assumed historically that it was within the rights of the monarch to undertake military contests to settle conflicts with his or her neighbours. The experience of the Great War changed that, particularly when British politicians reflected on their failure to neutralize a defeated Napoleon in the 19th century.

The assassination of Archduke Ferdinand, heir to the throne of Austria-Hungary, in June 1914 by a Bosnian Serb nationalist group prompted the Austrians to initiate hostilities against the Serbs. Serbia's Russian and French allies intervened. In support of the Austrians, German Kaiser Wilhelm II declared war on both states in August. The United Kingdom was drawn into the conflict to protect Belgian neutrality after Germany occupied Belgium to invade France through her northern border. The Turks joined the axis in protection of the Ottoman Empire with its ties to Austria-Hungary. The western front became a stalemate by November 1914, and remained that way for most of the war. Millions of young men were slaughtered on all sides. As the tide began to turn against the Germans, the Allies discussed among themselves the need to bring the outrages of war before an international judicial body to condemn the perpetrators. The British war cabinet reviewed the Napoleon file, and searched for a more constructive post-war solution for defeated belligerents. Anger focused on Wilhelm for his role in initiating armed aggression against neighbouring states. But there was also anger arising from the use of German U-boats against civilian targets such as the British passenger ship *Lusitania* which was sunk in 1915 with the loss of 1 198 lives, including 128 Americans. Evidence suggests that the ship was carrying armaments to England— making the ship a legitimate target of war—despite Britain's use of non-combatants as a shield. In addition, the British were deeply disturbed by reports of inhumane treatment of prisoners of war by both the Germans and the Turks. And finally, there was outrage over the massacres of Armenians in Turkey by the Young Turks under the pretext of war that were reported widely in 1915 and thereafter.

The Europeans had already begun to articulate the *limits to aggression* in the Geneva Conventions of 1864 and 1906 (later modified in 1929, 1949, and 1977), which spelled out the obligations of combatants to wounded soldiers and civilians, shipwrecked sailors, and prisoners of war. In addition, the Hague Conventions attempted to limit the use of specific weapons and techniques of war. The 1899 Convention led to an agreement to prohibit the use of exploding bullets (dum-dums), the use of asphyxiating gases, and the use of weapons projected from balloons. In 1907 the convention renewed only the last of the three limits, but extended the convention to other military procedures. What these conventions signalled was a desire among 'the civilized nations' prior to the Great War to identify a normative framework for armed conflict that would limit its barbarity. The contemplation of a judicial response to the perpetrators of the Great War reflects this normative context. The Geneva and Hague Conventions reflected a growing resistance to the excesses of war, a consensus about how they might be curbed through international conventions—international law—and a replacement of militarism with diplomacy as a key to conflict resolution. When war broke out despite such changes, reinforcement of the rule of law became a priority.

The Case for Liberal Legalism

In *Stay the Hand of Vengeance*, Gary Bass (2000) provides a history of European attempts to address the significance and success of judicial responses to war, war crimes, as well as massacres of minorities under the cover of war, particularly genocide and 'crimes against humanity'. Bass reviews the Napoleonic case alluded to earlier, as well as the attempt after the Great War to undertake prosecutions of war criminals at the German Supreme Court at Leipzig (1920–22), the attempt to prosecute the Young Turks in Constantinople (1919) and Malta (1920), the landmark Nuremberg trials of axis military and political leaders (1945), and the more recent UN ad hoc court at The Hague to prosecute war criminals from conflicts in the former Yugoslavia. This development of a judicial interest in the aftermath of international conflict represents a revolution in the methods of peace making. In the post-war context, it replaces generals and diplomats with judges, and formally marks the aggressor, not as much as a military strategist as a colossal criminal. The irony is that what we refer to as a 'legal system' usually presupposes a sovereign with access to the legitimate use of force, an independent police and judiciary, and a fair and transparent set of laws and procedures—all operating within a secure geographic territory. The international context has virtually none of these except for 'the laws of war' that consist of several international conventions, and a history of customs about limits to violence during politically inspired armed conflict. In place of sovereign or national justice, there is 'victor's justice'. The fly in the ointment is that the *victim* (read *victor*) plays all the roles of prosecutor, judge, and executioner, usually controls the venue of the trials, the types of procedures (adversarial versus inquisitorial), and, most importantly, the names on the docket. While acknowledging this, Bass is unfazed. Despite the claims about 'victor's justice', the proceedings exemplified by the Nuremberg trails were historically defensible, and represented a sea change in international law. A victor's response *could* be wholly realistic and expedient.

Victorious leaders have come up with an impressive array of nonlegalistic fates for their defeated foes. One could shoot them on sight. One could round them up and shoot them en masse. One could have a perfunctory show trial and then shoot them... One could (as both Winston Churchill and Franklin Roosevelt suggested) castrate them (Bass 2000: 7).

This is entirely a function of the political executive. Summary execution of the Nazi leadership was in fact the strategy initially proposed by Churchill and Stalin during the war. Bass argues that, particularly at Nuremberg, liberal legalism triumphed over expediency and realism, and that this signified a long-term shift in the dynamics of international law and accountability. What is his evidence?

First, the tribunals to which he refers, even if initiated by the victors, were preoccupied with the rule of law. They were not show trials. They were based on rules of evidence; the burden of proof was on the prosecution; convictions were not a foregone conclusion; the accused were entitled to a defence, and to challenge the evidence; and punishments were proportional to the magnitude of the crimes. The panel of judges represented an international body of jurists, and the accused were subject to humane treatment in custody. Not only that, the proceedings were open to the public, and had an educational effect by putting the facts of war on the record. In addition, states often pursue legal remedies in ongoing conflicts in order to undermine the political credibility of war criminals among the combatants. He mentions Prosecutor Goldstone's indictment of Serbian President Milošević, Bosnian Serb President Karadžić, and General Mladić at the ICTY. This undermined their political leverage at home—or rather, it was thought it should. In other words, political currency can be deflated or inflated by contexting it within international *legal* norms, and the latter can be valued so highly that they can constrain misconduct independent of the use of force. Finally, he notes that post-war judicial proceedings would hardly have been imaginable if the *Allied leaders* had been in the docket at Nuremberg instead of the Nazis, since the

latter had never developed strong legal norms and procedures independent of political manipulation during their reign from 1933–45.
There may have been show trials but their conclusions, like the
Soviet show trials of 1937–38, would have been a foregone conclusion. Bass's point is that the legitimacy of the entire proceedings
derived from *the rule of law*, and was assumed to transcend all
combatants.

International Law and Hegemonic Power

In his study of *Global Justice*, Kingsley Moghalu (2008) tackles
many of the same issues of legal liberalism raised by Bass. He
focuses more on the contemporary war crimes courts: Milošević,
the ICTY, and the Balkans, Charles Taylor and the Special Court
for Sierra Leone, the Iraqi Special Tribunal for Saddam Hussein,
and the politics surrounding the ICC. He argues, 'liberalism is *not*
the dominant motivation for the establishment or support of international war crimes tribunals by states, liberal or otherwise' (2008:
8). He offers an alternative conceptual framework that he describes
as 'an international society' perspective that is advanced by the
English School. This view is owed to Hedley Bull (2012), and it
posits an international order comprised of 'a society of states' that
have established institutions of cooperation as a result of some
common values, but are not subject to an overall political sovereign, and remain primarily self-interested. This is called *The Anarchical Society*. 'It is this unpredictability of actors in the international
realm, which stems from primordial self-interest, that is referred to
as "anarchy"' (Moghalu 2008: 8). Order exists precariously in the
international realm because independent sovereigns sometimes
find it in their interests to cooperate with other sovereigns, and even
undertake to participate in conventions that limit their sovereignty,
particularly in the area of international conflict, because the benefits outweigh the costs, not because they have succumbed to a philosophical conversion to liberalism. Where Bass sees the emergence
of an international 'community' based on liberal sentiments,
Moghalu sees competing sovereigns with unequal power and
resources jockeying for alliances to advance self-interests, even
where this entails altruistic contributions to the world order, and
subscription to international institutions that otherwise intrude
on their sovereignty, primarily the UN and its various judicial
and human rights organizations.

Michael Mandel (*How America Gets Away with Murder* 2004) addresses the apparent hypocrisy that arises from the immunity enjoyed by superpowers in the face of their breach of international law (assassinating foreign leaders, toppling governments, torturing terrorist suspects, etc.). For Bass this is an uneven development of liberalism, usually relegated to superpower misadventures overseas (Bass 2000: 108). For Moghalu, following the anarchistic view, this is to be expected. In respect of the international anarchic order, 'the exclusion of the crimes of powerful states from the sphere of international justice is one of its features. It is not just an unfortunate sideshow to liberalism's claim to export its values abroad. This is not the exception; it is the rule' (2008: 10). Though the international states may lack a common government, they often subscribe to common interests, and even common values that can influence their international conduct. Indeed, international law may express what competing nations agree on, but at core there is 'an absence of solidarity among the members of the international society' (2008: 11). This absence of solidarity (i.e. community) 'makes the prospect of a world justice that transcends the states' system a distant one indeed'. As a consequence, 'international law is a weaker kind of law than national law … [and] it is for this reason that international law often binds the weak more effectively than the strong' (2008: 12).

Moghalu's perspective does not return us to Bass's nemesis—the idea that nations act solely on the basis of realism and expediency. For Moghalu, a purely realist position ignores the ideological value of the advocacy of liberal values, supporting globalism, transparency, free trade, human rights, accountability, emancipation of women, denunciation of slavery, poverty, piracy, international drug cartels, and advocacy of war crime tribunals—while simultaneously enjoying a hegemony over the international rivals. In Moghalu's world, the rule of law has strategic ideological importance. It is a source of prestige and confers political credibility, particularly in the society of nations, even if it is honoured only when it serves sovereign self-interests. In the search for international prestige there is a certain amount of entrepreneurship in the creation of new norms. For example, advocacy of the abolition of landmines and cluster bombs can be viewed as a further cultivation of international prestige since the objectives are intuitively unassailable. Moghalu would not deny that these are policies worthy of international attention. He would require us to ask whose arms industry are we planning to eliminate, and which countries are we prepared to invade to provide security? If Libya, why not Syria or Tibet? In other words, how do our 'liberal' interventions mirror the balance of international power? How does this apply to the law of genocide? To what extent was it a liberal ideal adopted because of the evolution of liberalism in the West? And to what extent was it a product of international politics?

Lemkin's Genocide

Raphael Lemkin was a Polish jurist with a deep interest in account- ability for politically motivated mass murder. In the 1930s he began to write about the need to create an international agreement to curb 'race murder'. In 1933 he was preoccupied with the case of the Turkish annihilation of the Christian minority of Armenians in 1915. His analysis focused initially on two concepts: *barbarity*— 'the premeditated destruction of national, racial, religious and social collectivities'—and *vandalism*—the 'destruction of works of art and culture, being the expression of the particular genius of these collectivities' (Lemkin 1933). For Lemkin, a people could be obliterated through outright physical annihilation, but their iden- tity could also be erased through a destruction of their culture. Or their historical continuity could be eroded by control of their fertil- ity. His paper was presented at an international criminal law con- ference in Madrid in 1933 arguing that murderers could not stand behind sovereign immunity by killing their own citizens, and that a collective international agreement was required to ensure 'univer- sal repression' of barbarity and vandalism. Ironically, this was the same year in which the Nazis assumed power in Germany. After the invasion of Poland in 1939, Lemkin made his way across Russia to Japan, and ultimately to the US in 1941. Most of his family was killed in the Holocaust. He lobbied tirelessly to convince American intellectuals and politicians that the Nazi conquest of Europe was not only a contest between armies for territory, but was also aimed at the total annihilation of the Jewish people of occupied Europe. Except for those with contacts in the Polish community, no one believed him. Until the Allied liberation of Germany, news of the deportations, the death camps, and the mass executions tended to be treated as unsubstantiated rumours.

In 1944 Lemkin published *Axis Rule in Occupied Europe*. It documented the various decrees and laws that were introduced under Nazi occupation with the express intent of expunging the legal protection of Europe's Jews. It was also the work in which he introduced the term 'genocide' combining the Greek root for 'geno', meaning race or tribe, with the Latin root for 'cide', meaning killing. 'Lemkin had hunted for a term that would describe assaults on all aspects of nationhood—physical, biological, political, social, cultural, economic, and religious' (Power 2002: 40). It was recognized by lexicographers at *Webster's International Dictionary* in 1944, and commended by the publisher of the *Washington Post* as the most appropriate term to describe the millions of murders at Auschwitz-Birkenau in the 1940s. It conveyed the gravity of offences against civilians that had occurred in Turkey in 1915, and in occupied Europe in the 1940s, in a way that mere murder could not. At the Nuremberg trials, there was no crime of genocide per se since it had not been established by any international convention. The charges involved the 'supreme crime' of making aggressive war (crimes against peace), war crimes, and crimes against humanity. The term 'crimes against humanity' had initially appeared in a joint Allied communiqué issued in 1915 condemning the atrocities against the Armenians, and threatening to hold Turkish leaders personally responsible for such outrages. The pretext for making aggressive war the 'supreme' crime was based on an opportunistic reading of the Kellogg-Briand Pact of 1928 (also known as the Pact of Paris). This was a multilateral treaty in which sixty-three nations agreed to repudiate war as an instrument of conflict resolution. However, it was not compelling positive law since it provided no penalty for nations that failed to honour it, or a court with competent jurisdiction to investigate complaints. When US Secretary of State Kellogg presented the treaty to the US Senate, he noted that the signatories did not feel that they had obligated themselves to anything with legal traction. During the Hearings before the Committee on Foreign Relations in December 1928, Senator Claude Swanson questioned Frank Kellogg, who negotiated the treaty about the obligations arising from it:

Senator Swanson: As I understand from what you say, if this multilateral treaty is violated by any other nation, there is no obligation, moral or legal, for us to go to war against any nation violating it?
Secretary Kellogg: That is thoroughly understood. It is understood by our Government; and no other government made any suggestion of any such thing. I knew, from the attitude of many governments, that they would not sign any treaty if there was any moral obligation or any kind of obligation

to go to war. In fact, Canada stated that. The other governments never suggested any such obligation (Yale: Avalon Project 1928).

Moghalu wrote:

the legal principle *nulla poena since lege* (no punishment of a crime without pre-existing law) has been a cardinal rule of criminal law in many countries for several centuries... The Nuremberg Trials violated this fundamental legal norm when they included 'crime against peace'... as one of the crimes for which the Nazis were put on trial (2008: 34).

The Nazi defendants claimed that the pact lacked the force of positive law, a defence that the tribunal rejected (Glueck 1946). Notably, the UN affirmed the Nuremberg Principles and Judgment in a unanimous post hoc vote at the General Assembly in 1946. And the Convention on the Prevention and Punishment of Genocide was adopted by the United Nations General Assembly in 1948. Most parties ratified the convention within the year. The US did not ratify it until 1986 (Chalk and Jonassohn 1990: 44). Although the passage of the law was greeted as a landmark in international law, no genocide charges were to be laid before the UN tribunals for Rwanda and the former Yugoslavia until the mid-1990s. If there was a liberal shift in international jurisprudence of the sort identified by Bass and symbolized by the Nuremberg trials, it seems to have gone dormant for four-and-a-half decades throughout the Cold War.

The Genealogy of Genocide

In bringing a legal definition before the member states of the UN, diplomats negotiated the protected heads covered by the treaty. The Soviet Union had already undertaken systematic starvation of the Ukraine in 1932–33, resulting in the extermination of 2 million peasant farmers, the Kulaks (Gutman, Rieff, and Dworkin 2007). The convention was negotiated by those with blood on their hands to exclude such atrocities. Nationality, ethnicality, race, and religion were specifically protected areas, but mass extermination on the basis of political affiliation, social class, or gender did not enjoy protection (see Nersessian 2010). The rationale for this focus was that the protected categories are ones into which individuals are born, which are not chosen, and hence for which they are not responsible, whereas class, profession, and/or political party are more transitory forms of identity. This of course does not explain the exclusion of gender (Jones 2010a: 325ff).

The convention also entailed an obligation on the part of signatories to prevent the crime once identified. What became accepted as 'genocide', which Churchill had deemed during the Second World War as 'a crime without a name', became fixed, however arbitrarily, through the convention. Genocide brought a precision to the definition of the crime previously absent, but it lacked the generality of previous common sense usages that recognized something more than mere murder that was captured by such terms as 'mass murder', 'extermination', or 'atrocities'. In *The Complete Black Book of Russian Jewry* (2002) written during the Second World War, Russian journalists Ilya Ehrenburg and Vasily Grossman referred to the Nazi policy against Russians and Jews as 'annihilation'. This included the mass murder of civilians due to race (Jews) and/or political status (soviet commissars), the calculated murder of Russian POWs, peasants killed in reprisal murders, and individuals killed capriciously for defying Nazi authority. The legal concept of 'genocide' that emerged from the record of Nazi atrocities, and the UN Convention designed to bring such acts before international justice, captured only a subset of the appalling cases of annihilation that had marked prior human history. Certainly, other heinous activities are captured by different laws established for UN courts such as the proscription against crimes against humanity and war crimes (and all the violations by which they can be established, such as slavery, murder, rape, kidnapping, etc.), but the terms of reference of these crimes do not create a positive duty to prevent them. While there is a temptation to view genocide as more serious than crimes against humanity or war crimes (Hagan, Rymond-Richmond, and Parker, 2005), this view is weakened by the arbitrary limits placed on which types of annihilation are proscribed by treaty, and by the overlap in such crimes as described by Akhavan in the last chapter.

The issue of genealogy is highlighted by a recent analysis of the 'cosmopolitan' nature of the new international courts designed to deal with genocide, crimes against humanity, and war crimes. David Hirsch (2003) makes the case that the Genocide Convention represents the appearance of cosmopolitan law. The concept of 'cosmopolitan law' was advanced by Kant in his *Cosmopolitan Theory of Right and Peace* (Höffe 2006). Kant envisioned the rise of international forms of justice that transcended sovereign states, and flourished as a result of international social progress. Hirsch argues that in the International Criminal Tribunal for Rwanda (ICTR) and the

ICTY cosmopolitan law 'is coming into being' (2003: 159). For Hirsch 'the logic of cosmopolitan law is to tie the idea of universal human rights to a legal structure that can give those rights some concrete reality independently of the state' (2003: 11). 'In cosmopolitan criminal law it is possible for universal values to find a worldly existence that is not wholly subverted by power and interest' (2003: 155). Hirsch holds further that the legal process can produce 'authoritative narratives of the crimes' that may become the foundation for 'a cosmopolitan social memory' that will destroy the ideologies behind deadly political violence.

The Kantian perspective advocated by Hirsch has been the subject of extended criticism by both Nietzsche (1967) and Foucault (1979). Both reject the enlightenment idea that societies are on a trajectory of modernization marked by greater freedom through knowledge of the truth. In particular, Foucault's 'method' of genealogy is designed to identify the contingent, and often contradictory, sources of what passes for truth, and particularly, the role of power in conveying the status of truth on legal discourses. Hirsch's analysis, while far from being naïve, is contradictory in places. On the one hand, he acknowledges, 'the narratives produced by cosmopolitan courts are not, in some absolute sense, "the truth". But neither do they claim to be. They claim to be "judgments"' (2003: 146). Nonetheless he claims that the narratives created by the cosmopolitan judgments can establish 'a true picture of the events under investigation' (2003: 141). In my view, the case should be made that the cosmopolitan memories created by these courts are in part amnesia since they omit the conditions under which the courts were created, and funded, and the narrow construction of the protected heads.

Consider atrocities that the convention expressly excludes. In the introduction to *The Black Book of Communism*, Stéphane Courtois et al (1999: 8) quote the order from one of the first leaders of the Soviet political police on 1 November 1918: 'We don't make war on any people in particular. We are exterminating the bourgeoisie as a class. In your investigations don't look for documents and pieces of evidence about what the defendant has done...The first question you should ask him is what class he comes from.' This policy led to 'the execution of tens of thousands of hostages and prisoners without trial, and the murder of hundreds of thousands of rebellious workers and peasants from 1918 to 1922' (1999: 9). Untold millions were subsequently detained for forced labour in the gulag archipelago, an institution that was created in the first months of soviet communism, and which remained in place until 1956, and was, by all accounts, calculated to bring about the physical destruction of the bourgeoisie, in whole or in part, through utter disregard of human life (Solzhenitsyn 1985). The group was a class or political group, not a national, racial, or religious group. 'Vladimir Bukovsky...cried out in protest in *Reckoning with Moscow*, demanding the establishment of a new Nuremberg tribunal to judge the criminal activities of the Communist regime' (Courtois et al 1999: 27). Courtois estimates the murders and untimely deaths during the rule of soviet communism at 20 000 000. He puts the estimates of those killed in Mao's rise to power and rule over China at 65 000 000 including some 38 000 000 who died of starvation in 1959–61 as a result of collectivization of peasant agriculture, and export of the harvests to raise hard currency. Margolin (1999: 487ff) described this as the 'greatest famine in history'. Harvest quotas were set insanely high. The irrigation schemes designed to boost harvests were ineffective. Cannibalism became widespread, and desperate people tried to survive on grass and tree bark. Mao refused international help for ideological reasons, and was prepared to sacrifice 'half of China' to raise the funds for his weapons programme (Chang and Halliday 2005: 426ff). The harvests recovered when the peasants were permitted to return to traditional forms of agriculture. Both China and the Soviet Union initiated dictatorships that led to far higher losses of human life than anything attributed to Hitler, but in neither case is there any remedy under the Genocide Convention. Whole populations were decimated with impunity by political elites.

Genocide: The *Mea Culpa* Convention

A second point that should be made is that the convention appears to have been underutilized. Note that the UN Convention 'does not provide for the exercise of universal jurisdiction over the crime of genocide' (Moghalu 2008: 85). In other words, it cannot be tried anywhere by any national court (as can piracy). It can be tried in the territory where the act occurred, or in an international tribunal created by the contracting parties, and usually financed by them. Chalk and Jonassohn (1990) reviewed several cases that were actionable under the convention, but were largely ignored by the international community. Not all the cases reflect the protected heads, and are similar to the political cases we have just reviewed. But they raise grave questions about the utility, or rather the futility, of the convention. The first case involves the retaliation of the Indonesian army against members of the Indonesian Communist Party (PKI) after a failed coup in 1965. The army initiated the killings against unarmed PKI cadres and party members, and subsequently recruited civilian groups to follow suit. Chalk and Jonassohn estimate that the numbers killed throughout the archipelago was a staggering 500 000, and another 500 000 arrested within a six-month period. No US or UN intervention. No prosecutions in Indonesia. In Burundi, in 1972, the Tutsi army exterminated an estimated 200 000 Hutus, claiming that it was responding to a coup designed to overthrow the Tutsi-led government. The army targeted well-educated Hutus, persons of some wealth, and those employed in the civil service, wiping out fully half of the Hutu teachers, and other professionals in a period of months. 'The U.S. government never publicly rebuked the Burundi government' (1990: 391). Only Belgian Premier, Gaston Eyskens, condemned the massacres as 'veritable genocide'. However, no one was ever called to account, and the UN failed to act (Lemarchand 1994).

The third case was the massacre of citizens in Bangladesh in 1971. 'Between one million and three million were killed' by the Pakistani army before the latter was defeated by the Indian Army (Chalk and Jonassohn 1990: 396). Two million people were made homeless, and 10 million became refugees. International reaction was diverse. 'It ranged from intervention by India to the refusal by the United Nations to even discuss the case' (1990: 397). Chalk and Jonassohn's fourth case was the Cambodian genocide of 1975–79 in which 1.7 million people were murdered by the Khmer Rouge after Pol Pot's occupation of Phnom Penh. Most of the targets of the massacres were Cambodian nationals. A joint national-UN tribunal was created at the Extraordinary Chambers for the Courts of Cambodia thirty years after the defeat of the Khmer Rouge.

The last case was the invasion of East Timor in 1975 by Indonesia. The Indonesians supported a small pro-Indonesian political party that opposed the main parties seeking political independence from Portugal. The Indonesians conducted a campaign of murder and terror against the indigenous people, including massacres of citizens and carpet-bombing of villages and towns to exterminate the armed opposition to the invasion. There was a policy of starvation pursued to neutralize opposition to the forced annexation of the country. Kierman (2007: 578) estimates that these policies led to the death of over one-fifth of the population. In addition, the Indonesians sponsored a transmigration programme to replace the indigenous people with immigrants from Java and Bali. In 1999 the rebels declared independence, and the nation's autonomy was recognized in 2002. The UN repeatedly passed motions to criticize the illegal Indonesian occupation of the country, but these actions were always blunted by Indonesia's ally in the Security Council, the US.

In 2011 Rene Lemarchand updated Chalk and Jonassohn's list in a book called *Forgotten Genocides* that added several more contemporary and historical cases. What all these cases have in common is the wholesale massacres of civilians by national or colonial armies and militias. Most post-dated the Genocide Convention, but none attracted a speedy judicial remedy as provided for in the UN Convention—except for Cambodia after a delay of three decades (and not always for genocide), and a dysfunctional court in Dili, East Timor that was shut down prematurely. As indicated earlier, the first tribunals to apply the convention were created to deal with the genocides in the former Yugoslavia and Rwanda. There are good reasons to believe that the tribunals were an attempt to repair the damage to the UN's credibility, and the political failure of the major Western players—the US, France, Britain, and Belgium—to honour their obligations under the convention. According to Carla Del Ponte 'it was a diplomatic *mea culpa*, an act of contrition by the world's major powers to amend for their gross failure to prevent or halt the massacres' (2008: 69). Cruvellier comes to a similar conclusion. 'The ICTR was created by powers that failed...Thus, it had to render a justice in their image. It had to be a court of remorse' (2010: 167).

In forty-five years following the convention, the terms of reference appeared to apply only rarely. This was frequently because the victims were not always within the protected categories, a fact that reflects the political limitations of the convention. There may be another conceptual problem at the heart of the convention. This is suggested in the controversy over Darfur. In *Darfur: The Ambiguous Genocide*, Prunier (2005) labels Darfur as the 'first genocide of the twenty-first century', a view shared with Totten and Markusen (2006), and Hagan and Rymond-Richmond (2009). For Mamdani (2007, 2009), and de Waal (2004), the naming of genocide was more problematic.

Naming Genocide: The Darfur Debate

Mamdani (2007, 2009) argues that Western coverage of the events in Darfur has been simplistic and moralistic. Mamdani notes that the estimates of casualties in the hundreds of thousands reported in Nicholas Kristof stories in the *New York Times* from Darfur fluctuated widely from 2004 to 2006. The stories were cast as 'bad' Arabs killing and raping 'good' Africans. In 2004 the US government, following an alert from the Washington Holocaust Memorial Museum, declared the violence in Sudan as genocide. However, the UN investigation in January 2005 failed to come to that conclusion. That the Sudanese government inflicted violence deliberately and indiscriminately on civilians was very evident, but this did not constitute evidence of a plan to commit genocide. As Mamdani points out, the main fact missing in Western reports was that Darfur was undergoing an insurrection, and the Sudanese government was using the Janjawiid tribesmen to suppress the insurrection. The UN report found 'that many Arabs in Darfur are opposed to the Janjawiid, and some Arabs are fighting with the rebels...at the same time, many non-Arabs are supporting the government and serving in its army' (UN 2005). The conception that one ethnic or racial group was implementing a scheme to annihilate another distinct group—and were doing so to eliminate the group *as such*—takes on a different significance when viewed from Mamdani's counterinsurgency perspective. There may have been evidence of war crimes and crimes against humanity, but not genocide, and hence no treaty obligation to intervene.

In July 2008 the prosecutor of the ICC issued a warrant for the arrest of the president of Sudan, Omar al-Bashir for crimes against humanity and other war crimes. The warrant claimed that al-Bashir polarized Darfur into Arab and Black factions, turned the 2003–05 insurgency into a pretext for removing the Black tribes from their lands, and subjected survivors to slow death from malnutrition, rape, and torture in the camps for the internally displaced. According to Mamdani, 'none of these allegations can bear historical scrutiny' (2009: 271). The ICC prosecutor, Moreno-Ocampo, initially shared the UN conclusion that the events in Darfur did not amount to genocide, but reversed his position, and indicted al-Bashir for genocide in 2010.

Hagan and Rymond-Richmond (2009) and Hagan and Kaiser (2011) defined the events in Darfur beginning in 2003 as genocide.

Their data were based on the US State Department's survey of over 1 100 respondents displaced from homes in Darfur to refugee camps in Chad. Survivors reported killing of neighbours and family members, theft of livestock, bombing and burning of villages, and widespread sexual violence that was frequently accompanied by racial or ethnic slurs, suggesting intent to remove a protected group. Hagan and Kaiser raised another aspect of the conflict. When most accounts of genocide focus on extermination of the group's members, the actions of the Janjawiid amount to genocide by 'inflicting on the group conditions of life calculated to bring about its physical destruction', to whit: by destroying their wells and agriculture, by physically displacing them off traditional lands, and by undermining their group life. The numbers of refugees is estimated at two to three million, many of them exiled internally in Darfur. However, the special intent would have to demonstrate that the groups being removed were targeted *because* of their ethnicity, not because of conflicts between farmers and pastoralists over land use, conflicts over access to petroleum wealth, or competition for political dominance. In an exchange in the *British Journal of Sociology*, Tim Allen (2011: 35) responded that this approach lowered the bar for genocide by equating it with forced displacement. Use of the g word escalates the opprobrium that the ICC wants to attach to Sudan's bellicose behaviour. Charging suspects with genocide is like awarding them the Nobel Prize for evil. The charge is easier laid than proven. Another problem is that the charge makes a negotiated settlement of the insurrection more difficult by labelling one of the parties a *génocidaire*, and ignoring the massacres perpetrated by the insurgents. This case highlights the precariousness with which extremely violent events are framed as genocide, particularly when they arise in association with war and civil war (Shaw 2003).

The Politics of Genocide: A Typology

In this chapter, we have raised the issue of the genealogy of genocide. This concept forces us to consider the legal foundations of genocide definition and recognition, and the political contexts in which such claims appear. Claims of genocide activate obligations on members of the 1948 Convention to prevent and punish it. The result is a politics of claims making, claims recognition, and claims denial. Some atrocities escape labelling. Others attract it. But the distinction between these alternative assessments may have more to do with geopolitics than actual victimization, a fact that might reflect the process of conventionalization described earlier. This situation was explored by Herman and Peterson (2010a, 2010b) in an assessment of the ideological treatment of atrocities by US political elites and the mainstream Western media. They distinguished between four kinds of genocides based on the moral worthiness of the victims, and the client status of the perpetrators in US foreign policy. First are those that are 'constructive' in the view of the elites. The leading illustration is the massive fatalities of Iraqi children as a result of sanctions against Saddam Hussein following the first Gulf War. Some half a million Iraqi children died from starvation and disease created by the economic isolation of Iraq. US Ambassador Madeline Albright reported, 'the price was worth it' (Herman and Peterson 2010a: 32). Obviously, this situation, though regrettable, would not meet the *actus reus* of genocide by a stretch, even if it was atrocious.

The second category included the 'nefarious genocides' in Rwanda (1994) and Srebrenica (1995) that resulted in near universal condemnation. These events met both the *actus reus* and *mens rea* criteria at the ad hoc tribunals in Arusha and The Hague, but Herman and Peterson argue that neither was really genocide, and that perception as nefarious mass murder resulted from political agendas in the alleged manufacture of news. The third category included 'benign bloodbaths' where the victims got what they deserved, such as the massacre of the exiled Palestinians in Sabra and Shatila in 1982 during the Israeli invasion of Lebanon. And finally, Herman and Peterson consider 'mythical bloodbaths', atrocities that were staged for geopolitical advantage. They discuss the alleged Serbian massacre of Kosovars in Racak in 1999, which provided the pretext for NATO's attack on Serbia to end aggression against the Kosovars.

Herman and Peterson's work would be a significant contribution to genealogical studies of genocide, except for their own political biases. Gerald Caplan, a well-known Africanist (2008), pointed out that their analyses of the Bosnian and Rwandan genocides were simply inconsistent with accepted fact, and amounted to genocide denial. Herman and Peterson expressed considerable scepticism about whether the Bosnians killed after the fall of Srebrenica were actually executed, or died in military conflicts with the Serbs. Also, they suggested that the main victims of the Rwandan genocide in 1994 were members of the Hutu majority, and that Paul Kagame's defeat of the Hutu-led national army was part of a US military plot to displace the French influence in the Great Lakes region. They claimed, 'in reality, Rwanda's Paul Kagame is one of the greatest mass murderers of our time' (2010a: 68). Caplan (2010) challenges this historical revisionism at length (also see Jones 2010b). There is some controversy about the extent of the Srebrenica killings attached to questions about the reliability of one of the chief witnesses, Dražen Erdemović (Civikov 2010). Erdemović claimed to have participated in the mass execution of 1 200 Bosnians at the Branjevo farm in a five-hour period with a squad of seven other shooters. Civikov, who observed Erdemović's testimony in court, casts doubt on whether so many could have been killed in the manner that he describes, and suggests that these murders were probably better described as a war crime, reprisal killings for Bosnian incursions into Serb villages, as well as regular casualties from conflict. He also argues that the recovered human remains fell far short of expectations based on claims of the number of fatalities. Erdemović was sentenced to five years for his part in this massacre. None of the seven co-conspirators was subpoenaed to corroborate his evidence.

Even if we reject Herman and Peterson's lead, there is nonetheless some merit in developing a typology of genocide in the context of genealogical analysis. From a criminological perspective the key issue is the tension between the objective nature of the phenomenon—whether the elements of genocide are actually present or evident in the event—versus whether the event was labelled as genocide or not (Becker 1963). This suggests a typology that is useful in capturing the range of reactions to atrocities, and whether they are actionable under the 1948 Convention. This typology highlights the issue of contested statuses for genocide, including the possibility of deliberately false claims, mistaken claims, genocide denial, genocides that escaped detection or were forgotten (Chang 1997), and what Karganović et al (2011) describe as 'virtual genocide'.

The obvious categories in Table 3.1 are events that *are* genocides and *are seen to be* genocides or, alternatively, events that are not genocidal and not labelled as genocides. The more interesting cases are those where the perception and the reality are inconsistent. Earlier I referred to the example of the staged massacres of civilians by the KLM in Racak. That event probably does not actually qualify as genocide, even if it had occurred as initially reported, since there is no evidence of specific intent to eliminate a protected group as

Table 3.1 Genocide and genocide perception

		FACTS	
		a. Elements of genocide are present	b. Elements of genocide are not present
PERCEPTIONS	a. Event is labelled as genocide	• **True** genocide: Holocaust of European Jews 1941–45 Murder of Turkish Armenians and Turkish Greeks in 1915	• **False claims** of genocide: KLM staging of Rack assassinations in Kosovo • **Mistaken/contested** claims of genocide: Case of Herero extermination in SW German Africa (Poewe 1985)
	b. Event is *not* labelled as genocide	• **Genocides denied:** Turkish denial of Armenian massacres in 1915 • **Genocides unacknowledged:** Guatemalan massacres of Mayan peasants Massacres of Hutus in Burundi in 1972 Destruction of conditions of Native life through residential school Japanese mass murders and rape in occupied Nanking 1938 Ukrainian famine of 1932 Irish famine of 1845–49	• **Non-genocides:** War crimes Individual homicides Collateral damage in war

such. Murders of civilians occurred with stunning regularity throughout the Balkans during the civil wars. False claims differ from contested claims. Chalk and Jonassohn (1990: 230ff) describe the genocide against the Hereros of German South West Africa based on Horst Drechsler's history of the native African struggle against German imperialism. The revolt of the Hereros lasted from 1904 to 1907. The German response was led by General Lothar von Trotha who vowed to destroy the rebellion by shedding rivers of blood, and forcing the entire Herero population into the Ome-heke desert, refusing the surrender of anyone, including women and children. In his 'extermination order' of 2 October 1904, von Trotha vowed to shoot every remaining member of the race. Gewald (1999) referred to this as a 'genocidal war', a view consistent with Drechsler's interpretation. Karla Poewe (1985) conducted field-work in Namibia among the Hereros, and gathered information passed from generation to generation about the conflict. She concluded that they suffered tremendously, but that the German forces were incapable of conducting a genocide given their limited resources, and that the claims of genocide were based on the German rhetoric at the time, not on what they could accomplish. Rudolf (2010) makes a similar argument.

This is not the same as the genocide denial associated with Turks and the mass exterminations of Christians during the First World War, including the Armenians, as well as Turkish Greeks. Genocide denial is also different from genocide that has escaped definition. There has been a long-standing neo-Nazi denial of the Holocaust which has attracted legal consequences (Lipstadt 1993; Hennebel and Hochmann 2011), couched as historical 'revisionism', something no serious scholar acknowledges (Wistrich 2012). Wright (2000, 2005) makes the case for the secret state destruction of the Mayans in Guatemala, and Chiapis, Mexico. The Ukrainian famine of 1932 was brought about expressly by soviet state policies designed to destroy the Kulaks as a class, and constituted a genocide not recognized as such at the time. Similar arguments have been made regarding the Irish Famine of 1848. While it was brought about by the potato blight, the only place where it led to the starvation of a million people and the involuntary emigration of two million more was Ireland, where British landowners extracted all the other crops from Ireland under armed escort. Francis Boyle (2012), a well-known American human rights lawyer, has suggested that leading British politicians openly exhibited hatred of the Irish, and sought their removal because of deep religious animosity. This is a view shared by historian Tim Coogan (2012; The Economist 2012). A similar contentious case is that of the Canadian residential schools that were aimed at eradicating native cultures and language, and forcing the assimilation of Canadian first nations, a policy that inadvertently resulted in widespread dysfunctional behaviour among survivors. While the government may not have meant this outcome, motive is not intent. Bryce (1922) seems to think that there were some senior civil servants who were not uncomfortable with the thinning of the Native population because they *were* savages. Again, whether this fits the UN's definition of genocide is a matter of opinion. One of the implications of the typology is that it shows how attachment of the term, 'genocide' to a crime heightens its social significance, and may be more indicative of the political objectives of the claim-makers, than of the underlying events they seek to describe.

Conclusion

There is an interesting parallel between the politics of prosecutions at Nuremberg and the politics of contemporary global justice. The defendants at Nuremberg were deeply involved in acts of criminal aggression, but they were not the only ones who acted contrary to the laws and customs of war. The Allied bombing campaign led by 'Bomber Harris' specifically selected civilian targets with enormous quantities of incendiaries to kill the German civilian population, and to break their will to fight. The Americans pursued a similar programme of destruction of Japanese cities. None of this conduct resulted in formal charges or administrative discipline (Grayling 2006). Indian jurist Radhabinod Pal dismissed the prosecutions in Tokyo as 'victor's justice'. For Pal, the prosecutions had no foundation in international law or convention, and the activities of the Allied war efforts vis-à-vis non-combatants were as remarkably indifferent to civilian injury as that of Imperial Japan. If we look at the contemporary UN tribunals, we notice a similar asymmetry. Although the terms of reference of the ICTR covers all war crimes in Rwanda committed in 1994, there have been virtually no prosecutions of RPF Tutsis at the ICTR who engaged in widespread reprisal murders of thousands of civilians when they occupied Rwanda. Parenthetically, a 1999 trial of four RPF officers in Rwandan criminal courts for the massacres of civilians at Kabgayi resulted in the acquittal of a general and a major, and guilty pleas of two captains who were sentenced to five-year terms of imprisonment (Cruvellier 2010: 162). Michael Mandel's brief to Prosecutor Louise Arbour argued that the prosecution of Milošević for militarist aggression in Kosovo seemed to ignore the culpability of NATO leaders whose aircraft attacked civilian Serbian targets during the same war—and undertook crimes against peace by initiating aggression without Chapter VII support of the UN, thereby breaching international law. Although Arbour's successor, Carla Del Ponte, indicated that the case would be investigated, she dropped it when the US, a major diplomatic backer of the Hague court, objected.

This obviously takes us back to the competing ways of understanding 'the judicial turn in peace-making' with which this chapter began, and the contrasting perspectives of liberal legalism in Bass and political anarchy in Moghalu and Bull. Roscoe Pound, the great American jurist, argued that law in common law societies is structured around four ideals: politicality, uniformity, specificity, and penal sanction. The evidence suggests that there is a profound conflict between a system of justice that has politically responsive dimensions, and a system that applies equally and uniformly to all those suspected of breaching the law. Kant's cosmopolitan law would appear to be possible only as the world evolves in ways that reduce the power disparities between those who control and are controlled by the international order. If the judicial turn in post-conflict societies is to evolve fruitfully, it must move from the politics of victor's justice to what Mamdani refers to as survivor's justice (i.e. peace making and the rehabilitation of communities).

4

Explaining Crime and Genocide: The Control Perspective

Genocide, Atrocities, and the Control Perspective

This chapter is based largely on the control perspective pioneered by Norbert Elias. In criminology, control theories, generally speaking, have been limited to the explanation of ordinary street crimes. Nonetheless, the case can be made that self-control has a much broader application, and is at the very roots of Western civilization. Within contemporary criminology, control theory is most associated with the work of Travis Hirschi. His *Causes of Delinquency* (1969) elaborated the idea that strong social bonds between adolescents and their parents and teachers minimize the vulnerability of adolescents to the attractions of crime and delinquency. There is strong evidence that effective intergenerational bonds are critical for the development of self-control (Gottfredson and Hirschi 1990; Hirschi 2004; Hirschi and Gottfredson 2008; Lehrer 2009), and are inversely related to participation in crime and delinquency (Glueck and Glueck 1950; Loeber and Stouthamer-Loeber 1986; Sampson and Laub 1993; Moffitt 1993).

The application of control theories in the area of delinquency created the impression that self-control was a trait more or less divorced from the social context. Levels of self-control are not only subject to individual variations, but may be collective, and this may explain long-term trends in violence including genocide. The foundations for these historical arguments are derived from the work of Norbert Elias in *The Civilizing Process* (1939; 2000) and *The Germans* (1989; 1996). The first volume traces the curtailment of aggression from feudalism through to the modern absolutist states in Europe, and the emergence of the legitimate use of force as the sole prerogative of the absolute sovereign. The second volume deals with the circumstances in Germany that contributed to the reversal of the civilizing process that laid down the conditions for the

Holocaust in one of the most cultivated nations of Europe. Elias complements contemporary control perspectives by placing individual differences in self-control into larger social and historical contexts.

Self-Control in Historical Perspective: The Norbert Elias Thesis

The Civilizing Process is a study of the changes in the political structure of Western European countries (primarily Germany, France, and Britain) as well as changes in the emotional lives of their citizens. It appeared initially in 1939 in two volumes: *The History of Manners* and *State Formation and Civilization*. Although the publication was marginalized by the war, by the 1980s it was recognized as a classic contribution to social theory. Elias's account moves from a time before the nations were recognized as distinct countries with determined borders and separate languages. The changes are analysed as a *process* of 'civilizing', i.e. making people civil or polite. In Elias's sociology, there is no assumption that the Western version of *civilization* is superior to other forms of social and emotional change in different parts of the world. There is no assumption of a universal process of immanent development to which humans and their social formations are predisposed. There is also no assumption in Elias's work that the long-term changes in social structure were necessarily planned by specific parties to bring about the shifts he records. Both the macro-sociological changes and the emotional adaptations occurred because of changes in population density, the rising complexity of the division of labour, and the evolution of competition within and between the classes.

At the individual level, the changes that Elias reports are in the area of subjectivity: how persons react to one another emotionally. Elias argues that over the last 800 years, Europeans became more governed by 'impulse control'. As the social structure changed, Europeans became more vulnerable to feelings of shame, repugnance, and disgust to curb vile behaviour, and more inclined to display feelings of delicacy, sensitivity, and courtesy. He calls these 'psychogenetic changes'. At the collective level, the changes that Elias reports are in the area of the evolution of the 'absolute state' from feudalism to the renaissance and thereafter, and the consolidation of 'power figurations' under mechanisms that included the monarch's eventual monopolization of the right to use force and the right to collect taxes. These are 'sociogenetic changes'. Psycho-genetic changes and sociogenetic changes co-evolve. As the warri-ors and knights were absorbed into the courts of the feudal lords, their predisposition for spontaneity and violence became increas-ingly inhibited. The social organization of court life put a premium on diplomacy and negotiation. Courtly societies cultivated 'courte-ous' behaviour. *Courtesy* was superseded by general *civility*, which became the hallmark of Western *civilization*. In the case of psycho-genetic changes, these are attributed, as in Hirschi's control theory, to 'conditioning' primarily by parents who are reacting to changes in the division of labour.

The socially patterned constellation of habits and impulses of the parents gives rise to a constellation of habits and impulses in the children ... Behav-iour and words associated by the parents with shame and repugnance are very soon associated in the same way by the children, through the parents' expression of displeasure ... in this way the social standard of shame and repugnance is gradually reproduced in the children (Elias 2000: 159).

The changes in Western subjectivity followed profound changes in objective social structures. These sociogenetic changes included the monopolization of territories by powerful clans and alliances, the eventual demise of open land in Europe, the replacement of barter by money, increased social and economic differentiation with the rise of towns, and the development of export and international trade.

For Elias, the course and direction of conduct towards civiliza-tion was and is not guaranteed, nor was it uniform. Many factors can result in a reversion to 'barbarism'. Also, what is defined as 'civilization' was not uniformly shared among the leading Euro-pean states. In the 18th and 19th centuries, German intellectuals viewed the French model of courtly civility with contempt. It valor-ized sycophantic behaviour, and occluded the sense of inherent worth and virtue captured by the concept of 'Kultur'. Elias points out that the German aristocratic courts were small and dispersed, unlike the court at Versailles. The German aristocracy was land-rich, pre-industrial, and cash-poor. There was little prospect of social advancement in the German courts for the sons of tradesmen and petty manufacturers, and hence little value attached to civility as such. By contrast, in France the monarchy was no barrier to social advancement of the bourgeoisie. There was an intense inter-action between the bourgeoisie and the ruling elite, and there were numerous opportunities for social advancement by a partial abatement of class differences through the adoption of court culture.

The European pursuit of civility occurred in two phases. The first affected the emerging aristocratic classes as power struggles within the medieval warrior classes resulted in a feudal hierarchy. The second resulted in an appropriation of the same lessons of pacification to the entire population. At the core of his evidence is the work of Desiderius Erasmus, and his explicit mission to teach manners. Erasmus published *On Civility in Boys* in 1530. It underwent 130 editions, and enjoyed numerous translations and many imitators over the following 200 years. It was dedicated to a nobleman's son and focused on 'outward bodily propriety'. There was phenomenal interest in the book throughout Europe. Its advice was fairly modest— there should be no snot on the nostrils; a well-laid table includes a goblet, a well-cleaned knife on the right and bread on the left; do not wolf down food; do not share food from your own mouth; do not re-dip bread into the communal sauce bowl after eating it, etc. What is the significance of this? For Elias, *On Civility* signals a change in moral standards, and an upsurge in impulse control. The cultivated behaviour associated with the aristocratic courts was exported to the masses throughout Europe.

There had been 'etiquette books' in the medieval period. Many books in the 12th and 13th centuries were written in vernacular languages for courtiers in the emerging feudal courts of the warring nobilities and medieval knights. Like the books of the 16th century, they gave specific advice on how to behave well in courtly settings. According to Elias, they had a more naïve or simplistic tone—do not touch your nose or ears at table; do not put your elbows on the table; show a cheerful countenance; do not talk too much, etc. What is it that marked off the social world that Erasmus is advocating from the medieval world of manners? The world of Erasmus is more nuanced: it is not merely a book of commands, but a way of presenting the self that is more sensitive to the effects on others.

[T]he increased tendency of persons to observe themselves and others is one sign of how the whole question of behaviour was now taking on a different character: people molded themselves and others more deliberately than in the Middle Ages...People, forced to live with one another in a new way, became more sensitive to the impulses of others (Elias 2000: 68–9).

Elias surveys etiquette sources from the early feudal period to the late 17th century. The sources cover not only such public behaviours involving bodily functions, but behaviour in the bedroom, use of cutlery at meals, sexual attitudes about prostitution and promiscuity, and changes in aggressiveness. When Elias compares the sources over time, the evidence suggests that social control of impropriety was increasingly replaced by self-control or self-censorship. For example, the medieval guides indicated that spitting in the presence of 'people of rank' was permitted if the person concealed the spit with his foot. Later guides suppressed the impulse entirely, suggesting that spitting was itself 'quite unnecessary'. Impulse control was not limited to this. Medieval entertainment extended to public executions, torture, and animal cruelty. The medieval period that Elias paints was marked by a spontaneity that would become inappropriate in bourgeois or town society. People 'vented' emotions openly, both amicable and hostile.

A moment ago they were joking, now they mock each other, one word leads to another, and suddenly from the midst of laughter they find themselves in the fiercest feud. Much of what appears contradictory to us—the intensity of their piety, the violence of their fear of hell, their guilt feelings, their penitence, the immense outburst of joy and gaiety, the sudden flaring and the uncontrollable force of their hatred and belligerence—all these, like the rapid changes in mood, are symptoms of one and the same structuring of the emotional life (2000: 168).

This form of emotional spontaneity was curbed as a greater premium was placed on impulse suppression, and as the 'right' to use force to resolve conflicts migrated from individuals to absolute monarchs and their delegates. These psychogenetic changes in emotions became increasingly required as the division of labour changed dramatically, and as communities of individuals became increasingly interdependent, competitive, and cosmopolitan. The implications of the Elias thesis are profound. The changing levels of social control over time became second nature, *habitus* (Garland 1990: 222). By implication, the spontaneous actor of the feudal warrior class was not acting pathologically when he entered conflict on the smallest pretext. In the absence of the state, the ability to explode emotionally on the slightest challenge may have been a key to self-preservation in a world where there was a strong likelihood of being attacked without warning through the course of daily life. Capitalism and international sea trade fostered a longer-term horizon, and a greater ability to delay gratification. Under these conditions, a short fuse, emotionally speaking, was retired from the emotional repertoire of the new classes. Europeans were learning to manage the long-term consequences of their actions.

There is compelling evidence that patterns of homicide changed significantly in England and Europe during the period studied by Elias. Research in historical criminology suggests that the feudal period was far more violent than those that followed. Estimates of homicide in England by Ted Gurr (1981) based on court records and other sources from 1200 to 1900 suggested that the rate of homicide declined significantly during this period. Manuel Eisner (2003: 95) came to the same conclusion based on 390 estimates of homicide in Europe during the same period. James Q. Wilson (1985: 229–223) made a comparable argument for the decline in homicide in America. Evidence suggests that social investments in 'character', i.e. sobriety, fidelity, and self-reliance reduced homicides throughout the 19th century and into the middle of the 20th century. Elias's thesis on the civilizing process is a common element in the explanation for the decline in violence in all three sources. Pinker (2011) provides a thorough overview of these trends.

The Germans (1989)

The civilizing process helps to explain the decline in crime, not its resurgence. Exactly fifty years after *The Civilizing Process*, a year before his own death, Elias published *The Germans*, an account of the Holocaust. In this work he dealt explicitly with the reversal of the longer-term trajectory towards self-control, and the rise of civilization laid out in the first book. *The Germans* is a key text for any student of genocide because it juxtaposes the case made for the development of self-control in Western civilization with the incivility found at the heart of the Third Reich. How does one reconcile these two analyses? Elias argues that every modern European nation's history is incorporated into the psychological outlook of its citizens as neophytes learn their history, literature, and culture. To some extent, history becomes embedded into personality as people acquire myths about themselves and stereotypes about the other peoples with whom their ancestors struggled. However, in the industrial period the German people were scattered across Eastern and Western Europe. They never experienced a coherent state, or an absolute monarch with whom they could collectively identify, until much later than either France or Britain. The German-speaking peoples, like the Italians, were organized into small states, provinces, duchies, and independent political units occupying an enormous land mass that resisted centralization. The unification of Germany as a second Reich followed the conquest of France in 1871. According to Elias, 'the victory of the German armies over France was at the same time a victory of the German nobility over the German middle class' (1989: 145). The political development in the decades thereafter was decidedly reactionary. Prussian militarism became a societal ideal in public life, since the military signalled the reappearance of empire. In contrast to the middle classes in France and England, who carved out large integrated financial and manufacturing associations in urban centres, the German entrepreneurs turned their backs on the cities. As Max Weber noted in his analysis of the Junkers, successful businessmen in Germany were inclined to invest their wealth in rural estates, and to emulate the lifestyles of the aristocracy. Weber (1968: 211) likewise notes that the German university students adopted quasi-military codes, where duelling was practised with zeal, and where facial scars were worn with honour. By the late 19th century, the university militia fraternities had become a key to social advancement in professional life for ordinary Germans.

According to Elias, 'for many Germans the defeat of 1918 was an unexpected, highly traumatic experience' (1989: 7). Worse still, the terms of the peace negotiated at Versailles in 1919 were humiliating because they included reparations, exposed German military leaders to prosecution for war crimes, and presumed the collective guilt of the Germans as a whole. In fact, the Germans had *not* been defeated; they signed an armistice to cease hostilities. Freikorps, the post-war paramilitary groups, organized against communists and liberals. They staunchly opposed the democratization of Germany as the Weimar Republic pushed the nation towards representative government. They fought to defeat the Bavarian Soviet Republic, and the Baltic, Silesian, and Prussian states to suppress left-wing politics. Hitler's appearance on the political scene had great appeal to this section of German society. Hitler's promise of reviving the nation by protecting its racial superiority—its blood—replaced the collective appeal of the Prussian military with a dictatorship by the 'Volk' through the strong leadership of the Nazi party. The idea of making the Germans masters of all Europe through popular dictatorship appealed to the people who had fallen from grace. Hitler signalled the renewal of German nationalism, and a return to the greatness to which they were destined (1989: 321).

German humiliation made the public highly vulnerable to Hitler's extravagant visions for the future. This vulnerability reflected a national character that had evolved as a result of Germany's historical development:

In most of the German states, the habituations of many centuries had produced a tradition of attitudes and beliefs which was attuned to strong rule from above, with very little or no participation at all from the ruled. People had become more or less accustomed to all decisions touching on the control of the state being in the hands of small, autocratic elites who held the reins of power in a far-reaching system of control. This pattern of external control had been internalized (1989: 338)

The development and traditions of German society often produced a weak individual conscience. Even among adults, the functioning of an individual's conscience remained...dependent on someone outside watching and reinforcing the compulsion, the discipline which individuals were incapable of imposing unaided on themselves...Many Germans cheerfully shed the burden of having to control themselves and shoulder the responsibility for their own lives' (p. 383).

At least in the context of state matters, state control superseded self-control (p. 384). In the areas of private life touched by religion, literature, and music, personal autonomy continued to flourish for the average German. In the Nazi state, there was never any widespread political opposition to the racial politics of anti-Semitism since the self-control of the mass of the German people was assumed by the state and its rulers (p. 386). 'The Germans never ceased to obey' (p. 387). According to Elias, the Führer became a shaman, a rainmaker who took the burden of failure in 1919 off the back of the German masses, and promised them historical fulfilment.

National development in Germany did not produce the vibrant middle class found in Britain and France, where the emergence of the absolute monarch had balanced the class competitions between the aristocracy and the bourgeoisie, where political struggles were pursued in democratic institutions, and where conflicts required diplomacy and negotiation of competing interests, things Elias equates with heightened self-control and responsibility. By contrast, dictatorial rule in Germany was based on the absorption of the middle class by a nationalist culture that valorized duty and militarism. The Germans never acquired a bourgeois democracy comparable to Britain or France. The memory of 'Deutschland' evoked the sense of loss of an earlier empire that had united all the German-speaking peoples, subsequently scattered throughout

Europe. The defeat of the Second Reich at the Treaty of Versailles in 1919 made the German public vulnerable to a total restructuring in which the political fantasies of racial superiority, a *Lebensraum* or future development 'in the East', and the total subjugation of Europe, were ideas that went unchallenged in a culture based on conformity to power. Where England and France increasingly had made heightened levels of self-control a prerogative of the individual, the German sociogenesis, for Elias, placed impulse control in the hands of elites, not through self-control, but through social control.

In summary, Elias's account is broadly consistent with the idea that what causes crime generally also caused the Holocaust. Crime or violence is suppressed by self-control, and the trends in European civilization have been associated with increasing suppression of emotional spontaneity on the one side, and a general decline in violence on the other. Despite the long-term momentum in European crime abatement, the Holocaust was a reversion to barbarity that occurred as a result of a specific trend in national development in Germany, in which self-control was superseded by a social control that made the population vulnerable to political manipulation. In the project to restore Germany's empire, people were asked to pillage and kill, to conduct war and racial elimination. And they appeared to do so, at least initially, with enthusiasm and pride. This was not the banality of evil, but the thirst for historical renewal. In this exceptional state, public conscience had no political currency, and before Valkyrie, opposition to the state was scattered and ineffectual.

There are several problems with this account. The first concerns Elias's explanation of the Holocaust in terms of a reversion to barbarity. I question what barbarism means in these two accounts, and question the continuity of meaning between the two works. Was Nazi Germany barbaric in the sense that medieval Europe was barbaric? The second point is the relationship between control as it appears in the historical account, and control as it appears in the more recent studies of street crime. In the arguments that follow, I identify significant differences between the two perspectives in terms of the relative stability of self-control in contemporary and historical perspectives. This leads to a third point: a proposal to mediate these differences by exploring their common roots in Durkheim's analysis of social pathology. Neither the contemporary control perspective, nor that of Elias, pays full heed to the varieties of pathology that Durkheim initially brought to light in his analysis of suicide. A re-examination of Durkheim promises to mediate these discontinuities. I develop the 'Gillis Thesis' that some pathologies occur due to a pathological *excess* of control. Finally, I return to the question of the banality of evil raised earlier, and reconsider it in terms of the conclusions suggested by the control perspective.[1]

Nazi barbarity versus the Age of Barbarism

Elias repeatedly characterizes the Nazi crimes as an expression of 'barbarism', and he describes this in terms of 'the breakdown in civilization'. This juxtaposition of changes in affect and social structure, then and now, seems to imply that civilization is in some sense 'cumulative', and that barbarism consisted of a reversion to a level of pre-modern existence which was more or less underneath it, or lurking below the surface. This is contrary to Elias's initial perspective. In his earlier work, Elias argued that medieval society was not a beginning, nor a 'bottom rung' in the process of civilization, nor did it represent 'the stage of barbarism', or that of 'primitiveness' (2000: 54). It represented a period in which the pleasures arising from eating, drinking, sexuality, and cruelty were relatively unencumbered. In this sense, 'barbarism' has no moral valence that would make it inherently reprehensible. Nor was 'barbarism' associated solely with aggression. Although Freud had suggested that different drives (food, sexuality, violence) were independent psychic processes, Elias argued, on the contrary, in favour of 'the unity and totality of the life of drives, and the connection of each particular drive to this totality' (2000: 161). In other words, the lack of restraint in medieval society was not confined to aggression, and tended to find expression across the range of human experiences including love, loyalty, and sport. In medieval society 'rapine, battle, hunting of people and animals...were vital necessities...were visible to all. And thus for the mighty and the strong, they formed part of the pleasures of life' (2000: 162). Unrestrained indulgence in food and wine, and communal bathing without regard to

---

[1] Over the last few years, Ron Gillis has suggested to me that control theorists should pay more attention to the phenomenon of over-control in opposition to the idea of self-control. My re-analysis of control theory in terms of Durkheim's description of altruism and fatalism is owed to those conversations.

modesty, went hand in hand with communal violence uninhibited by codes of war. The war hymns of the medieval minstrels cele-brated the love of the mêlée as the charging horsemen crashed with the arms of opponents, smashed the helmets of the footmen, and trampled the fallen under hoof. The vanquished found themselves in chains, their estates plundered, plantings uprooted, their wells buried, and their serfs butchered. For the survivors, Elias notes that a particular pleasure was taken in the mutilation of prisoners. The minstrel recounts the habit of severing the noses, ears, feet, or arms of the defeated, and severing the breasts of women and tearing out their fingernails to make them incapable of work.

To what extent were such barbaric excesses a *necessity* of conflict i.e. rational? In communities prior to the general circulation of money, where few captured enemies could pay a ransom for their release, the vanquished were of no material value to the conquer-ors. Mutilating the survivors made them useless for further military service, and made them a burden on their clans. Destroying the baron's crops and fields, and harvesting his forests took the immov-able wealth away from the opponents, and crippled their long-term prospects for repeated warfare. So in this respect, the 'strong affec-tivity of behaviour was to a certain degree socially necessary' (2000: 164). This would suggest that the barbarity of medieval warfare was rational, premised on the calculation of long-term benefits, and hence a mark of high self-control. However, Elias does not fully endorse this line of reasoning. In the examples cited from Luchaire's history of early France, the victims of violence were just as likely to be widows and orphans, nuns and priests, none of whom was a combatant. Their destruction could not be justified as rational. On the contrary, torture and mutilation were a way of shaming the van-quished, and turning their suffering into a form of sport or enter-tainment, especially when their defeat could not be turned into money through ransom.

Elias also notes several other things that suggest a broader read-ing of these excesses. The violence that marked medieval society was not confined to the warring knights. The propensity for vio-lence pervaded medieval society. 'The little people too—the hatters, the tailors, the shepherds—were all quick to draw their knives' (2000: 168). Despite the apparent 'bonhomie and gaiety of social relations' among the common people in the 15th-century towns, conflicts typically exploded with brutal passions. This emotional lability was also evident in the public spectacles.

One of the most vivid examples was the Midsummer Day celebration in Paris in the 16th century. The populace would gather to witness the ceremonial burning of the cats. Several dozen animals would be suspended in bags or baskets on a scaffold over an enormous pyre, and would wail pitifully as the flames leapt up and set the bags on fire, causing the prey ultimately to drop alive into the blazing coals. The spectacle was accompanied by solemn music, and among those attending were typically the nobility. Today, we find such events so offensive 'because the joy in torturing living creatures is revealed so nakedly and purposely, without any excuse before reason', and would be seen as abnormal in our times (2000:171). The same emotional appetites for cruelty were stoked, whether in the mutilation of defeated opponents, the disfigurement and torture of criminals condemned to the rack and suspended from the gallows, or in the festive celebration of cruelty to animals. Such excesses were considered normal (see Pinker 2011: 129–48).

Elias makes several key observations that reinforce this interpretation. The cruelty was conducted in the open. No punitive system existed to condemn such behaviours. Perpetrators of such acts were not shunned by society as a result of their activities. The activities enjoyed the patronage of the elite. And the pleasures were unrestrained by the religiosity of the population. As Elias notes, the Christian faith did not constitute a counterbalance to the excesses of cruelty. 'It did not prevent them from savouring to the full the joys of the world; it did not hinder them from killing and plundering' (2000: 166). Religion never has in itself an affect-subduing consequence (2000: 169). The Age of Barbarism was a period of emotional expressiveness that ebbed and flowed with the changing patterns of affiliation of late medieval society, but it was not 'barbaric' in the modern sense. Does the account of Nazi mass murder given in *The Germans* really suggest a return to barbarism? On this point, Elias appears to be ambivalent. At one point, he describes the attempt to eradicate the entire population of European Jews as 'a *regression* to barbarism' (1989: 308 emphasis added), using the Freudian term that suggests a reappearance of a base instinct that had been successfully repressed by civilization through the course of history, and repressed by socialization through the life-course. For his part, Freud viewed such instincts as primal in either framework. Was Nazi race hatred an expression of such a base instinct? If we equate feudalism and Nazi barbarity, this would suggest that pre-modern Europe was instinctually primitive, and generally lacking the sort of self-control prevalent in society more recently. At one point in *The Civilizing Process*, Elias (2000: 169) says that 'because emotions [during feudalism] were expressed in the manner that in our world is generally observed only in children, we call these expressions and forms of behaviour "childish"'. That is not quite the same as acknowledging that medieval barbarism in effect expressed unrepressed primal instincts. That would make feudalism a lower rung on the ladder to civilization, a position he rejects. But even if we concede that point, in respect of the Nazis, Elias speaks of the atrocities in unambiguous moral terms that equate evil with what is base nature. When discussing the vulnerability of civilization to contemporary change, Elias warns that 'processes of growth and decay can go hand in hand but the latter can also predominate relative to the former' (1989: 308), suggesting that Nazism was a form of decay, i.e. nature as it succumbs to illness and decomposition, if not a reversion to primitive instinct. Since Elias had explicitly rejected historicism, this suggests at minimum a discontinuity in the sense of barbarism in the two books.

Several arguments support the idea that barbarism has different meanings in each book, and that in the Nazi (i.e. the modern) case, the term carries none of the implications associated with medieval society. Note that during the key period of German development (post-1871), there is no aberration in the general rate of crime. If medieval barbarism and Nazi barbarism were equivalent, such an aberration would be expected if the affect state had shifted significantly to circumstances that promoted higher levels of disinhibition across all forms of pleasure and expression, and if there was 'a unity and totality in the life of drives' (as was mentioned earlier) that would result in a society-wide rise in impulsive behaviour. Zehr's (1976) analysis of national development and crime patterns in Germany and France shows no trends in crime uniquely attached to German political developments. In addition, the 'Final Solution of the Jewish Question' was conducted, as much as possible in secret, unlike the medieval atrocities. The extermination camps were built in the wilderness in Poland. Only when the eastern offensive was underway did mass murder occur *in situ* in Russia, the Baltics, and Ukraine under the cover of war. Furthermore, the Holocaust was undertaken as an industrial challenge that called upon the professional expertise of architects, engineers, chemists, statisticians, demographers—not to mention professional soldiers—persons not characterized by emotional lability, recklessness, and low self-control. This was the aspect of the Holocaust that Bauman equated with modernity (1989). This suggests that the Nazi crimes did not have the same character as the excesses Elias associates with feudalism. In addition, the 'breakdown of civilization' does not appear to refer to the cohesiveness of everyday life in Nazi Germany during the war. If anything, the Allied bombing campaign caused the common Germans to rally around their leaders, and increased their resolve to survive. In my view, it is an error to equate the barbarism of feudalism with Nazi barbarism. In order to emphasize this point, I digress briefly to consider contemporary control theory to illustrate how it helps us think about crime, particularly on the issue of self-control, in order to contrast that with the picture conjured by Elias.

Contemporary Control Theory

One of the leading illustrations of control theory is contained in Gottfredson and Hirschi's *General Theory of Crime* (1990). Their argument starts with classical action theory: people choose things that give them pleasure, and avoid things that give them pain. Among the important restraints on actions are those imposed by laws that penalize particular choices. However, *informal* social controls are just as, if not more, important. People are restrained by families and friends, and are governed by the anticipated reactions of those they hold dear. However, there is an important caveat to this general tendency. People vary to the degree to which they are restrained by the consequences of their acts. There is significant variation in self-control. Evidence suggests that the disposition towards self-control is acquired relatively early in life, and tends to be highly persistent over the life cycle. The parental bond teaches the young child to delay gratification, to become responsive to the reactions of others, and to anticipate consequences of conduct as well as misconduct. External social control in the form of supervision, direction, affective bonding, and moral injunctions becomes internalized. Habits acquired through social control persist as self-control. A failure to establish self-control during youth elevates the risk of a life-course trajectory marked by impulsive behaviour. Another finding is that a significant percentage of the offender population is characterized by high rates of recidivism, because such persons are indifferent to the consequences of misconduct, including censure. Without the habit of registering consequences of misconduct, they are vulnerable to the attractions of the moment.

A further finding is that persons who have difficulties restraining their impulses do not specialize in any particular form of crime, but are relatively versatile, and engage in a range of hedonistic offences undertaken with little planning, reflecting whatever opportunities present themselves at hand. And finally, interpersonal problems for persons with low self-control are not limited to crime, but show impairments in other areas of life: school failure, accidents, unemployment, drug and alcohol dependencies, family conflicts, and residential insecurity. The consequences of low self-control are both profound and independent of the other well-known effects of age (the spike in crime in the late teenage years) and gender. These findings have been corroborated in other fields (see Lehrer 2009).

When considered in this light, what Elias describes as the loss of self-control is totally inconsistent with the contemporary view. Elias's barbarians are barbaric only in respect to one area of their lives: the political. They appear to function effectively in social life without committing crimes elsewhere. Rather than being social failures and school dropouts, the leadership of the SS, for example, appears to have consisted of a large number of well-educated, socially successful participants. After the war, despite their alleged barbarism, they miraculously desist from further crime, and return to society as constructive citizens (Drumbl 2007: 8). None of this would be possible if they were characterized by a persistent deficit in self-control. What does this suggest? The acts of the Nazis were barbaric, and unspeakably evil, but they have nothing to do with the profile of the typical offenders in modern criminology who recurrently exhibit the trait of low self-control. Nor do they have anything in common with the emotional lability found in medieval society. In my view, Elias is mistaken to explain Nazi behaviour with respect to this concept. It is neither barbaric in the sense of generalized medieval spontaneity, nor is it evidence of a 'weak' executive function. In accepting this, we do not reject his analysis of the peculiar nature of Germany's national development, and the attraction of dictatorial rule to a large section of the German public. How do we make sense of this 'barbarity' theoretically if it is not low self-control? In the next section, I propose that the Nazi case of compliance in mass murder results not from a lack of self-control, but from quite the opposite: over-control. The case for pathological behaviour resulting from over-control is found in Durkheim's analysis of altruism and fatalism in his classic study of suicide.

Durkheim and social pathology

In 1897 Durkheim published *Suicide: A Study in Sociology*. At the time of writing, most observers thought that the impulse towards self-destruction was a wholly psychological or individual phenomenon, and had to be understood in terms of personal psychopathology. Durkheim argued that persons who experienced suicidal ideation, and who suffered deep anguish about the purpose of their lives, were inhabitants of a social structure that was pathological, and which was unnerving them. Patterns of affiliation and life world events were capable of throwing individuals out of their zone of comfort, and making them question their self-worth. In his analysis, Durkheim observed systematic variations in the social distributions of suicide that varied by religion, marital status, and political conflict. Similarly, social upheavals that unite people around a common cause drive away the impulse to commit suicide by making individuals close ranks to confront a common danger. Extreme deficits of attachment (more common with Protestantism or non-married status) created a pathological condition marked by *egoism*; at the other end, excesses of attachment were similarly problematic, inasmuch as they smothered individuality in favour of a pathological condition described as *altruism*. These two conditions arose when social attachments created stress due to their intrusiveness on the one side (altruism), and their complete absence on the other (egoism).

Durkheim suggested that a second dimension in social life—regulation—created similar liabilities in its extremes. Persons undergoing disturbances in their material fortunes, either favourable or unfavourable, faced an increased risk of self-destruction through the displacement from regulation that was caused by such disequilibria. 'The higher rate for those of independent means (720 per million) show clearly that it is the better off who suffer most' (Durkheim 1985: 112). The abrupt removal of their day-to-day regulation creates a state of *anomie*, or lawlessness, that detaches them from their routines and obligations, and undermines their security. Similarly, divorce, or widowhood, particularly for males, prunes the individual from the quotidian obligations of daily life, leaving the survivor floating without direction, and prone to losing any sense of purpose. In a footnote, Durkheim added a fourth and final type of pathology associated with an excess of regulation and supervision that so curbed the individual's freedom as to make suicide appear preferable. He described this state of pathology as *fatalistic*, and offered the case of the slave so burdened with obligation and regulation that life becomes futile.

Durkheim employed suicide to illustrate how aberrations of regulation and attachment disrupted healthy patterns of adjustments. He proposed that the four conditions (egoism, altruism, anomie, and fatalism) yielded separate forms of pathology. His analysis has been extended beyond the case of suicide to all sorts of problems, including crime and illness. Durkheim introduced a paradigmatic way of thinking about pathology that redirected the focus away from the individual, and his or her inherent characteristics, to his or her circumstances. This paradigm later extended to a sociological approach to epidemiology known as 'the social determinants of health'. Needless to say, there have been some methodological issues in his work that required further research. For example, there is some debate as to whether Durkheim's four types are mutually exclusive. Kushner and Sterk (2005) suggested that Durkheim's analysis of the altruistic suicide of the military men who lay down their lives for the leaders, the country, and the greater good, would be better described as fatalistic, since their combat roles often give them little choice. Indeed, the question of the mutual exclusiveness of the types is a common criticism. Also, Durkheim's measures of association were not based on individual measures of traits (i.e. the religion and cause of death of individuals), but ecological measures (jurisdictions which have levels of certain religions correlated with high levels of suicide). Though valid, these methodological questions are less relevant for our purposes than the theoretical issues. Criminologists usually depict the typology as a cross with four points representing the separate kinds of suicide based on regulation and attachment as shown in Figure 4.1.

The problem with this common depiction is that it implies that regulation and attachment occur independently of one another; indeed they appear to be at right angles from each other. In my view, there are good grounds for thinking that they co-vary, and that such co-variance corresponds to different levels of self-control. For example, Hirschi's bond theory explains delinquency, surely a form of Durkheimian pathology, in terms of four processes: attachment, commitment, involvement, and belief. The first two processes are elements of integration between the youth and the parents: personal identification, emotional attachment, and commitment of the youth to objectives held in common with the family (school achievement,

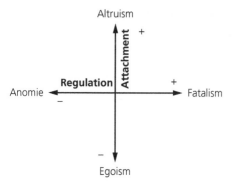

Figure 4.1 Four types of pathology based on Durkheim's suicide

civility with family and neighbours etc.) The latter points, *involvement* of youth with parents and transmission of their *beliefs* are issues of regulation, i.e. exposure to parental supervision, and acceptance of moral instructions and norms provided by parents. A youth who is closely attached to parents typically is also pressured to adopt their regulations. Similarly, an adolescent whose bond to parents is weak is not liable to acquire many of their morals or regulations. As noted earlier, persons who do not absorb these processes tend to exhibit impulsiveness and low self-control. What about the other extreme? What neither Elias nor the contemporary control theorists consider is the original Durkheimian paradigm that captured the consequences when individuals experienced excessive pressures towards attachment (pathological altruism) and excessive regulation and control (fatalism). This is captured in Figure 4.2.

What Figure 4.2 suggests is that low self-control individuals experience both egoism—a preoccupation with the self and a disregard for others—*and* anomie—a sense of lawlessness and a disregard for authority. What is more interesting is the opposite extreme. I have used the term 'pathological altruism', following Oakley et al (2011), because the examples Durkheim used differ from the usual connotations of altruism that suggest virtuous actions based on unselfishness and generosity. His three other types—egoism, anomie, and fatalism—all have negative connotations. Durkheim's usage of altruism refers to actions based on a sense of duty or obligation that entails self-destruction, or at least the risk thereof. These included the suicides of men approaching old age to remove their

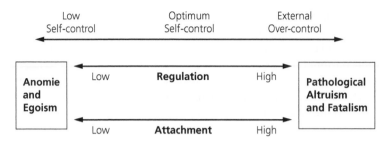

Figure 4.2 Pathological consequences of extremes in self-control

dependence on kin, women on the death of their husbands in Hindu communities, or slaves on the death of their masters. All these cases were drawn from pre-industrial societies. Among the modern nations, this form of suicide is most prevalent in the army. It is not associated with soldiers who kill themselves rather than face humiliation and defeat at the hands of their enemies, but warriors who fight without regard to their personal survival, and embrace valour and death in the service of the larger society.

In my view, it is into this particular pathology that we should place the 'barbarism' that Elias attributes to the Nazis. Elias was well aware of the extraordinary appeal of the 'Motherland' to the rank and file German soldier, and the extraordinary spell that the Führer held over the ordinary Germans. According to Elias, it was regarded as essential for the protection of the state 'that every individual should be prepared in times of emergency to kill the enemies of the nation and sacrifice his own life' (1989: 342). The state had acquired such an intense emotional aura as to appear as something so valuable that it deserves to be venerated. 'This feeing usually extends to everything which can be said to belong to the nation or to be in the national interest, including the use of force, of fraud, deception or, if it comes to that, of torture and of killing' (1989: 147). Again: 'everywhere in national crises...people are urged...to join the armed forces and subordinate their own ambitions, goals, hopes, even their own survival, to the survival of the society to which they belong' (p. 334). Members of all classes 'came to be tied to their country as much through "inner" ideas and beliefs as through "external" controls' (p. 355). Elias captures in detail and colour what Durkheim had scarcely anticipated in respect of what might be called genocidal altruism.

In addition to the compunction towards altruism that is prominent in the Nazi mentality, Elias also provides strong evidence for the related dimension: fatalism or futility. 'Few other peoples had in their national mystique, in their poetry and in their songs so many allusions to death and self-sacrifice as did the Germans' (1989: 331). If national duty required an unquestioning commitment that dictated the destruction of the other, so be it. Likewise, if one had to die in the service of the nation to achieve that objective, so be it. The theme of death and defeat was recurrent in the songs sung by the German troops marching to battle. The death lyrics had 'a strange fascination for the Germans'. Even when they were victorious, the Germans 'never seemed quite able to silence the feeling that they would lose the last battle' (1989: 332). When called to arms once more in defence of the third empire, the Germans presented with enthusiasm, but suffered from fatalism. But they were 'burdened by the memory of earlier generations who, like them, had marched loyally, unquestioningly and with similar faith in Germany's victory, towards defeat and death' (p. 332). This was a major theme that ran throughout the cultural tapestry that accompanied Germany's imperial expansion from Berlin to Stalingrad, and from the euthanasia programme to the chimneys of Auschwitz. This was not a legacy of impulsive barbarism, but over-control.

Conclusion

When Hannah Arendt attended Eichmann's trial in 1962, she saw an individual stripped of his military and cultural trappings, and presented in isolation from the historical events that had gutted the European landscape two decades beforehand. He was characterized as an inauspicious, low-brow non-entity confined behind a glass cage. The Holocaust was laid at the door of universal bureaucracy manned by indifferent civil servants or persons coerced to participate. The picture that one gathers from Elias requires us to update this interpretation. The followers of the Führer were swept up by a politics that reflected the highest human aspirations, the highest honour that individuals could bestow on their country and its legacy, that called on superhuman efforts to achieve superhuman goals. Elias notes that the political legacy of Germany did not cause these outcomes, nor make them inevitable (Elias 1996: 331). However, it made them possible, and Hitler conjured a dream of empire that required extraordinary sacrifice. By all accounts, the masses were mesmerized. Just as a person enters a state of hypnosis or a delirium that severs his or her direct knowledge of reality, an emotional politics can blind those who are seduced by them, and can influence their perceptions and feelings. They are less able to engage in reality testing when they have imbibed a whole history and culture, with all its self-congratulatory stories, myths, inherited grievances, and senses of entitlement, all assumed as natural, however extravagant or maniacal. Instead of labelling this as the banality of evil, we should recapture the spirit in which it was originally conjured up by Hitler and his inner circle: the colossal triumph of the will to power, the transubstantiation of ordinary Germans into historical giants, the transcendence of German subservience into total political and moral mastery of all of Europe. That is the subtext that Arendt seems to have overlooked—the very magnificence of evil, and its seductive appeal to all the Eichmanns large and small. In retrospect, it appears naive to have attempted to hang the entire barbarity of the Nazi state on such a tiny hook—banality.

In this chapter garden-variety offences are attributed to low self-control. These appear to be well understood in terms of breaches in development arising from aversive and/or unsupportive social environments. On the other hand, political crimes, such as genocide, appear to derive their spell from collective events that put individual choices at the disposal of the sovereign, the leader, or the larger social collective. Arendt attributed this to the banality of evil. In retrospect, I would suggest that *the splendour of evil* would be a more accurate epithet to Hitler's nightmare. In the next chapters, I extend Elias's approach to the Rwandan genocide.

5

The Psychogenesis and Sociogenesis of Genocide in Rwanda

Introduction

How useful is Elias's framework in understanding recent genocides? In this chapter I explore the historical context of the events that culminated in the 1994 genocide in Rwanda, and explain them in terms of his concepts of sociogenesis and psychogenesis. It is based in part on observations in Rwanda as well as at the ICTR in Arusha, Tanzania in 2004 and 2005. It builds on reports gathered from the Rwandan government, as well as from various non-government organizations, both local and international.[1] The point of departure in this chapter is a focus on two of the most peculiar features of the massacres. These constitute the psychogenetic or subjective features of the killing, looting, and rape. The first perplexing feature is the large-scale mobilization of perpetrators who, for the most part, had no previous record of violent behaviour. The evidence suggests that participation in the killings was widespread, that those who did not

[1] During my trips to Rwanda and Arusha in 2004 and 2005, I spoke with numerous people to learn what they could tell me about the genocide. And I collected those documents, often in the public domain, that I thought relevant. These included maps of the killing sites (from the Department of Monuments), maps of the secteurs and provinces (from the census office), a copy of the 1991 census describing the population prior to the genocide, a copy of all the gacaca (and related) laws which had been gazetted, Martin Ngoga's report on the Rwandan judiciary, reports from the 2004 preliminary gacaca trials describing locations and numbers of cases, the Ministry of Local Government estimate of victims, Ibuka's Kibuye Dictionary Project, a copy of the Amnesty Law from the 'Codes et Lois du Rwanda', field reports from Penal Reform International, RCN Justice et Democratie, ASF, African Rights, GTZ, and others. Nicholas Jones used some of the materials gathered in this research in his book, *The Courts of Genocide: Politics and the Rule of Law in Rwanda and Arusha* (Routledge 2010). Jones completed his doctoral training under my supervision, and is now Associate Professor at the University of Regina.

participate directly were supportive of it, and that killings took place in the open, and were undertaken by ordinary people working in concert with members of the militias, the police, the army, and the gendarmerie. There were many people who opposed the killing and protected their neighbours, but these cases were the exceptions (African Rights 2003f). Similarly, there was also some short-term military opposition (Dallaire 2003: 292). In addition to the general participation in the killing, Romeo Dallaire (2003), who witnessed the events first-hand, reported that the speed of killings was much more intense than even that of the Holocaust. Alan Kuperman (2001: 16) similarly noted 'perhaps the most remarkable and least appreciated aspect of the genocide was its speed . . . [the] rate of killing would make it the fastest genocide in recorded history'. According to the conventional wisdom, the entire killing spree was accomplished within three months. The estimates of those killed vary. Des Forges (1999) offered a figure of 550 000 killed. A government of Rwanda report from the Ministry of Local Government put the estimate at over a million (MINLOC 2002), a number probably higher than the entire Tutsi population.[2]

The second psychogenetic feature is the frequent observation by NGOs that the perpetrators showed few signs of remorse or contrition in the aftermath of the genocide. Mamdani (2001: 8) says 'it is the "popularity" of the genocide that is its uniquely troubling aspect'. According to some accounts, perpetrators openly admitted their murders, although they tended to use euphemisms (Hatzfeld 2005). In subsequent years, the jails were full of *génocidaires* who typically denied having participated, and many who denied there even was genocide. Mamdani expresses the situation this

[2] The 1991 census gave a total population of 7 162 565, and estimated the Tutsi composition as 8.4 per cent (i.e. 601 655), three years before the genocide (Rwanda 2004: 14, 125)—suggesting that the majority of Tutsis were eradicated. The total population included citizens 'absent' for the census (265 153) as well as 'visitors' (270 167). The actual number of 'résidents présent' was 6 892 398. As for the ethnic distributions, the Tutsi figure of 8.4 per cent in 1991 contrasts with the figure of 17.5 per cent in 1950. The Hutu Revolution reduced the Tutsis by 50 per cent, by this measure. In 1991 respondents were not required, as before, to show identification cards to verify ethnicity, and after the demise of the monarchy in 1961, many Tutsis and Twa represented themselves as Hutu (Rwanda 2004: 126). These issues make it difficult to draw accurate estimates of population loss. Verpoorten's comparison of the census with population data from Gikongoro Province suggests that the Tutsi population may have been underestimated in 1991 (Verpoorten 2005).

way: observers need to understand how people not only could set apart a group as an enemy, but also could 'exterminate it with an easy conscience' (2001: 13). The sense of guilt and responsibility was made an issue by the gacaca process, which put an onus on the offenders to confess their crimes, and to seek forgiveness from the surviving victims in order to expedite their release from prison.

When the confession and guilty plea procedure was first instituted, very few genocide suspects opted to take part in it…A conspiracy of silence about the genocide was maintained…Some prisoners regard themselves as innocent of the charges against them, while others still believe that the genocide of Tutsis was justified (African Rights, 2000: 5).

Penal Reform International similarly observed:

Prisoners and other accused persons tend to present the genocide as being the result of a bad policy of the former government…They do not seem to accept responsibility for their acts, even when they confess and ask for pardon…The manner in which the confessions were often made…lead us to believe that remorse has little effect and that many guilty persons do not feel responsible for the crimes they have committed (PRI 2003: 9–10; also see Hatzfeld 2010).

Drumbl (1997–1998: 607) says 'it was this sense of moral ambiguity that struck me the most…I had thought that…someone would come forward and confess, wishing to seek some closure or redemption. Instead, the prisoners inhabit a world where no-one feels guilty.' Prior to April 1998, some 1 000 inmates in Rwandan prisons being held for their role in the genocide had offered confessions. This changed after 24 April 1998 when twenty-two men convicted of genocide were executed in public. Within two months, 5 000 had confessed. The number of confessions reached over 8 000 by the end of 1998 (African Rights 2000: 11).

How many people participated in the violence? There is no certain answer. Scott Straus (2004) studied incarcerated inmates who confessed to genocide, and determined how many killings they participated in. He concluded there were 175 000–210 000 killers. Another indication comes from the number of cases brought to court on all charges. After ending the conflict in 1994, the government of President Pasteur Bizimungu and Vice-President Paul Kagame pursued a policy of 'maximal accountability'. Everyone who had participated was to be identified and brought to justice, not simply the elite, and not simply the killers. However, the judiciary in 1994 had been nearly obliterated. According to Martin

Ngoga's 2004 presentation to the ICTR prosecutors, before the genocide, there had been an estimated 758 judges, seventy prosecutors, and 631 support staff. Since the Tutsis were over-represented in the legal profession, their eradication was particularly devastating for the country's legal institutions. By November 1994, about 75 per cent of the legal personnel had been lost (Ngoga 2004). The government created specialized chambers presided over by lay magistrates. They frequently presided over trials in which there were large numbers of co-accused implicated in the same murders. By way of illustration, RCN Justice and Democratie (2004) recorded 595 genocide cases from 2000 to 2003: these involved nearly 5 493 accused (i.e. 9.2 persons per case). For the same period, prosecutions for ordinary criminal law violations suggested a ratio of 1.6 accused per case. Much of the aggression had been carried out by mobs.

Under the immense pressure on the criminal courts, the government initiated the gacaca process through laws enacted in 2000 and 2004. Gacaca was modelled on the ideal of a traditional dispute resolution mechanism, but the contemporary process employed several lay judges, again without more than rudimentary legal training. It was devised to prosecute the enormous backlog of cases (Jones 2010). How many cases were brought to the gacaca jurisdiction?[3]

In March 2008, the Republic of Rwanda, having operated the gacaca nationwide for several years, issued a report that summarized the total numbers prosecuted: 818 564, approximately 10 per cent of the population (Rwanda 2008b). This figure omits thefts that were eventually diverted out of the gacaca jurisdiction and resolved by arbitration. However, as Table 5.1 indicates, just over half of perpetrators were followers or accomplices to murder

---

[3] In 2004 Nick Jones and I reviewed the results from the findings from pilot courts in some 1500 locations. Each had 75–80 prosecutions. The gacaca jurisdiction estimated by linear projection that if the 9 100 cells nationwide were to experience similar caseloads that there would be some 682 500 to 728 000 cases. After checking maps which depicted the major sites of violence, and computing the populations for all the secteurs with information from the census, we suggested to Domitilla Mukantaganzwa that this range was probably a gross overestimate since several northern prefectures had relatively *fewer* violent incidents, and since the trial courts were held in jurisdictions associated with urban centres with relatively *larger* average caseloads. She projected that the caseloads would be *much* larger. She was correct, but that suggests something dramatically enlarged the net cast between the pilot courts and the nationwide implementation. As Schabas (2005: 4) observed, the mushrooming of charges is 'staggering'. 'Charging 1 000 000 Rwandans with genocide amounts to an indictment of perhaps one-third of the country's adult population.'

Table 5.1 Summary of gacaca prosecutions for genocide

	Category One (Planners, authorities, notorious murderers)	Category Two (Accomplices to murderer)	Category Three (Persons who committed assault)	Total
Number	77 269	432 557	308 738	818 564
Percentage	9.4%	52.8%	37.7%	100%

(apparently in contrast to Straus's focus on primary perpetrators). This figure, 818 564, reports the number of persons prosecuted, not convicted. Recent reports suggest that there were well over a million cases (RNW 2011; RNW 2012b). The actual breakdown of such cases has never been published.

How were such a large number of people mobilized? I argue that the scales of participation, and the speed of the crimes, were the result of the legacies of colonialism that I describe as 'administrative closure' and 'racial closure'. These were the evolving social structures that made over-control possible. The first kind of closure explains the ability of the system to quickly mobilize the masses. The second kind of closure points to the processes by which the two groups, previously interdependent, became so deeply alienated in Rwandese political culture, and how elites could exploit these feelings in their pursuit of self-interest through genocide. How does this tie to Elias and control theory? These two points follow Elias's analysis of sociogenic, and the corresponding psychogenic, changes. Through the historical development of Rwanda, persons in authority were able to cultivate intense levels of external control over the population in a process that cascaded from pre-colonial, to colonial, and post-colonial domination. During the same period, the main constituent groups—Hutus and Tutsis—were progressively alienated from one another in terms of perceptions and feelings.

Administrative Closure: the Sociogenesis of Hierarchical Dependencies

In the 1920s, Belgium introduced a rigid administrative system to implement colonial policies. It built on the pre-colonial legacy of administration by chiefs on the individual hills. Gourevitch (1998: 49) describes the organization of the kingdom at the time of the ascent of King Rwabugiri (1860):

The Rwandan state, having expanded from a single hilltop chieftaincy, administered much of what is now southern and central Rwanda through a rigorous, multi-layered hierarchy of military, political, and civil chiefs and governors, subchiefs and deputy governors, sub-subchiefs and deputy-deputy governors. Priests, tax collectors, clan leaders, and army recruiters all had their place in the order that bound every hill in the kingdom in fealty to the Mwami [king].

When the first German administrator arrived in the country, the Nyiginya lineage enjoyed a system of kingdom-wide administration that spanned two centuries (Vasina 2004: 3). There was a constant competition between the clans to acquire and expand wealth in the form of cattle and pasture. This was done through warfare, political alliances, as well as by contracts under which subordinate lineages were given cattle in exchange for obligations to chiefs in terms of work, gifts, and loyalty. In the 19th century, the terms Tutsi and Hutu were meant primarily to indicate group wealth and power. Clans operated in semi-autonomous principalities linked through alliances. At the time of European contact, there was a single dominant mwami or king, and a political structure that extended state control over much of the current boundaries of Rwanda. The mwami was a divine being in Rwandan culture, and he *or she* stood at the apex of an economic system that extracted tribute from subservient lineages throughout the kingdom.

This hierarchical state was refined by the Europeans as a way of rationalizing the collection of taxes, the planting of export crops, and the recruitment of corvée labour. Towards the end of the 19th century, the mwami had usurped control of virtually all the land. All subjects were required to pay some form of tribute. A large bureaucracy emerged to collect these payments. A council of ministers was under the direction of the mwami, under them the provincial chiefs, and the subchiefs. The Hutu guardians of the traditions and rituals were the mwami's spiritual advisors, the abiiru ritualists (Mamdani 2001: 63–4). The mwami delegated his authority to the chiefs of the great families who delegated control to those subservient to them. 'In a similar way, the mwami distributed land and cattle among his subjects, who in return administered regions, paid the tributes, and provided military services ... this system of obligations and tributes descended from the mwami to the most common farmer' (Louis 1963: 111). 'The traditional relationship between the patron and the client, and the chief and the subordinate, was mutual, in the sense that the chief owed the subordinate protection and assistance as the subordinate owed the chief subservience' (Kroslak 2008: 23).

In the 19th century, one of the most common forms of affiliation was organized around the *umuheto* chiefs who raised men to serve in the mwami's armies. An *umuheto* chief was entitled to collect prestations (obligatory 'gifts') from lineage heads, often in the form of cows or luxury items (fine mats, fibre bracelets, honey etc.) annually or biannually on behalf of the mwami from both Tutsi and Hutu families. Army service was a source of social recognition and status. The client clan's expression of loyalty was usually separate from prestations presented to the provincial chiefs that were paid as a form of land tax. During Rwabugiri's reign a new form of relationship was introduced called *ubuhake*. 'Unlike early umuheto clientship, which usually involved the gift of a cow at regular intervals from a client lineage to its patron, ubuhake involved the transfer of one or several cows from patron to client' (Newbury 1988: 98). The gift consisted of the use of the cow (milk, calves), not ownership. Also, the *ubuhake* patron–client relationship was individual, not collective, and individuals could enjoy relationships with several patrons, all of whom would receive some service and loyalty in exchange for the relationship. Where *umuheto* clientship tended to reinforce small-scale horizontal ties, *ubuhake* tended to undermine lineage solidarities. Finally, the *ubureetwa* relationship was a more exploitative form of clientship. It consisted of obligations on the part of the poorest peasants to perform service for the chiefs on whose lands they lived, at the risk of losing access to the land's gardens and pasture. This could involve two days' service in every five days, and usually consisted of the most menial tasks: collecting firewood, serving as night watchman at the chief's hut, fetching water, and cultivating the chief's field (Newbury 1988: 141). This 'traditional obligation' was unpaid, and was viewed by those entailed to do it as humiliating. It also fell almost exclusively on the backs of the Hutu. Memory of such exploitative obligations lingers to this day (McDoom 2012: 148).

The German colonial period (1898–1916) made little impact on traditional Ruanda-Urundi social structures (aside from military intervention in 1912 to defeat Hutu opponents of mwami Musinga in the north-west). However, the occupation of Ruanda-Urundi by the Belgians in 1916 saw the start of significant administrative interventions. A head tax on adult males was introduced in 1917. In 1926 the position of *umuhetu* chiefs and the prestations owed to them were abolished (Newbury 1988: 112). In 1934, prestations owed to land chiefs in the form of agricultural tributes were replaced by cash payments. Also, the previous obligations that arose from patron-client relationships between lineages were transferred to individual adult men. This included a universal corvée called *akazi*. However, the new Belgian administration did not treat all groups equally. 'Supposedly every adult man was liable to pay taxes and perform corvée; ubureetwa, however, was imposed specifically on Hutu' (Newbury 1988: 112). *Ubureetwa*, the most asymmetrical obligation, was the only traditional obligation that continued to enjoy legal status. The rationale was that it reinforced the political ascendency of the traditional Tutsi chiefs. However, there was an economic rationale as well. When the Belgians introduced a market economy and crops for export, it required chiefs to plant quotas of coffee plants and new forests. The *ubureetwa* obligations guaranteed them access to unpaid labour, and made them richer through the marketing of exportable agricultural products. According to Newbury (1988: 143) 'the elevation of ubuteetwa to colonial law meant that it affected more people in a more burdensome fashion than in the past'. In addition, the elimination of the threefold level of chiefs on the hills (for agricultural land, for pasture, and for the army) removed the ability of average farmers to form alliances to advance their self-interests through playing off the various chiefs and subchiefs against one another. This was a more starkly hierarchical bureaucracy that motivated a lot of Rwandans to migrate to the Congo to escape the privations created by the new administrative structures associated with Belgian colonial rule.

Administrative changes in the First and Second Republic

Beginning in 1960, the central government introduced an administrative system that provided very tight vertical linkages across levels of community. Initially, the country was divided into ten prefectures or provinces comprised of 140 different communes or districts. Each commune would be composed of four or five secteurs, and each secteur would be divided into ten cells. The cell was the basic level of community, and consisted of ten households comprising some eighty people, although there is some variability in the size of the population in each administrative unit (Mamdani 2001: 144 and 314).

During the second republic, Habyarimana created a single political party, the MRND (National Revolutionary Movement for

Development), and made all citizens members at birth. The administrative system was further refined, and the political consequences of the hierarchical system were profound.

Under the presidency and the interior ministry, the country comprised ten préfectures administered by préfects (roughly equivalent of governors) appointed by the President of the Republic. The préfectures were subdivided into sous-préfectures, each combining 4–5 communes and run by the sous-préfect. Below the sous-préfect there were 145 communes (counties) with a population of approximately 40 to 50 thousand persons, each run by a burgomaster, also appointed by the President of the Republic (Twagilimana 2003: 161).

The communes were divided into sectors of about 5 000 persons each, governed by an elected councillor. Below the secteur were the various 'cells' with a population of about 1 000 persons governed by a group of five cell members, one of whom was designated the head or the 'responsible' that reported to the secteur council. Every political appointment ensured the implementation of presidential policies. The reorganization of the administrative structure abolished the electoral reforms that had brought the first president, Kayibanda, to power through mass Hutu support in 1961. 'The prefect was like the colonial chief: he decided how many acres of coffee should be cultivated in each commune…He alone was responsible for public order and tranquility' (Mamdani 2001: 144). The burgomasters were like colonial subchiefs demanding 'gifts in return for administrative services, from settling a case to penning a signature'.

Twagilimana reports that, in the aftermath of the October 1990 invasion, an even lower level of control was established: the 'nyumbakumi' (Swahili for '10 houses'). The nyumbakumi was the head of the ten households, and reported on all local movements. Residents were required to inform the nyumbakumi of any guests they were hosting, report the name and identity from the individual's registration card, and were required to inform the responsibles if their presence was suspicious. Indeed, administrative control over ordinary Rwandans was intense. It became necessary for everyone to obtain the burgomaster's permission to apply for a job or schooling outside the commune. Individuals had to produce 'a birth certificate; a certificate of complete identity specifying the date of birth, place of birth, and residence (cell, commune, and prefecture), parents, ethnic group, marital status, and employment position, if any; certificate of good conduct, life, and morals…and a marriage certificate' (Twagilimana 2003: 162). As a consequence, unless he or she had access to an authority more highly placed, anyone who alienated the burgomaster could not apply for anything. The burgomaster was a gatekeeper for individual advancement through education and employment. As a result of the administrative structure, privacy and autonomy were not paramount features of Rwandan society for the majority of citizens. The pre-colonial patron-client dependency had devolved in post-colonial society into rigid micro management, i.e. external control.

The consequences of the administrative structure for peasants cannot be underestimated. It provided a direct line of political control from the president's office right down to the individual hamlets. The line of authority could be used to facilitate the mobilization of hundreds of thousands of ordinary people at very short notice in what, by 1990, was a densely populated country. The préfects, sous-préfects, and burgomasters owed their status and power directly to the president, and could be expected to deliver the compliance over those whose lives they administered. In addition, all the prefectures were connected to Kigali by roads paid for by foreign aid. They were, in the words of Gourevitch (1998: 32), 'the best roads in central Africa'.

In Rwanda, because of population growth and intensive settlement, there were few places to hide, either for the victims or the potential perpetrators. Nor was there any restraint on government policies arising from a free press. The national radio was an official state-controlled institution. The first private broadcaster, RTLM (*Radio and Télévision Libres des Milles Collines*), and independent newspapers such as *Kangura*, were owned and operated by extreme Hutu groups that broadcast virulent hate propaganda that incited violence. Also, there had been little political opposition to check the powers of Rwanda's dictators, either under Kayibanda or Habyarimana. Habyarimana's one-party state moved to multiple parties in 1991. The other major institution in Rwandan society, the Catholic Church, was politically supportive of both regimes. The administrative closure created a tightly administered society, and the other institutions that could potentially mitigate its control were absent or compliant.

Racial Closure: the Cultivation of Division and Resentment

Prior to colonialism, there is little evidence of warfare between Hutus and Tutsis as such. Certainly, by the end of the 19th century, the Hutus were considered as vassals, and the Tutsis as aristocrats. However, historically, most conflicts were between rival clans that were made up of Bantu farmers, Nilotic pastoralists, and Twa hunters. Oral histories suggest that for a period of several centuries a pattern of mostly Tutsi chiefs administered control over clans that occupied land inherited through lineages. However, the clans historically had tended to integrate Hutus, Tutsis, and Twa, by assigning traditional roles in warfare, government, and agriculture. As noted earlier, the rise of *ubureetwa* obligations was an irritation between the groups in the decades before the European contact. Nonetheless, the people were Banyarwandans with a common language, religion, and culture. The legacy of colonialism was to 'racialize' the differences between the groups. The early Europeans believed that the tall, fine-featured chiefs were racially distinct, and probably were migrants from the horn of Africa. The Hamite hypothesis, developed by the Europeans, suggested that Tutsis were the descendants of Ham, the lost son of Noah, and had innate superior talent that made them born to rule. The Belgian colony was founded on a system that privileged them, and increased the marginalization of the great Hutu majority. Jefremovas (2002: 68ff) refers to this period as 'the time of whips', when chiefs resorted to corporal punishment to extract Hutu compliance in forced labour. While prior to colonial contact people could move into and out of Tutsi status depending on their economic success, this ended with colonialism. The issue of racial identity cards largely prevented movement across the lineages in 1933. The racial differences became a self-fulfilling prophecy as Tutsis moved differentially into the emerging roles of power and prestige in the new colonial society, and came to dominate in the economy, the political administration, and the Church. In addition to the native Kinyarwanda language, the Hutus were instructed in Swahili, the language of the mines and the fields and, as explained earlier, were required to perform unpaid labour for the Tutsi chiefs. Tutsis were taught in French, and were free of this corvée service. What had originally been an economic and political difference in pre-colonial times among competing clans became a form of political apartheid premised on inherent difference. The previous client–patron relationships became raw exploitation. The petite Tutsis still enjoyed goodwill on the hills. Intermarriage was not uncommon, and neighbours attended both religious services and markets together as commoners. However, the elites became sharply divided in the political imagination.

After Belgium lost political control of the Congo to independence elements in the mid-1950s, the Belgian military attaché in Rwanda, Colonel Guy Logiest, was instructed to steer Rwanda onto the course of republicanism, thereby removing the potential influence of the Tutsi royal family and its unifying function, and switching allegiance from the Tutsi elite to the newly emerging Hutu elite. The aspirations of this new elite were expressed in the Hutu Manifesto signed by eight Hutu intellectuals in 1957. It bluntly presented the historical exclusion of the Hutu by the 'political monopoly which [was] held by one race, the mututsi' (Newbury 1988: 191). At the time, Hutus had about 6 per cent of the representation on the High Council, despite their overwhelming dominance of the population. Prunier (1997: 27) notes that they were altogether excluded from the chief system of government: 'by the end of the Belgian presence in Rwanda in 1959, forty-three chiefs out of forty-five were Tutsis as well as 549 sub-chiefs out of 559'. Lemarchand (1970: 134) contrasts the relationship in the post-war period with the pre-colonial period: 'Social differentiation between Hutu and Tutsi was actually greater in the post-war years than at any time during the pre-colonial period.' The Belgians were intent on reversing the Hutu fortunes.

In 1959 the Umwami Mutara Rudahigwa died suddenly after medical treatment in Burundi. Conservative Tutsi politicians chose his successor, Kigeri Ndahindurwa, without input from the Belgians. As part of the transition to responsible government, Belgium announced elections for the end of 1959, and new political parties emerged to stake out their respective claims for political change: the Hutu PARMEHUTU party—party of the movement for the emancipation of the Hutu, on the one side, and the Tutsis UNAR party—party for the national Rwanda union, on the other. Following an attack by Tutsi youths against a Hutu sub-chief, Dominique Mbonyumutwa, on 1 November, Hutus rose up in rebellion. Although the rumours of Mbonyumutwa's death were false, gangs of Hutus burned the homes of scores of Tutsi chiefs over the next week, and forced them to flee. This provoked violent counter-attacks by Tutsi against Hutu political figures who were kidnapped and tortured. A state of emergency was declared on 11th November, and Colonel Guy Logiest, with aid from the Congo Force Publique and Belgian paratroopers restored order. After the November uprisings, there was widespread mass opposition to Tutsi chiefs.

Logiest instructed local Belgian administrators to depose as many such chiefs as possible. Other Tuutsi chiefs and subchiefs fled from their posts...Logiest and his delegates then appointed new, interim chiefs, who were supporters of the Hutu parties...Logiest's policy was intended to prevent a return to power by Tuutsi (Newbury 1988: 197).

By the following March, Hutus held half the chiefdoms and over half the sub-chiefdoms. In the 1961 elections supervised by the UN, the Hutu parties won an overwhelming majority of votes, and abolished the monarchy through a referendum. In a period of months, the minority Tutsi was annihilated from the political land-scape. The Belgian administrator, Colonel Guy Logiest

was clearly and outspokenly in favour of the Hutus and declared that it was the duty of the colonial administrators to 'disfavour the Tutsi element...[and to] favour the Hutu element.' Far from being neutral or passive the Belgium administration thus legitimized Hutu domination and the practices employed by certain groups to attain this domination. Hatred and violence could be capitalized upon (Kroslak, 2008: 24).

Hatzfeld reports that after the death of Mwami Mutara Rudahigwa in 1959, the colonial authorities deported many Tutsis internally. 'Desperate Tutsis, fleeing the deadly pogroms celebrating the aboli-tion of their monarchy, were herded onto the wooden beds of trucks provided by the Belgian colonial administration and, after traveling all night, were abandoned on the banks of the Akanyaru River' in Bugesera (Hatzfeld, 2005: 18). In urban areas, fights broke out between gangs of young Tutsis and Hutus that led to assaults, arson, and murder. A mass exodus of Tutsis occurred, the first of many. 'Hutu peasants burned down Tutsi chiefs' houses with no reaction from the colonial authority...Native authorities [i.e. Tutsi chiefs]...faced increasingly violent attacks from the White Fathers' missions, which, with the hardly disguised complicity of colonial civil servants, encour-aged the subversive scheming of Hutu peasants' (Semujanga 2003: 179–80).

Hutus were groomed as the new Belgian clients. Colonial author-ities were complicit in violence against the Tutsis to consolidate ties to the political leadership of the majority Hutus. When thousands of Tutsi homes were burned down, and Tutsi chiefs murdered in the Hutu revolution between 1959 and 1962, the Belgian security forces seemed incapable of bringing the offenders before the law, and encouraged the diaspora of the Tutsis. They orchestrated admin-istrative elections to force their former clients out of positions of authority. Mamdani notes (2001: 125): 'the colonial government literally surrendered control over local government to the insurgents'. Lemarchand says similarly that, without the Belgium administration, the events following 1959 would have been a revolt, not a political revolution. The transfer of power polarized the groups, encouraged animosity, and empowered the majority without any protection of minority rights.

How did administrative and racial closure come together in the genocide?

Evidence from the African Rights reports

African Rights (AR) is a Kigali-based human rights group formed in 1992 by Alex de Waal and Rakya Omaar. After the 1994 genocide, it researched a mountain of evidence documenting the events that transpired in Rwanda in 1994 and thereafter. Of specific interest here are local histories of the genocide at the level of specific sectors from across Rwanda. The histories were based on interviews with persons in prison, as well as survivors, and witnesses from over forty cells within six sectors from across the country (African Rights 2003a–e; 2005). There are recurrent themes from these micro-histories about how such large numbers of persons were recruited for genocide. The accounts report detailed information about who was killed, identifying them by name, and indicating who participated in the murders, when the activities started, and who played a role in orchestrating them. Frequently, neighbours formed large groups that collectively undertook arson, murder, rape, and looting. What comes across in every report is the personal nature of the killings. Each cell had only a few Tutsi families, all known by name. The marshalling of violence against them was not spontaneous. In every sector, it was orchestrated by the army officers, councillors, préfects, sous-prefects, bourgmestres, judges, and teachers (e.g. African Rights, 2003a: 15; African Rights, 2003b: 13, 33; African Rights, 2005: 7–8). The local people were hectored by their politicians to participate. If locals showed a lack of initiative, killings were precipitated by more enthusiastic militias from other communes and provinces. As Jefremovas observed (2002: 119) 'the so-called spontaneous violence can be shown to have been systematic and cold-blooded. It did not arise out of ancient hatreds but through overt political manipulation, ruthlessly orchestrated by a morally bankrupt elite.' Having said that, it is important not to miss the emotional consequences of the invasion of Rwanda by Ugandan Tutsis in 1990, and the subsequent assassination of the president, a person referred to repeatedly as 'the father of the nation'. Fear, anger, and resentment are critical in understanding the psychogenesis of the genocide, that is, the emotional mentality of the masses recruited into the acts of mass murder. In a study of female génocidaires, Adler et al (2007) argued that the assassination created a 'disaster mentality' and 'confusion'.

After the initial incursion of the Rwandan Patriotic Front into Rwanda from Uganda in October 1990, there was tremendous alarm about the threats to individual security attributed to the Inyenzi (cockroaches) and their Tutsi collaborators. McDoom (2012: 144) reports interview data that showed that there was a step-wise decline in inter-ethnic relationships, and a loss of personal security following the 1990 invasion, which declined more sharply after the assassination of the president. The invasion was immediately exploited by Hutu extremists in political rallies and mass media broadcasts to justify a righteous slaughter in the defence of the political emancipation that the Hutus had achieved under the first two republics. This drew on racial closure in speeches such as that of Leon Mugesera who advocated the deportation of Tutsis back to Ethiopia via a short-cut, the Nyanboronga River, a tributary of the Nile. The invasion was represented as a return to traditional exploitation.

A second point raised in the African Rights investigations was the role of the 'self-defence committees' and night patrols created by local politicians immediately following the murder of President Habyarimana on 6 April. These were organized at sector and cell levels to screen all travellers on major roads and paths to identify potential enemies. Initially, Tutsis in the south joined these patrols prior to the president's death (McDoom 2012: 151) but discovered that *all* Tutsis had become suspect thereafter. In addition, the 'responsibles' and councillors were strategic in generating lists of victims beforehand to indicate who was to be eradicated. This proved relatively simple given Rwanda's administrative structure, and the intimate knowledge neighbours had of one another. Third and relatedly, the hierarchy of officials from 'responsibles' to councillors and 'bourgmestres' distributed guns, grenades, and machetes, and coached the ordinary citizens that it was their duty to eliminate the invaders, and their Tutsi collaborators, and ultimately supervised the murders by scheduling when and where the common people were to meet in order to undertake their 'work'.

The killings were rationalized as a form of self-defence, a continuation of the political revolution under which the feudal yoke of Tutsi domination had been originally cast off in 1961. It was organized as traditional corvée labour called *umuganda*—unpaid labour to support the state that had been the traditional obligation of Hutus. *Umuganda* under Habyarimana's republic had replaced colonial *akazi* labour, and obligated every adult to contribute to community projects. Rooting out the threat to security was imposed on every peasant, usually under threats of small fines and verbal rebukes by local political figures (Hatzfeld 2005; African Rights 2003a–e), although in Gishamuvu cell the councillor suggested that 'any Hutu he found at home after 7:00 am on Saturday [9 April] would face terrible consequences, including the possibility of being shot' (African Rights 2003a: 5). The officials organized squadrons of peasant killers to comb the bushes and marshes, using whistles to start and stop the operations to 'hunt down the inyenzi'.

The officials were also instrumental in the immediate distribution of the booty of the victims. Army and gendarmerie seized cars and trucks, if they existed. The militia carted away furniture and household goods. The neighbours seized the tile roofs and corrugated tin siding. And the least powerful in the community, often old women, raided the gardens and harvested the crops. In some places, the price of meat cratered as so many Tutsi cattle were butchered immediately after the murder of their herdsmen. This created material incentives 'from the bottom', aside from any ideological justifications for mass murder. This material incentive is often overlooked, not least by Osiel (2009: 214). For a period of time, a festive atmosphere marked every evening as *génocidaires* feasted on meat, and got intoxicated with Primus and banana beer. Hutu families celebrated their newly acquired booty. Because of the disruption of society, the Church stopped administering the sacraments. There were no marriages, masses, baptisms, or Christian burials for weeks. And when the national army failed to defend Kigali, millions of people picked up their possessions, and walked into exile, primarily to Zaire.

The AR interviews with those imprisoned indicated little sense of individual responsibility. They blamed the petty political officials who mobilized and coordinated murders on the ground, and the political militias who pressured them to kill. Hatzfeld's interviews (2005) with *génocidaires* in Bugesera supports the same finding. It was as though people were not responsible actors. They were recruited to kill, and they did what was required of them. In some cases, there were issues of personal antagonism, and settling of old conflicts. There was also an enthusiasm for acquiring new land for gardens inherited from the departed neighbours. But there was little evidence that those who took the lives of their neighbours experienced much in the way of shame, contrition, or embarrassment. Nor was the threat of force on them all that grave. Loyle (2012) suggests that common people, at least initially, were caught up in an emotional 'tsunami' as a result of the assassination.

The diffusion of murder after 6 April: evidence from Ibuka's Kibuye Dictionary Project

Semujanga (2003) makes a startling claim about the speed of the genocide. 'By some estimates more than a million and a half people were killed in Rwanda during just two weeks in April 1994.' Most experts offer a lower death toll, and a longer time frame. However, there is evidence that corroborates at least part of what he claims. Ibuka is the name of a group that advocates on behalf of Rwanda's genocide survivors (Rwanda 2008a). In the late 1990s, Ibuka undertook a survey of victims of genocide in Kibuye Province. Kibuye is a western province that borders Lake Kivu, and had traditionally a high percentage of Tutsis (some 15 per cent of the population). It was the site of several places of resistance where people gathered in the mountain forests to defend themselves, primarily Bisesero. The Kibuye Dictionary is a massive book that contains the names of all those killed (over 59000 single entries) in April to July of 1994 based on interviews conducted door to door throughout the province. The interviewers also gathered information about the gender, age, and lineage of the victims, the date they were killed, their occupations, and the methods used to kill them.

The African Rights study of Nyarugunga Sector, which is located adjacent to a military base, and home to the Presidential Guard just outside Kigali, suggests virtually all of the Tutsis there were murdered in their homes overnight within hours of Habyarimana's plane crash. 'By sunrise, the great majority of Tutsi families had already been killed' (2003b: 4). The report lists the names of almost fifty victims. What does Ibuka report for Kibuye? Kibuye is a half-day drive from the capital. The murders there began immediately, but killing took longer throughout the entire province. By the end of the first week of the genocide in Kibuye (12 April 1994) already

20 per cent, or 12 000, Tutsis living in Kibuye had been killed. The perpetrators killed another 25 per cent, or 15 000, of the resident Tutsis on 13 and 14 April. By the end of the second week, 20th April, already 80 per cent or 48 000 of the Tutsis of Kibuye had been massacred (Ibuka 1991: 10). This is consistent with Semujanga's estimate. The mobilization of the population in Kibuye was immediate, and the eradication of the Tutsi population was nearly instantaneous. Straus (2006: 256) points out that the killings commenced in all prefectures on the 6 or 7 of April, except in Gitarama and Butare where the killings commenced on 14 April. Figure 5.1 shows the daily pattern of murders based on the original Ibuka survey. Although 59 050 victims were identified, dates of death were only known precisely for 12 716 individuals. The graph is based on Philip Verwimp's published projections for all 59 050 victims over the first twelve weeks.

The graph shows that the murders were concentrated over the first two weeks. Over 10 000 Tutsis had been concentrated in Kibuye town by 15 April. Some 5 000 were murdered in the

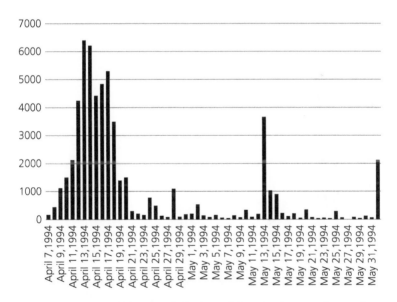

Figure 5.1 Date of death of Tutsis residing in the province of Kibuye

Sources: Ibuka (1999: 10); Verwimp (2004: 241).

Gatwaro stadium, and a similar number in the grounds of the Catholic church. The massacre at Bisesero started on 13 May. The spike on the far right of the graph represents all the deaths up to 2 July. The first United Nations Security Council (UNSC) Motion on Rwanda—Number 912—was proposed on 21 April; it reduced Lt General Romeo Daillaire's peacekeeping force from 2 500 to 270. The second motion on 17 May (UNSC Motion 918) called for a new force of 5 500 troops. No troops were available. The third (UNSC Motion 929, 22 June) reflected France's proposal to undertake a peacekeeping operation (Operation Turquoise). What the Ibuka evidence suggests is that the vast majority of the victims were already killed before the UN undertook *any* action.

A second datum of information from the Ibuka report in Figure 5.2 is instructive in understanding the Rwandan genocide. How were people killed? Were they murdered by bullets from the army? Were they cut down with traditional weapons? The evidence suggests that over half of all victims were killed with machetes (52.9 per cent)—reflecting the popular participation in the killings. Another 16 per cent were killed by nail-studded clubs. The

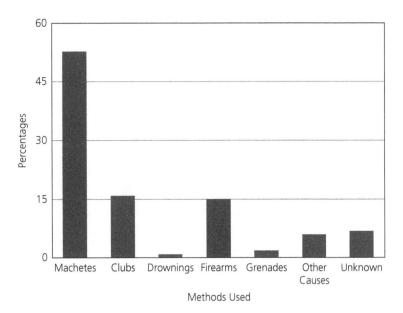

Figure 5.2 Methods used in province of Kibuye

Source: Ibuka (1999: 9).

Kibuye Dictionary Project put the figure of persons killed at some 59 000. The subsequent study by the Minister of Local Government, Information and Social Affairs (MINLOC 2002: 19) put the figure for Kibuye at 84 341 declared victims and 72 688 identified victims. The Kibuye report refers only to Tutsi deaths. The MINLOC Report did not distinguish lineage.

The Post-Colonial Legacy: The Culture of Complicity for Massacres (1959–1994)

The MINLOC Report provides some compelling evidence of how the Belgian colonial power, however inadvertently, planted the seeds for the pattern of massacres, and legal impunity that preceded the 1994 genocide. Having just been ousted from Congo by Patrice Lumumba, the Belgians were determined to hold on to their other colonies in Rwanda and Burundi, even if that required making Rwanda a republic by unseating the Umwami Mutara Rudahigwa. The king died suddenly of anaphylactic shock after receiving penicillin from a Belgian doctor in Burundi in 1959. In 1962, Belgian colonial officers engineered Rwandan independence under the rule of Gregoire Kayibanda, and an abolition of the monarchy by referendum. When Rwanda gained independence, there was widespread burning of Tutsi property, and massacres of thousands of Tutsis, prompting a mass exodus. When exiled Tutsis attempted a military raid back to Rwanda from Burundi in December 1962, there were some 10 000–14 000 reprisal murders of Rwandan Tutsis (Twagilimana 2003: 75). During the period of the Hutu revolution (1959–63) over 150 000 Tutsis fled Rwanda for safety elsewhere. The Belgians were complicit in these atrocities. Indeed, Colonel Guy Logiest warned at the time that if the exiles returned to Rwanda to provoke an insurrection, the consequences would be fatal for all Tutsis. 'If such a movement be called into life by the Tutsi, it will be the prognostication of their massacre by the Hutu. I think that the Tutsis, as a whole, realize this' (MINLOC 2002: 13 (translated from French)).

The same kind of messages were found in speeches by the first and second presidents of the new republic, suggesting that European diplomats would have known about the ideological orientation of the top leaders, as well as the ongoing massacres in the period from 1963 to 1990. In a March 1964 speech, President Kayibanda foretold the genocide addressing the Tutsis: 'Supposing the impossible that you come to take Kigali by storm, how would you assess the chaos in which you will become the first victims? You will say among yourselves: "this will be the final and hurried end of the Tutsi race." Who is exterminated?' Likewise in 1976 President Habyarimana reiterated the same warning: 'According to the History of Rwanda, we observe that the Tutsi say they are the descendants of heaven...these Tutsis who provoke the Hutu forget that if the hour of massacres should come again, it will be them to pay the price' (MINLOC 2002: 13). At some point after the Ugandan Tutsis invaded in October 1990, a section of the Hutu power circle started to plan the total annihilation of the Tutsis in earnest, but massacres of minority Tutsis had been a leitmotif of the republic since its inception. What is especially interesting is that there was not merely a culture of impunity with respect to the massacre of the former 'feudal' overlords. It was embedded in the law.

The amnesty laws

The first law was passed in May 1963 and covered the period from 1 October 1959 to 1 July 1962. This was one of the bloodiest periods of anti-Tutsi violence, often undertaken with support of the security forces and Hutu politicians. In November 1959 Belgium recognized the Hutu uprising against the Tutsi chiefs and placed Rwanda under military rule. As noted earlier, thousands of Tutsis were massacred (Kroslak 2008: 281). The first amnesty law appears to have been responsive to this crime wave. It appeared in the Appendix to the *Codes et Lois du Rwanda* until 1994. Table 5.2 reports the key sections in the original French and in English translation (from Brannigan and Jones 2009).

However, the massacres continued beyond this initial period. 'In Nyamata, the Rwandan army carrie[d] out the first widespread massacres of Tutsis' in Bugesera in 1963 (Hatzfeld 2005: xi). Although the laws provided for a political amnesty commission, there is no record of its proceedings. The amnesty decree was renewed in 1974.[4] These decrees are important because they provided a legal foundation to the wider culture of impunity that permitted the political marginalization and physical eradication of the Tutsi

---

[4] Martin Ngoga (2004: 2) suggests that the 1974 addition occurred in response to anti-Tutsi violence in 1972, but the law itself refers to breaches of 'state security' on the night of 18–19 September 1968.

Table 5.2 Amnesty law, *codes et lois du Rwanda*, 1991

DISPOSITIONS COMPLEMENTAIRES AMNISTIE	COMPLEMENTARY PROVISIONS AMNESTY
20 MAI 1963-Loi	20 MAY 1963-Law
Amnistie général des infractions politiques commises entre le 1er octobre 1959 et le 1er juillet 1962.	General amnesty for political infractions committed between 1 October 1959 and 1 July 1962.
1. Amnistie générale et inconditionnelle est accordée pour toutes les infractions commises à l'occasion de la Révolution Sociale pendant la période du 1er octobre 1959 au 1er juillet 1962 et qui, en raison de leur nature, de leur mobile, des circonstances ou des motifs qui les ont inspirés, rentrent dans le cadre de la participation à la lutte de libération nationale et revêtent ainsi un caractère politique même si elles constituent des infractions de droit commun.	1. Unconditional and general amnesty is given for all offences committed during the Social Revolution between 1 October 1959 and 1 July 1962, that due to their nature, their motives, their circumstances or what inspired them, are part of the fight for national liberation, and take on a political character even though these offences are an infringement of the common law.
2. Son écartées du bénéfice de l'amnestie accordée par l'article premier de la présente loi les infractions commises durant cette période par des personnes qui ont lutté contre la libération des masses opprimées par la domination féodo-colonialiste.	2. Offences committed during this period by people opposing the liberation of the oppressed masses from feudal-colonial domination are not covered by the amnesty given in the first article of this law.

minority. In his interviews with former perpetrators operating in the Bugesera region in April and May 1994, Hatzfeld reports that the killers operated without any sense of individual accountability. One reports, 'it gave me no pleasure, I knew I would not be punished, I was killing without consequences' (2005: 51). In the Bugesera case, instructions for the massacres were transmitted from the local judge, and the coordination of the killing parties who were searching homes, the bush, and the swamps was undertaken by the local mayor, councillors, policemen, and army officers. All this gave the killings the 'form' of law, if not the content, and that form was arguably reflected in the amnesty laws. The genocidal events that occurred in the spring of 1994 had been occurring on a smaller scale throughout the history of the Republic, and had never attracted punitive judicial condemnation.[5] In *Confessing to Genocide*, one of the most common points of resistance to confession was the belief that there would be a general amnesty, as in the past (African Rights 2000: 17–20).

The 1990 invasion and the subsequent massacres

The dictatorship of Gregoire Kayibanda ended in a *coup d'état* led by Juvenal Habyarimana in July 1973. He had been one of the first officers to train in the national army academy. There had been political friction due to cronyism associated with Kayibanda's contacts in Gitarama Province, as well as a concern with the ongoing violence against the remaining Tutsi elites. Habyarimana represented northern interests, and he instituted a relatively peaceful social transition. That situation changed dramatically in October 1990 with the invasion of northern Rwanda by elements of the Rwandan Patriotic Front (RPF), led by Major General Fred Rwigyema and Major Paul Kagame.

Reprisal massacres occurred almost immediately. On 11–13 October, in Kibilira, Tutsi civilians were attacked by army and militia units resulting in the death of an estimated 400 civilians. Five hundred homes were set on fire and 10 000 Tutsi 'suspects' were rounded up, imprisoned, and tortured (Wallis 2006a: 58). In 1991,

---

[5] Twagilimana (2007: 22) notes that in the Bugesara massacres of March 1992, 'even though there were about 466 persons arrested, they were all sent home after some months without any indictment'. In 1963 after an estimated 14 000 Tutsis were murdered, Bertrand Russell described the event as 'the most horrible and systematic massacre since the Holocaust'.

from mid-January to mid-March, several hundred more people known as the Bigogwe (a regional group of north-western Tutsi pastoralists) were murdered (Twagilimana 2007: 9; Dorsey 1994: 179). In March 1992 there was a large-scale massacre of the Tutsis of Bugesera, sometimes thought of as a 'dress rehearsal' for the genocide (Des Forges 1999: 70). 'Two more landmarks were the massacres at Kibuye in August 1992 and at Gisenyi in February 1993' (Kroslak 2008: 38). Mamdani (2001: 92) estimated that 3 000 were murdered from 1990 to 1994. Wallis (2006a: 57) put the figure at 15 000. Human Rights Watch claims there were sixteen attacks against civilian Tutsis prior to April 1994 (HRW 2006b: 7). During the period leading up to April 1994, Hutu extremist political parties created militias of young men to kill civilians with traditional weapons. These included the MRND's *Interahamwe* and the Coalition for the Defence of the Republic's (CRD) *Impuzamugambi*. Secret training camps were created and operated by the Presidential Guards and French military instructors to train these militias (Wallis 2006a: 54–5). They were enlisted in the massacres prior to April 1994.

Remarkably, the killings were the subject of two international reports. After a brief visit to Rwanda in 1993, UN Special rapporteur, Bacre Waly Ndiaye, concluded that the post-invasion massacres constituted genocide (UN 1993, paras 78–81) and that they had been precipitated by Rwandan officials. 'The role of such officials (prefects, sub-prefects, mayors, councillors, sector leaders, or cell leaders) in the massacres of civilian populations consists chiefly in encouraging, planning and directing the operation, and in some cases in actually participating in it' (para 37). A similar report was published in 1993 by the International Commission of Investigations of Human Rights Violations in Rwanda (USIP 2012); it also concluded that genocide was taking place in Rwanda that year. Despite repeated major massacres, no one was held accountable for these acts of mass murder. The amnesty laws reflected the assumption that mass murders could be undertaken with impunity. The other lesson here is that genocide prevention cannot be premised on the existence or credible, prior expert knowledge since, in this case, there was no shortage of that.

Conclusion: The Psychogenesis of Genocide

If people have a high level of autonomy and great latitude in choices, when they choose badly, guilt is common since it represents the failure of self-control. In a society where control is exercised primarily through political hierarchy, as external control, high levels of compliance in murder do not produce a comparable sense of guilt. *Yes, we acted badly. But we did it to serve the leader. We resorted to the machetes because you ordered it. And we stopped when you said it was enough. Why is everyone angry with us now? We only did what was expected of us. No one can escape his obligations or his duties.* This is the mentality of the surviving *génocidaires* who have displayed such an emotional insensitivity to their role in mass slaughter. They are deeply compelled by communitarian obligations and hierarchically denominated choices in which Western 'individualism', and its corresponding culpability, cannot be presupposed (see Lugan 2003: 167–8.)

6

Catalysts and Accomplices

Introduction: Complicity in Mass Murder

Most inquiries into genocide and similar crimes begin by conceptualizing the stakeholders in juxtaposed categories corresponding to perpetrators and their victims. We classify the opposing parties in terms of their innate power or vulnerability, and explain crimes primarily in terms of the motives of the former against the latter, and the chasm of power and vulnerability between them i.e. Young Turks vs Armenians, Nazis vs Jews, Guatemalan Army vs Mayan peasants, Khmers vs urban Cambodians. This post hoc bias overlooks the context and process under which crimes are realized, and overlooks the complicity of other key actors (Grunfeld and Huijboom 2007). The issue that I explore in this chapter is the role of 'small fish', bystanders, and third parties, as well as inanimate events, as catalysts that help shape the outcomes that we recognize as genocide or analogous behaviour. I approach this process at three levels. At the first instance is the issue of enlisting the participation of individuals who are actually deployed to carry out the sovereign's plans for mass aggression. I have devoted considerable attention to understand how this was possible in the Rwandan case. Here I explore the dynamics of this in light of some field studies that document the contingencies of this process in greater detail. At a second level, I emphasize the role of technical, scientific, and bureaucratic processes that expedite the sovereign's plans, and give the key actor leverage without which the genocide could not attain global consequences. Finally, I raise the issue of the ideological work done to mask, or expedite, the processes of genocide and war crimes. Evidence for this latter perspective is based on an analysis of the role of the UN and leading European powers, particularly France, in the near total annihilation of Rwandan Tutsis in 1994. This perspective likewise points us to the role of the UN in the Bosnian massacres and genocide during the partition of the Balkans.

Where history generally tends to focus on primary agents, the thesis advanced here attempts to capture agency in the *periphery* of genocidal intent, i.e. in the role of an accompanying partner, the bystander, or collaborator with the capacity to escalate a massacre into a holocaust, or to emasculate it altogether. Such parties have agency or capacity to act without the *explicit* intent to initiate genocide. Their culpability is ambiguous, or may have no subjective element of agency, because of the diffusion of responsibility among actors and institutions (Cohen 2001). Sociological complicity is more an issue of capacity to act, and to intervene, in a situation where the accomplice, in a 'state of denial', aids and abets a scheme authored primarily by others *without sharing the same genocidal motivation as the principal actors*. In short, genocidal intentions among elites at times can only be realized by the complicity of actors who are often indifferent or impartial to the intentions of the perpetrators. Bystanders can be catalysts. By the same token, interveners can be spoilers.

This analysis points to the role of social complicity in murder. The approach to complicity stands in contrast to the very explicit construction of *mens rea* or intent in the Genocide Convention. The international convention on genocide adopted by the ICTR and ICTY requires 'specific intent' to establish culpability for genocide. By way of illustration, to establish genocide, it is insufficient to recklessly kill civilians through indiscriminate aerial bombing of German and Japanese cities in the Second World War (Grayling 2006). In neither case was there 'specific intent' to destroy 'in whole or in part a national, ethnical, racial or religious group' as such. This is of course hypothetical since the Genocide Convention post-dated these events. Or, to draw on a more recent controversy from the Rwandan experience, the 'double genocide' theory associated with Hutu Power propaganda holds that in 1994 there was a plan of *mutual* annihilation by both Hutus and Tutsis attributed to a mythical history of tribal hatred (Prunier 1997: 297; Verwimp 2003; Davenport and Stam 2009). While the culpability of the Hutu Power parties for genocide has been well established, the culpability of the Tutsi for large-scale reprisal shootings during the invasion of Rwanda is less settled (Prunier 1997: 305). Specifically, there is no evidence to establish that, in 1994, the RPF was planning to annihilate the Hutu people in whole or in part. Without establishing evidence of such a plan, there is no case of genocide to meet, and no issue of 'specific intent'. Having said that, it is nonetheless true that the Ugandan Tutsis who comprised the RPF invasion force were shocked by the evidence of Hutu massacres of their families and compatriots, and murdered many civilians in reprisal (Lemarchand 2009a: 133). The cases of the Allied bombing campaign, the destruction of Japanese cities, and RPF reprisal shootings may meet the test of war crimes or crimes against humanity under international law, but they are beyond the specific *mens rea* requirements of genocide under the UN Convention, i.e. *dolus specialis*—control of a course of action expressly designed to eliminate in whole or in part one of the four protected groups. By contrast, the culpability of those *complicit* in genocide is a greyer area. In my view, sociological complicity is an even broader concept than 'complicity to genocide' as defined by the ICTR and ICTY. The ICTR defines complicity as follows: 'complicity to commit genocide in Article 2(3)(e) refers to all acts of assistance or encouragement that have substantially contributed to, or have had a substantial effect on, the completion of the crime of genocide' (*Prosecutor v Semenza*, Case No. ICTR-97-20 (Trial Chamber) 15 May 2003, para 395). In *Prosecutor v Akayesu* (Case No. ICTR-96-4-T (Trial Chamber) 2 September 1998, paras 533–7) the Trial Chamber described some of the defining elements of complicity. These included (a) procuring the means of destruction by providing weapons and advice, (b) knowingly aiding or abetting the perpetrators in planning or enabling the acts of genocide, and/ or (c) instigating genocidal behaviour in other persons or inducing compliance through gifts or coercion, or directly inciting genocide. Unlike aiding and abetting a crime, the *actus reus* of complicity requires a *positive* act, not simply an omission. For example, a crime could be abetted by failure to report the identity and location of a suspect. Complicity would require actively protecting the identity of a suspect. In addition, the *mens rea* for complicity requires that the accused *know* that the crime being supported was criminal, in other words, 'the mens rea ... required for complicity in genocide is knowledge of the genocidal plan' (HRW 2006a: 31). However, culpability of complicity does *not* require the special intent to commit genocide. A person may knowingly support the genocidal actions of others even though such a person does not share the specific intent to destroy a national, ethnical, racial, or religious group. *Mens rea*—yes. *Dolus specialis*—no. In addition, complicity can only be charged if genocide itself is established independently. Hence, no genocide, no complicity.

At the ICTR, there have been numerous charges of, and several important convictions of, complicity in genocide. Jean Kambanda, prime minister of the 1994 interim government of Rwanda created by the coup leaders in April 1994, was convicted of genocide, incitement of genocide, and complicity in genocide, in addition to crimes against humanity. Many of the same 'concise statement of facts' are used to support the different charges, i.e. genocide, complicity in genocide, conspiracy to commit genocide etc. (*Prosecutor v Kambanda*, Case No. ICTR-97-23 (Trial Chamber) 4 September 1998, paras 3.12–3.15). In paragraph 3.12, Kambanda is charged with public support of the genocide promotion by Radio Télévision Libre des Mille Collines. Elsewhere he is charged with promoting the genocide in speeches to préfects and other government functionaries and individuals in the militias, who were primarily responsible for the killings, and encouraging and congratulating those who were committing murder and rape. Through these actions and speeches, he became an accomplice (i.e. complicit) to genocide. Similarly, Laurent Semanza, bourgmestre for Bicumbo commune for twenty years before 1993, was acquitted of genocide *per se* but convicted of complicity in genocide for transporting members of the militia, and their weapons, to locations at which people had been concentrated for annihilation. Allegations that he planned and orchestrated the murders were unsupported on the evidence, hence no conviction for genocide, although he was convicted of crimes against humanity for rape, torture, murder, and extermination.

The ICTR cases of complicity have a number of common features. The charge of complicity is typically embedded in a series of related charges involving genocide and crimes against humanity. The accused are typically government officials or members of Hutu Power parties who engaged in various activities sometimes before and, almost invariably, during the widespread massacres of 1994. The accused are typically in an authority structure with ties to the hierarchy most closely associated with the planning and realization of the genocide. They are virtually all Rwandans. The charges sometimes appear as 'insurance charges' that create a secondary liability (of complicity) should the main charge (genocide) fail to meet the legal test. However, they nonetheless carry extremely serious penalties. Kambanda, convicted of both genocide and complicity in genocide, received life imprisonment. Semanza, convicted of complicity, and crimes against humanity, received twenty-five years.

There are no cases where the accused was convicted and sentenced solely for complicity, so the determination of the magnitude of the penalty owed specifically, and solely, to this crime is difficult to determine. However, in *Semenza* the Chamber did indicate 'that the appropriate sentence for the Accused for complicity in genocide (Count 3) and for aiding and abetting extermination as a crime against humanity (Count 5) is two terms of fifteen years imprisonment' to be served concurrently (*Semenza*, para 585). This suggests that the tariff for complicity *per se* on these facts is one term of fifteen years' imprisonment—an extremely grave penalty.

The inchoate crime of complicity, like aiding and abetting, conspiracy to commit genocide, and attempted genocide, recognizes the spectrum of culpability surrounding the crime of genocide, and provides legal tools to call to account those who played a supporting function in these crimes. It may ultimately function to deter future actors from behaving in a similar fashion by widening the net of culpability, although the deterrent effect of law generally is weak for garden-variety crimes. Nonetheless, it recognizes the peculiar structure of this form of murder. Unlike garden-variety murders that can be perpetrated solo with little planning beforehand, or contemplation of consequences, genocide is the work of many hands that typically entails command responsibility and participation in a joint criminal enterprise, factors that make it vulnerable to control (Osiel 2009). It is characterized by a coordination of action in an authority structure, often with a propaganda function designed to make the activities socially defensible, and often orchestrated and realized over a long period of time and across many events. The peculiar structure of genocide may provide legal devices for attenuating its development by restraining not only the principal architects of mass murder, but the enormous supporting cast whose activities contribute to, in the wording of *Semenza*, 'the *completion* of the crime of genocide'.

Level I: Attracting Perpetrators

In complicated crimes such as genocide, complicity may be critical for ensuring that the crime is completed by those to whom it is delegated, that it receives material support for its success, and that it is ideologically justified. In fact, the success of the crime may be entirely contingent on the cooperation of exogenous parties. This raises an important theoretical issue in genocide studies that concerns the doctrine of 'intentionality' versus 'contingency' in the explanation of genocide. Do genocides and analogous offences occur because the leaders plan annihilation of their enemies a priori? Or do they happen due to emergent and contingent events only loosely associated with a master plan? Scott Straus argues in favour of the case for contingency and cumulative radicalization: 'I argue that Rwanda's genocide was not necessarily "meticulously planned" well in advance' (2006: 12). He points out that, following the crash killing President Habyarimana, several senior army officers opposed Bagosora's military coup following the evening of 6 April (2006: 46), and elected to pursue the Arusha accords. Colonel Léonidas Rusatira, interim chief of staff of the Rwandan government forces, opposed the coup d'état, personally aided Tutsis to escape capture, and attempted to create a cease-fire with the RPF to create the broadly based government of national unity proposed by the Arusha accords (Dallaire 2003: 251–4). He and others were almost immediately marginalized, and departed Rwanda under French military escort. The Kibat record of the Belgian peacekeepers suggests that at the time of the crash the armed forces at Kanombe military base were asleep (Belgium 1994)—in contrast to the Presidential Guard who secured the airport crash site within minutes. Obviously, there were different stakeholders jockeying for control over events, and Rusatira's men were out of the loop. Straus's view downplays the previous existence of a plan to murder the entire Tutsi population, to assassinate Belgian peacekeepers to hasten the departure of the UN peacekeeping force, and to train militias to kill Tutsi civilians—things related to Lt General Dallaire, commander of the UN peacekeeping force, months before the assassination of the president in April (Dallaire 2003: 141–4). Verwimp argues, 'most scholars writing about the Rwandan genocide are convinced that the plan to commit genocide was developed in the period between November 1991 and August 1992' (2006: 3). Others suggest they developed soon after the first incursion of Ugandan Tutsis into Rwanda in October 1990. As we saw in the last chapter, massacre and counter-massacre were features of the political landscape from the inception of the republic, but these events did not enjoy the unanimous support from senior army personnel. The early 1990s was a period in which several leading businessmen began to import large numbers of machetes and transistor radios for use in the massacres, all tracked through The Bank of Kigali. Contrary to the 'contingency' hypothesis, the African Rights (2003c) history of the genocide reported that mass killings of Tutsis by the Presidential Guard began in Nyarugunga Sector in Kanombe district within hours of Habyarimana's assassination—based on those lists of targeted victims that Lieutenant General Dallaire had been warned of months previously. Something was obviously meticulously planned beforehand. Moderate politicians began to disappear within hours of the crash. Straus may be correct that there were influential actors who were not architects of the plan, but who were conscripted as the plan was put into place, and others who opposed it from the start, and were subsequently neutralized as Bagosora pulled together an interim government dedicated to genocide.

Straus argues 'the Hutu hardliners fomented mass violence against the Hutu population in order to combat the RPF. But when the hardliners first gave the orders to do so—assuming that they did in fact issue an explicit private order to attack Tutsi civilians—is unclear' (2006: 49). That may be true in respect of mobilization of the peasants, but the orders to the Presidential Guard and the Para-Commando Battalion appear to have been issued almost immediately—and not privately—after the crash. On the night of 6–7 April, Théoneste Bagosora contacted Lieutenant Colonel Anatole Nsengiyumva 'to begin the massacres in Gisenyi' (*Prosecutor v Bagosora*, Case No. ICTR-96-7-1 (revised indictment) 12 August 1999, para 6.3). At 5:00 am on 7 April Bagosora 'personally ordered a group of Interahamwe from Remera, the INYANGE, to commence exterminating the civilian Tutsi population' (para 6.32). In addition, all the Hutu Power politicians were removed from their homes that evening and relocated to the Diplomat Hotel. The moderates were not evacuated, but slated for murder. The radio station RTLM broadcast names of Tutsis, along with their addresses and vehicle licence numbers, to be singled out for extermination. Prime Minister Agathe Uwilingiyimana's neighbourhood was sequestered, and she was murdered on the morning of 7 April within twelve hours of the murder of the president. Here there is little evidence for cumulative radicalization, and more a case for the 'third force' shedding the non-conformists. Straus is correct to point out that the perpetrators had to negotiate with many actors to realize the genocide. The prefect for Butare, Jean-Baptiste Habyalimana, was a Tutsi, and initially jailed the Interahamwe members, before being deposed, and disappeared, at the orders of the new prime minister. This delayed the massacres in Butare by two weeks.

Another illustration involved Jean-Paul Akayesu, former bourgmestre of Taba. With his eight police officers, Akayesu had valiantly opposed violence after the assassination of the president until 18 April when the interim government convened a meeting of all the republic's mayors and prefects, and sent the Interahamwe to expedite the killings. At a public meeting in May, he reluctantly read a list of names of suspected RPF supporters—effectively condemning them to death. Cruvellier summarized the effect:

[i]t was not a great criminal conspiracy set in motion through the actions of the former bourgmestre as the impromptu execution, so to speak, of a genocide legitimized by the interim government on the national level…and implemented in a disciplined manner by a local authority who clearly lacked criminal intent at the start (2010: 28).

It was a halting plan opposed by many middle-level politicians and senior army officers, usually unsuccessfully.

However, as we saw in the last chapter, overall the genocide proceeded like clockwork, and was completed swiftly. In this process, Bagosora and the other architects of the genocide relied on the complicity of other key figures—army officers, politicians, the clergy, the French allies, and the vast population of peasants. Rather than juxtaposing 'intentionality' and 'contingency' as *alternative* explanations of genocide, it appears that both factors were critical. Straus's 'hardliners' mobilized thousands of accomplices of varying degrees of culpability, from zealous butchers in the Interahamwe, to compliant peasants reluctant to refuse demands put to them by their political leaders. But the evidence of a long-standing plan is well established. What is less well established is how the architects of the genocide could count on the population for their cooperation. This has been examined by Fujii (2009) and McDoom (2005).

Fujii offers a radical situationalist interpretation of the dynamics of the mass murders that occurred in Rwanda in the early 1990s, culminating in the genocide of 1994. Fujii spent nine months in Rwanda in 2004 dividing her time between two secteurs in rural Rwanda—'Kimanzi' in Ruhengeri Province in the north, and 'Ngali' in Gitarama Province in the south. The sampling frame permitted access to people in different regions of the country, and to people who had participated in the murderous events of 1994, in one way or another, or who had desisted. Those in the north were brought into conflict with the RPF incursion by Ugandan Tutsis into northern Rwanda in October 1990. Those in the south felt few effects of the nascent civil war until the assassination of the president on 6 April 1994.

Fujii's analysis begins by examining 'the local narratives and explanations' of genocide employed by residents to make sense of the genocide. At the neighbourhood level, Fujii suggests that there was no evidence of systematic inter-ethnic hatred or fear in the north prior to 1990. In the south, things changed overnight with the assassination of the Rwandan president. The secteur leader organized night patrols, recruited men into killing groups, and prepared for defence against the RPF. Tutsi homes were immediately burned and pillaged. However, even in the south, not everyone participated in killing. Fujii argues that many people explained their participation in situational terms. 'Circumstances compelled people to do what they did. People had no choice' (Fujii 2009: 90). Why not? As one resident of Ngali explained: 'the mobilization by authorities...made the war escalate between the people'. Other informants noted that some neighbours transformed into Power Hutus instantaneously after the assassination (Fujii 2009: 91). According to Fujii, if the norm was that neighbours protect neighbours when things get tough, 'then the only explanation for the murderous transformation in some people was situational exigencies that were beyond anyone's control' (Fujii 2009: 93). Both Fujii and McDoom reject the idea that Rwandans were docile actors readily obedient to authority, but active agents in the genocide as it unfolded.

In 'The Logic of Groups' Fujii takes up the narratives associated with the rationale of the Joiners. Fujii suggests that the formation of groups that undertook violence was initially unplanned, but subsequently gathered a momentum. People joined groups whose character was initially spontaneous. However, once they joined they found themselves compelled to participate. They could not resist because 'they had no power...no one would listen to them' (Fujii 2009: 163). 'They did not believe they could affect the outcome in any way...there is little evidence that Joiners tried to hide, evade, resist, or free-ride in any way once they joined in the violence' (p. 166). 'For going along with the group at each step, from conducting night patrols to killing Tutsi, shifted the responsibility to act, and act purposely, on the group.' Fujii refers to 'the constitutive power' of killing in groups. The groups killed collectively, in public, intimately, and theatrically. Once created, the group identity overtook individual identities, and the larger the group, the weaker the sense of individual responsibility. Such group formations occurred throughout Rwanda, although the effectiveness of middle-level authorities in creating them varied from province to province. Wherever the locals were reluctant to act, the Interahamwe were often dispatched to take the lead.

McDoom (2005) also reports from fieldwork conducted in Rwanda in 2002 and 2003. Like Fujii, he notes dramatic differences in the regions, particularly the differences between the north and south. By 1994, the northerners were already mobilized against the Tutsis as a result of exposure to the Ugandan invasion. However, he argues that there was a great deal of negotiation among middle-level authorities before they committed themselves to the genocidal project. What was decisive was the perception on the part of the population that the Ugandan invasion threatened to reverse the political gains of the 1959 Hutu revolution, and that the genocide was endorsed by legitimate authorities. Once these conditions were met, the Hutu farmers were mobilized en masse. McDoom (2011) also reports that recruitment to killings was mediated by proximity to the sites of violence, and household and neighbourhood participation in the killing. Verwimp (2011) makes a similar point about the spatial element in the 1990–92 massacres; they tended to occur in areas under spatial reorganization, particularly in northern Rwanda where there was a deliberate policy of minimalizing pastoral allotments in favour of agriculture devoted to the preparation of export crops.

What lessons can be drawn from the situationalist thesis? They do not present a strong challenge to my emphasis on administrative and ethnic closure. What they provide is a picture of heterogeneity of participation within these larger structures. Fujii's radically independent agents pretty much did what they were told.

The crash intrigue

One of the most important and contingent aspects of the genocide was the event that set it in motion: the assassination of President Habyarimana. Who killed the president? Straus attributes the assassination to the RPF. 'The current balance of evidence suggests the RPF was responsible' (2006: 44). This was also the conclusion of Michael Hourigan's confidential August 1997 report to the UN. Hourigan wrote that a 'Network' with the assistance of a foreign government 'shot down the Presidential aircraft'. 'Major General Paul Kagame was the overall operations commander' (UN 1997). Straus notes that 'the extremist assassination theory is favored in many seminal works on the genocide'—including Prunier (1997). The extremists were presumably the army elite, who stood to lose considerably in the terms negotiated under the Arusha accords which would have allocated half the senior military positions to the RPF, and half to the existing army, the FAR. There is no credible evidence that the RPF was responsible for the assassination of Habyarimana. The 'extremist' theory appears most economical. Otherwise, we are forced to speculate that there were two coups d'état coincidentally separated by twelve hours: one against the president by parties unknown, another against the prime minister, which we know was the work of the Presidential Guard. Theoretically, one cannot discount the importance of this. Straus argues that the RPF–FAR conflict provided the context for the genocide. 'Without a war in Rwanda, genocide would not have happened. (By war I mean here the civil war that began on 7 April 1994, after the president was assassinated and which the hardliners were losing)' (2006: 7). This date contrasts with the commencement of hostilities dating to 1 October 1990, the date of the first incursion of Ugandan Tutsis into northern Rwanda. Was the destruction of Habyarimana's plane by his own armed forces part of their escalation of the conflict, or an attack by the RPF designed to decapitate the government? The destruction of the president who was, according to hardliners, betraying his military may have provided the pretext for action. Currently, there is a great deal of uncertainty about the crash. There was no international investigation. The original black box containing the last recorded information about the flight appears to have disappeared. French anti-terrorist Judge Bruguière indicted former RPF senior officers for their role in the crime. This indictment has been dismissed by a respected Rwandan expert (Melvern 2006) and by the ICTR itself (Musoni 2006). More recently, the government of France has concluded that Habyarimana was assassinated by his own troops (Karuhanga and Kagire 2012).

For our purposes, it does not matter who killed Habyarimana. What matters is that if a theory of genocide is to identify the catalytic circumstances that encourage it, then war or civil war must be at the top of such a list. This was Martin Shaw's conclusion in *War and Genocide* (2003). In the past century it is difficult to identify genocidal mass murder that occurs without open warfare. Harff (2003) adds that the other leading predictors of genocide include autocratic regimes noted for their ethnic exclusionary ideology, and regimes marked by ongoing massacres of minorities, neither of which are truly exogenous explanations. These are among the most important catalysts. But all of them are contingent on a successful mobilization of the actual perpetrators, and that cannot be taken for granted.

Level II: The Experts

If we accept the logic of mass participation along the lines I have suggested following Elias and the thesis of 'over-control', there is a second level of effect without which the major crimes would be impossible. I contrast the Eliasian level of how people were recruited with what I call the Baumanian level. Zygmunt Bauman (1989) argued, contrary to Elias, that the Holocaust was a logical outcome of modernity, that is, technical rationality and economic efficiency without a moral compass. Bauman's thesis is not consistent with the maniacal conquest of Europe espoused by the Hitler and the Nazis, which was profoundly irrational, but it resonates with the success of the Nazis in enlisting the genius of the German engineers and scientists in designing war and Aryan supremacy in Europe (Jarausch 2002). These are separate but independent effects. One of the most compelling analyses of how this evolved in the 1930s is evident in Edwin Black's analysis of *IBM and the Holocaust* (2001). Black documents the case for the culpability of intellectuals and manufacturers in realizing the Holocaust in the Second World War, which established the critical role of experts as catalysts for mass murder. Although there were no computers in the 1930s, the Dehomag company had invented a sophisticated punch card and card sorting system. Dehomag was IBM's subsidiary in Germany, and its engineers worked with the Nazis to assist them to reach their objectives. The machines were originally invented to assist the tabulation of information about population characteristics in the 1890 US census. A card could be punched to record a number of salient characteristics such as age, gender, religion, occupation, citizenship etc.—and the machines could then 'read' the information on thousands of cards representing unique individuals within minutes, and produce summary statistics.

When the Nazis first came to power in 1933, one of their first objectives was to estimate the Jewish population. Dr Friedrich Zahn, Chairman of the German Statistical Office, worked with the Reich Census office to design a national census that would identify the racial characteristics of the entire population. The objective was not to identify devout or practising Jews, but 'racial' Jews, including those of 'mixed race'. The race professors and the leading statisticians worked with the Nazis to supply expertise to 'correctly' identify those destined for eradication. Half a million census-takers swept across Germany to canvas the country and delivered thousands of boxes of census cards to be analysed by IBM Germany. The census was repeated in the expanded Reich territories in 1939. IBM USA supplied the high quality cards needed, and negotiated the rental of thousands of Hollerith card sorters until the end of the war. The 1939 census included a separate household lineage card to identify racial predecessors. When the Nazis began to deport European Jews to eastern ghettos and death camps, the coordination of the rolling stock across occupied Europe was made possible with precision by IBM technology. Six thousand victims could be assembled on a train platform at a precise hour and delivered to a death camp whose previous 'inventory' had already been liquidated. In addition, every concentration camp acquired card sorters to help the regime identify causes of detainment (Jewish, criminal, Jehovah's witnesses, POWs, etc.), language, country of origin, age, occupation, etc. in order to track the success of the Final Solution. Germany became IBM's largest overseas customer, and in 1937 the president of IBM New York, Thomas Watson, was awarded the Hitler Prize for his contribution to the Reich. He returned it after the invasion of Western Europe in 1940. The company received rent throughout the war paid into Swiss bank accounts, and enjoyed enormous sales of the high-quality American card stock. Black's thesis is not that Watson and his employees co-invented the policy of genocide. They simply permitted their products to be employed to expedite it. They were a catalyst that extended the efficiency of mass murder, and without which the racial war would have been relatively retarded. They may not have had the culpability of the engineers who designed the industrial gas chambers and crematoria in the Polish killing camps or manufactured the gas, but they were party to the design objectives for every different application to which their technologies were applied. At the end of the war, they retrieved their machines and, ironically, were awarded a contract as information managers for the mountains of evidence of war crimes introduced at Nuremberg.

The IBM case widens the scope of persons who might be considered sociologically complicit in war crimes, genocide, and crimes against humanity. The fact that a private company might sell products to a state that is engaged in self-defence would not raise an eyebrow. The fact that they provision states and dictators who are conducting aggressive war certainly would, and many were called to account for this at Nuremberg. But the fact that they are materially provisioning a state to commit mass murder of civilians is morally, and surely legally, indefensible. This larger circle of culpability includes businessmen, demographers, engineers, and other technical experts who help realize mass murder without necessarily having any specific criminal intent. They are complicit by positive action. The circle should also include those who control the legitimation of crime, whether in the mass media or in religious organizations. Critics of dictatorial regimes who were leaders of national religions in both Nazi Germany and Rwanda were remarkably indifferent to the extremist policies of the members of their flocks. These bystanders were complicit by omission.

The genocidal elite can also be constrained by other forces in society, the security forces, or the society's moral and religious institutions, and by forces external to the sovereign state—trading partners, civic organizations, international news media, etc. Powers that transcend the parties in national conflict can broker peace agreements that neutralize genocidal policies, or they can fail to act, hence hastening genocide. That was the case of the UN in the 1994 Rwandan genocide and the 1995 massacres at Srebrenica in Bosnia.

Level III: Realizing Genocide: The Role of Ideological Accomplices

The role of supporting actors in helping to constitute or realize the genocide extends to ideology, justifications, and excuses that can alter the credibility of intervention or the failure to intervene. In the following discussion, I focus on the role of the UN in the Bosnian and Rwandan genocides of 1994–95, and the role of the UN and France in creating conditions that escalated the conflict in Rwanda into genocide, both in terms of precipitating violent conflict and in controlling how it was labelled.

Adam Lebor makes the case against the UN in Bosnia and Rwanda in a remarkable book, 'Complicity with Evil': The United Nations in the Age of Modern Genocide (2006). The title borrows from a conclusion of the UN report published in August 2000 that reviewed the UN peacekeeping operations of the 1990s. UN adherence to a strict diplomatic policy of impartiality between warring parties proved to be catastrophic. The report noted that where one party is clearly violating the UN Charter, 'continued equal treatment of the parties by the United Nations can in the best case result in ineffectiveness and in the worst may amount to complicity with evil' (2006: ix–x). Reflecting the observations of critics of UN ineptitude during the Bosnian war, Lebor (2006: 83) concludes that 'neutrality and impartiality in the face of sustained, organized aggression did not mean steering a middle course: they meant de facto appeasement, the aiding and abetting of genocide and ethnic cleansing'. Resolution 836 was passed by the UN in June 1993, and provided that the United Nations Protection Force (UNPROFOR) 'deter attacks' from areas declared to be 'safe areas' by the UN. These were principally Bosnian towns and villages. However, when the resolution was drafted, it did not say the areas 'would' be safe, implying a duty to make them so, but 'should' be safe, allowing the permanent members of the Security Council to appear to be acting decisively, but in fact obligating no one. Bosnian Serbs throughout the period 1992–95 carried out a policy of ethnic cleansing of mainly Bosnian Muslims as the former elements of Yugoslavia scrambled to carve out ethnically distinct territories. The conflict was marked by atrocities on all sides, but the Bosnian Serbs distinguished themselves in an aggressive war on civilian populations. The war included shelling hospitals and markets with mortar fire, employing snipers to shoot children at play and people shopping, massacring civilians displaced from their villages, and operating concentration camps where POWs were starved and tortured. Of the 162-plus people indicted at the ICTY, barely 5 per cent were Bosniak commanders—the majority were Serbs.

UNPROFOR was organized under a Chapter 7 deployment that permitted peacekeepers to employ force to meet the mandate of the Security Council's resolutions. NATO had provided fighter jets to attack Serbian military targets, but even when these were requested repeatedly by the Dutch peacekeepers in Srebrenica in July 1995, the UN commanders would not consent to have the aircraft deployed for fear of creating the impression that they were choosing sides. There were other tactical considerations, including the kidnapping of UN peacekeepers, aid workers, and observers by Bosnian Serbs. The Bosnian Serbs effectively held the UN captive, and prevented the world body from carrying out the mandate of the Security Council. On 10 August 1995, barely a month after the massacre at Srebrenica, US Ambassador to the UN, Madeline Albright, presented photographic evidence of mass graves in Bosnian Serb-controlled areas. Evidence of mass murder, if not genocide, implicated the Bosnian Serb militias. On 28 August, Bosnian Serbs started re-shelling the Bosnian capital city, Sarajevo. Five mortars landed, killing thirty-seven civilians and injuring one hundred others. The UN commander, French General Janvier, who had rejected Dutch requests for NATO air strikes, was absent on personal business, and the request for retaliatory air strikes went to General Smith, his alternative. Smith pulled UN troops out of eastern Bosnia to prevent them from being taken captive. On 30 August NATO forces started a mass bombing of Bosnian Serb positions. The campaign, Operation Deliberate Force, lasted until 20th September. There were 3 500 sorties against Bosnian Serb ammunition dumps, bunkers, an arms factory, and command posts. The Bosnian Serb capacity to make war was ended. Two months later, Richard Holbrooke brokered the Dayton Peace Accords ending the Bosnian war (Lebor 2006: 130–32). Many observers at the time commented that previous UN policies of appeasement put the civilian population at risk of murder, rape, and displacement. José Maria Mendiluce, a senior official from the UN High Commission for Refugees (UNHCR) suggested that the UN force commander, General Janvier, 'shares the responsibility for the genocide' (2006: 118). He is viewed as an accomplice, not because he wanted the killings to come about (particularly in Srebrenica), but because he resisted intervention with the force mandated by the UN, as had the UN's most senior official in Yugoslavia, Yasuchi Akashi. As a result, massacres and war crimes were protracted.

Lebor compares Bosnia to Rwanda. In Rwanda there was similar evidence of professional ineptness. Lieutenant General Dallaire received communications in early 1994 that the Hutu extremists were planning a total extermination of the Tutsi minority. One informant identified the location of illegal arms caches that were being compiled to conduct the massacres. Dallaire's request for permission to seize the weapons and confront the political leadership was thwarted by Kofi Annan, head of the Department of

Peacekeeping Operations (DPKO) in New York. He wanted to preserve the UN's appearance of even-handedness during the conflict. Annan directed Dallaire to advise the Hutu president about the arms caches on the pretext that he did not know about them, or about plans for the massacre of the Tutsis. Briefing of the situation on the ground by UN staff in New York was inadequate with many diplomats suggesting they received more reliable information from NGOs such as Human Rights Watch and MSF, and news reports. When Habyarimana's plane was shot down, and the massacres commenced, the UN did not reinforce Dallaire's complement of 2 500 peacekeepers. It reduced them to 270 soldiers, making them almost completely ineffective in halting the genocide of the Tutsi population. There is reason to believe that had the DPKO given Dallaire a revised mandate, the genocide might have been averted, or its magnitude may have been attenuated. Lebor's evidence makes a compelling case of complicity, not in a legal sense, but in a sociological sense. The UN was party to the slaughter of the innocents in Bosnia and Rwanda, not so much by commission as by omission. There was no specific intent. Nonetheless, doctrinaire diplomatic impartiality cost lives among those the missions were designed to protect. When General Smith launched Operation Deliberate Force, the war crimes ceased. In Rwanda, the UN was an accelerant to the massacres, but not the only one, nor the most important.

The government of French President Mitterand had a close relationship with the Habyarimana dictatorship. The Anglophone army invaded from Uganda in October 1990 to enforce the right of return of Tutsi refugees, whose families had been forced out by ethnic cleansing during the period of independence in 1959–62. The Tutsis assumed many senior positions in Museveni's rebel army in Uganda. Despite their assistance in establishing Museveni's rise to power, they were denied political rights under the new regime. Return through force was their last option. In Rwanda, French diplomatic efforts provided political and military security for their Hutu clients over the next four years to prevent that return. The French provided direct military assistance after the October 1990 invasion of Paul Kagame's troops. Wallis (2006b) reported that the French eventually took effective command of the Rwandan army, supervised its massive expansion over the next four years (expanding it from 3 000 to 30 000 or more soldiers), trained the political militias that carried out the genocide, supervised the war against the RPF in the field, financed individuals to acquire weapons through loans, violated the UN sanctions against arming the combatants, and seized UN vehicles to evacuate its ex-pats to the Kigali airport when the genocide started in April 1994 (Buckingham 2006).

Similarly, Linda Melvern (2006) wrote: 'During nearly three years of civil war, in some instances senior French officers took operational battlefield control.' France was the first country to recognize the 1994 interim government after the coup d'état of April 1994 that led to the murders of both the president on 6 April and the prime minister on the following day. French diplomats and defence sources knew the government was conducting a carefully orchestrated murder of Tutsi Rwandans—indeed it hosted the murderers at the French embassy where extremist ministers were reviewing the progress of the killing from the various Rwandan provinces in the spring of 1994, when the ambassador was burning his correspondence with the prior regime in his yard (Wallis 2006a: 90; Melvern 2009). President Mitterand quipped, 'in countries like that, genocide is not so important'. This could be written off as ancient tribal conflicts.

In 2006 a Rwandan national inquiry under prosecutor Jean de Dieu Mucyo adduced evidence of French complicity in the 1994 genocide. Reporting in *The Independent* Linda Melvern wrote: 'The seven-person examining commission is hearing testimony from 20 survivors, some claiming serious human rights abuses, including rape and murder, by the French military....Human rights groups in France claim French soldiers tricked thousands of Tutsi survivors out of hiding, and abandoned them to the Interahamwe militia' (8 November 2006). Wallis (2006a: 136–41) provided evidence that during the supposedly humanitarian mission in June 1994 called 'Operation Turquoise', several thousand Tutsis behind the French lines were surrendered to the militias to be murdered. The French fuelled the FAR trucks to expedite their escape to Zaire. France continued to support the Hutu government on the supposition that the *génocidaires* would retake the country, and return Rwanda to the Francophone fold. Indeed, at the November meeting of the Francophonie convened at Biarritz, France snubbed the new broadly based government of Rwanda, which brought the genocide to an end in July 1994.

The Mucyo Inquiry (Rwanda 2008c) was created in 2006. It completed its investigations on 15 November 2007 and released its findings on 5 August 2008 (Mucyo Report 2007). What did it conclude? Evidence suggested that French authorities knew that genocide was being planned as a result of its intense military contact with the FAR leadership prior to 1994. France advocated strongly for the CDR party during the Arusha accords in order to secure it a seat in the proposed broadly based government of national unity, knowing that the CDR openly advocated genocide of the Tutsis. The French Minister of Cooperation claimed that France supported the Arusha accords, but called for all Rwandan opposition parties to unite against the RPF, the main proponent of Tutsi political rights. The French military actively supported the FAR, even in its creation of checkpoints to select out Tutsis for murder. The French military helped develop a programme of 'civil defence' to arm civilians to intercept RPF members, and anyone believed to be supportive of them. This became a chief mechanism for initiating the genocide. The French army also assisted in the training of militias in five army barracks to target civilian Tutsis for assassination. The French gendarmes created the electronic filing system to identify the country's Tutsis, so that lists could be created for their destruction. The French diplomats in Kigali were the first to support Bagosora, the commander of the security apparatus that initiated the genocide, and continued diplomatic and military support to the interim government, which openly committed genocide. The report identified the chief actors in these operations and the dates they acted. The report made a case for the culpability of thirteen senior French politicians, including President Mitterand (now deceased), several top ministers, and a series of ambassadors. In addition, it identified the names of twenty senior military leaders and their periods of active support of genocide or genocide preparations (RIE 2007; Kimenyi 2007).

The accusation against a European power of complicity in genocide is not new. For example, Dadrian (1996) makes a strong case for German complicity in the Armenian genocide in 1915–16. The chief evidence concerns the utilization of the Berlin to Baghdad Railway to deport Armenians to the Syrian desert, and the forced labour of the Armenians in completing sections of the railway. And certainly, there is evidence of at least one German military official ordering the deportation of Armenians into the desert. Bloxham (2005: 115) takes a more nuanced view. He points out that Germany was Turkey's main ally during the Great War, and that official German reaction was indifference, since a dispute over a population in which it had no interest might have split the alliance. Nonetheless, he too acknowledges the utilization of the German railway in the service of Turkey's policy of mass murder. Despite these differences, the point made here is that the accomplice does not have to have the intent to commit genocide or mass murder, merely knowledge that the main perpetrators are acting criminally. The bystanders become accomplices, not only by their indifference, but also by putting their railway at the service of an ally for the purpose of massacring a civilian population. This may have occurred before the creation of the Genocide Convention, but it reinforces the importance of the sociological complicity in the sociogenesis of such crimes.

Cameron (2011) and Melvern (2007) make a case for the culpability of the British government's complicity in the genocide. After the onset of mass killings, the British government received reliable information from Oxfam and other NGOs that the killings in Rwanda were escalating beyond imagination in April and May of 1994, but failed to convey this to the public in Parliament, and played dumb at the UN, contributing to the dismantling of Dallaire's peacekeepers in Rwanda. This amounted to complicity by silence.

Conclusion: The Legacy of Complicity

The evidence examined here points to the ominous role of complicity in genocidal sociogenesis. Even if we accept that animosity between Rwandan Tutsis and Hutus intensified during the Hutu revolution of 1959–62, the conflicts associated with the struggle of Tutsis to return after being exiled in the 1990s would arguably not have had the same scope in the absence of French complicity. Yet there is no evidence that any of the key French actors shared the specific genocidal motives of the architects of the killings. The main motive appears to have been to keep Anglo-Saxon influence at bay in French Africa, and to prevent a repeat of the Fashoda crisis (i.e. routing of the French presence in the Sudan in 1898 by a British army).

The effect of the UN in Bosnia, particularly the policies of strict diplomatic impartiality, worked as a catalyst that created the time and opportunities for the Bosnian Serbs to achieve an extensive programme of ethnic cleansing of Bosniaks, including the indiscriminate murder of civilians in Sarajevo. Again, the breakup of Yugoslavia was rife with potential for ethnic violence. The assumption of total UN impartiality made the UN complicit, and raised stakes considerably, particularly in respect of the so-called 'safe areas' in Bosnia.

A legal point to be raised in the context of complicity concerns how accomplices may help contribute to the evidentiary requirements to establish the mental state required to establish genocidal intent on the part of the primary perpetrators. Several trial chambers struggled with whether this mental factor was an objective or subjective construct, or a combination. In *Akayesu*, the Chamber wrote, 'intent is a mental factor which is difficult, even impossible to determine' (paras 523–4). However, in the absence of a confession, several considerations can tip the balance, including 'the scale of atrocities committed'. The evidence reviewed here makes a strong case for the contribution of accomplices in raising *the scale of atrocities* that bring mass slaughter into the conventional definition of genocide.

What this analysis suggests is that 'the completion of the act of genocide' requires coordination of action across various levels of society: the mobilization of the perpetrators, the logistical support conveyed to them in terms of arms, material support, and leadership, and the ideological reinforcement of their efforts. Each step is a transition point capable of escalating or attenuating the crime of genocide. Correspondingly, each has a potential role in deterring or preventing such crimes. The question of deterring such crimes is usually associated with the criminal law. In the next chapters, we address the legal responses to genocide and other crimes against international humanitarian law.

7

The Limits of the Criminal Law

Introduction: The Idea of Cosmopolitan Law

In the last decade, numerous studies have analysed the genocide courts and increasingly questioned the effectiveness of judicial responses to mass atrocities, and crimes against international humanitarian law. Ironically, their appearance coincides with the creation of the first permanent International Criminal Court at The Hague. As noted in an earlier chapter, for many advocates of the recent ad hoc UN tribunals for the Balkans and Rwanda, and the hybrid tribunals for Sierra Leone, Cambodia, East Timor, and Lebanon, as well as the ICC, the development of such transnational institutions is the fulfilment of Immanuel Kant's dream of 'cosmopolitan justice'. Cosmopolitan justice would abolish sovereign immunity for crimes and would hold the political and military elite accountable for atrocities against their own citizens, and for aggression against their neighbours. At the end of the Second World War, the Nuremberg trials and the International Military Tribunals for the Far East were colossal steps in this direction, and successfully prosecuted German and Japanese leaders for the supreme crime of 'making aggressive war', and crimes against humanity (Ratner and Abrams 2001). The UN provided an ongoing institutional home for the preservation of the hope for transnational justice throughout the Cold War. The 1948 Convention on the Prevention and Punishment of the Crime of Genocide was the single most important achievement in this regard, followed by the Universal Declaration of Human Rights in the same year. For many, the creation of the ICC following the decline of communism gave the world a permanent Nuremberg-like solution to genocide, war crimes, and crimes against humanity (Schabas 2007). How confident should we be that a legal response to such conflicts is the optimal one? In this chapter I examine some important 'report-cards' on the recent

* Sections of this chapter appeared in an earlier article: 'Is the Sun Setting on Cosmopolitan Justice?', published in *Society*, 2011 (48): 420–25.

UN and hybrid courts. To put them in perspective, I review a key historical trial—Auschwitz—that has recently attracted a great deal of attention among historians and legal scholars.

The Auschwitz Trials (1963–65)

At the end of the Second World War, numerous former Nazis were extradited to Eastern Europe to face trials for wartime atrocities. Within Germany, tens of thousands of former Nazis were 'lustrated', i.e. stripped of political rights to neutralize their threat to the emerging democratic institutions. The National Socialist ideology was subsequently discredited. However, there were complaints throughout the 1950s that concentration camp guards remained free in West German society, and their crimes in Poland were being ignored. This story was researched independently by two historians, Rebecca Wittman (2005) and Devon O. Pendas (2006). The Auschwitz trial was the most dramatic, and well-publicized postwar Nazi trial to be convened in the Federal Republic of Germany. Unlike Nuremberg, which was created, prosecuted, and adjudicated by the victors, this was a trial held under German law, prosecuted and tried by Germans. Because the events of the war pre-dated the 1948 Genocide Convention, persons charged with the mass murders, tortures and other indignities that occurred in Nazi-occupied Poland—the 'general gouvernement'—were tried under ordinary criminal law. Twenty-two persons were indicted before the Frankfurt criminal court. They represented a cross-section of the camp's administrative units, and ranged in rank from Major to Private, and included a single kapo (inmate-guard). The case arose from a local initiative in the Stuttgart prosecutors' office based on allegations from a petty career criminal who identified a local citizen, Wilhelm Boger, as a notorious torturer at the Auschwitz concentration camp. The case may have been dropped were it not for the involvement of the International Auschwitz Committee (IAC), a network of survivors who supplied authorities with the names of suspected war criminals and witnesses who might offer testimony to prosecute them. Despite the prickly interaction between the IAC and German prosecutors, the case eventually made it to the office of Hessian Attorney General, Fritz Bauer. He secured jurisdiction from superior courts to bring the matter before the Frankfurt court, and gathered sufficient evidence to initiate a preliminary investigation under Judge Heinz Düx. Düx interviewed over 1 500 witnesses, and an indictment was prepared against the twenty-two suspects (two escaped trial for medial reasons). The charges included murder. The crimes consisted of selecting persons on the ramp at Auschwitz for immediate gassing or enslavement for forced labour designed to bring about death through exhaustion and maltreatment. Other indictments dealt with the killing of hospital inmates by lethal injections of phenol. There were also periodic purges of units of workers within the camps, and individual executions for attempting to escape and disobedience, and deaths resulting from 'intensive interrogation' and torture.

For Fritz Bauer the purpose of the trial was 'ultimately pedagogical' (Pendas 2006: 52) in the sense that it would expose the deep reach of Nazism into the German psyche, and would contribute to the de-Nazification of German society. Bauer attempted to put the entire genocidal complex at Auschwitz on trial, and to demonstrate how the Holocaust was the outcome of widespread complicity of people from all walks of German life functioning under a complex criminal enterprise. Because the international Genocide Convention was *ex post facto* law, the defendants were tried under the 1871 German homicide law. That law limited liability for first-degree murder ('Mord') to those who were primary perpetrators, and who acted with base motives in taking the lives of others. Accomplices, while guilty, were considered to have significantly lower levels of culpability, particularly in terms of penalty. As a result, the routine activities of forcibly deporting millions of people from their homelands, imprisoning them in temporary ghettos, classifying them on the railway sidings for work or immediate death, and the subsequent act of gassing them, were viewed as regrettable, minor crimes ('Totschlag'), akin to manslaughter. The law took a sterner view in the case of torture, and individual atrocities based on cruelty, sadism, or hatred. These crimes overshadowed the genocide itself. What was the result? The crimes of Auschwitz were equated with individually culpable acts of subjective barbarity. The state-initiated acts of mass murder disappeared as a focal point. The extermination system was 'beyond justice' (in the words of Wittmann), and escaped 'the limits of law' (in the words of Pendas). Six accused were convicted of first-degree murder ('Mord'), but the majority of accused was convicted of being accessories to 'Mord' and received an average penalty of 6.3 years. Ironically, the 'Totschlag' convictions were implicated in the extermination of millions of victims, while the 'Mord' convictions were based on a few hundred deaths. Throughout the trials, the defendants acknowledged that crimes had occurred at Auschwitz, but denied their own guilt, since they had played 'only' a secondary role. In place of guilt, they often exhibited pride in the effectiveness with which they carried out their assignments.

According to Pendas (2006: 293), the trial 'was unable to articulate adequately a historical account of the Holocaust that fully incorporated or even sufficiently acknowledged the extent to which it was a "total social event," one in which every dimension of German society was implicated.' Wittmann (2005: 271) concluded similarly: 'The public gained a skewed understanding of Auschwitz. The sentences meted out to the defendants distorted the realities of the program of extermination [and] shifted the focus in the courtroom away from Nazi genocide towards individual acts of cruelty, suggesting that…the Nazi orders had been acceptable…' Hannah Arendt, whose riveting account of the Eichmann trial in Jerusalem appeared as the Auschwitz trial was winding down, also noted the failure of the proceedings to take hold in the minds of ordinary Germans: 'Exposure for twenty months to the monstrous deeds and the grotesquely unrepentant, aggressive behavior of the defendants…had no impact on the climate of public opinion' (cited in Wittmann 2005: 246). The trial failed to register the historical enormity of the events that created Auschwitz, including the explicit scheme of racial extermination, the plan to subjugate the entire continent of Europe, and the mobilization of the army, industry, and academy to bring this about. As far as the verdict at Frankfurt was concerned, most of the business at Auschwitz involved individual crimes that had little relevance for most of the Germans. Indeed, the majority of the crimes recognized by the Frankfurt trials, aside from genocide, were offences that would have been illegal under SS regulations.

One of the recurrent themes that runs through genocide trials, then and now, is that they are thought to be socially important by recording history through the testimony of witnesses and the examination of documents. The exposure of the lives of the accused, and of their victims, for the purposes of establishing guilt is equated with the historical task of establishing truth. The lesson of the Auschwitz trials is otherwise. The equation of guilt and truth is ill founded since such proceedings are adversarial and are arbitrarily limited by rules of evidence, procedure, and the slant of the laws. In this case, both Wittmann and Pendas laid the failure of the trial as history at the door of German law, particularly the procedural distinction drawn between perpetrators and accomplices and, in addition, the requirement of a base motive at the core of first-degree or capital murder charge. If the law had been written differently, the observers would have taken away an alternative lesson. There are two issues here. The first is that the legal lens will always shape and colour how events are portrayed, but so will the perspective of the historian. The second point relates to the limitations attributed to the specific German law. I offer an alternative reading to that of Wittmann and Pendas. The problem was not a deficit or oversight in the German penal code. A Durkheimian reading would suggest that the law follows changes in the collective consciousness of society. In *The Division of Labour in Society*, Durkheim (1893) argued that the forms of law (retributive, restitutive, commercial, and constitutional) reflected changes in historical patterns of affiliation, changing density, the rise of commerce, urbanization, etc. In this view, German law may well have reflected the hierarchical nature of German society by demarcating the role of perpetrators and accomplices so sharply. I would suggest that the subjective reactions of the accused during trial—smug indifference—reflected precisely the sort of mentality that Norbert Elias described in *The Germans* (1996). Elias notes that German civil society was marked by the substitution of strong leadership for individual autonomy in political and military matters. With the Prussian ascendency, national development occurred hand in hand with a deep aversion to democracy and individual political responsibility. The Auschwitz accused could not be shamed as a result of simply carrying out official orders, since they were not complicit in their design, although they followed them with panache, in accordance with duty. From this perspective, the 1871 law of homicide conceptualized accomplices as followers, in contrast to the Anglo-Saxon law, which viewed accomplices as associates, with near commensurate levels of responsibility.

The trial failed on two counts. It failed to capture the organizational nature of the Holocaust and the high level of complicity that it required, and it failed to awaken any sense of shame in the perpetrators. As I have noted earlier, we find the same absence of subjective guilt among the Rwandan *génocidaires*. The convention to prevent and suppress the crime of genocide created new international law without the limitations that Wittmann and Pendas attributed to domestic criminal law. How successfully has the 1948

Convention brought mass atrocities within the reach of the law in recent times?

In the shadow of the 'right' law

The Nuremberg trials did not prosecute the crime of genocide. However, the General Assembly of the UN in December 1946 held that 'genocide is a crime under international law which the civilized world condemns', suggesting that it was already customary law. As noted earlier, the term which formed the core of the 1948 UN Convention was only coined by Raphael Lemkin in 1944. Certainly, people had been horrified by massacres of civilian populations in political conflict from the time of Melos (487 BC), Carthage (146 BC), and the Thirty Years War (1648). The 1948 UN Convention created the first positive law that described the elements of the offence, as well as the special mental element, or *dolus specialis*, required to establish guilt. This special element appears to presuppose a high level of agency among the perpetrators of mass murder. Not only do they have to kill, they have to be motivated to exterminate certain categories of people, and to do so deliberately because they belong to such categories. However, one of the recurrent observations in the genocide literature is the neutral, vacuous, or evanescent mentality of the legions of persons recruited for acts of mass murder. In the Rwandan case, the amnesty laws justified mass murder as part of the Hutu revolution, and hundreds of thousands of *génocidaires* were typically reluctant to accept any sense of guilt or remorse. Their killings were righteous, like those of patriots defending The Good. The legal process in the current genocide courts is premised on the idea that offenders are morally sensitive, and that the legal process will result in their acceptance of a guilty verdict, that they will stand condemned, and that their conviction will expedite acceptance of responsibility. But the evidence from these courts suggests that those assumptions which are associated with individual forms of offence and prosecution (mere murder) are misplaced in trials for mass murder.

The Creation of the Recent Courts

We have been focusing on comparatively ancient history: the Auschwitz trials from West Germany in the Cold War period. To what extent have the weaknesses of earlier genocide trials persisted in the

more recent trials? The first ad hoc UN tribunal to investigate genocide, war crimes, and crimes against humanity was created during
the civil war in the former Yugoslavia in 1993 before the hostilities
had ended. If law had a deterrent effect, presumably that would be
evident from experience in the former Yugoslavia, since the combatants had knowledge of liability while conflict was ongoing. A second tribunal was created following the end of the Rwanda genocide
in 1994. The former was confronted largely with allegations of war
crimes, and crimes against humanity ('ethnic cleansing'). The latter
was overwhelmingly confronted with genocide, complicity in genocide, and incitement to commit genocide. The two ad hoc tribunals
were created to deal with breaches of international humanitarian
law separately for each conflict, one located in The Hague, the second in Arusha, Tanzania. A single prosecutor initially directed the
two courts. When this proved ineffective, a separate prosecutor was
designated for each court, although the appeal process was amalga-
mated under a single bench to ensure some continuity in the new
jurisprudence that arose from trials in each region. The courts were
initially under-resourced, and their progress was halting. However,
as they attracted more reliable funding, their caseloads expanded,
and they reported progress. Nonetheless, there were recurrent allegations of professional incompetence of tribunal staff, financial mis-
management, political interference, and disconnection of the legal
process from the post-conflict societies. When subsequent calls were
made for ad hoc tribunals for atrocities elsewhere in the world, the
UN adopted a 'hybrid' approach in which the legal process would
be based on international laws developed in the initial ad hoc tribunals, combined with input from domestic law and local judges, and
funded in part by the post-conflict states themselves, and by voluntary state donations. The aim of the hybrid courts was to better
integrate the stakeholders in justice: the victims, the national governments, and the United Nations. Unlike the Frankfurt court,
which conducted its prosecution under national criminal procedures, and national criminal law, the ad hoc courts attempted to
create something out of nothing. They were to act in specific regions
with a global mandate created by the Genocide Convention, and
consistent with the jurisprudence created famously at Nuremberg.
They were in a certain sense operating in the dark since Nuremberg
never prosecuted genocide. There was no settled jurisprudence for
genocide. There were no clearly determined operational rules for
criminal procedure comparable to those found in the nations that

had created them. This opened the chasm between Anglo-Saxon adversarial procedure and continental inquisitorial procedure. The selection of judges and prosecutors was eminently political since the parties at the UN who created the courts were averse to creating judicial processes to which they themselves or their countrymen might be subjected, while at the same time assuming responsibility for the costs. And there was no institution corresponding to the police. Apprehension of international suspects was fraught with challenges to sovereignty that could result in state-to-state conflict. Those who designed such courts presumed that there existed sufficient transnational communication, recognition, and cooperation that a new layer of courts could simply be added to the existing national, provincial, and municipal levels of society. The national systems evolved over centuries. Expectations that a higher level of justice could be achieved in a short period of time as a result of globalization were clearly over-optimistic.

Doubts about the ad hoc courts

Have the new ad hoc tribunals succeeded where the Auschwitz trials failed? After all, the new courts have had the advantage of legal doctrines that explicitly recognized liability, which the 1881 German homicide law lacked. Genocide does not require a base motive, but a special motive. Conspiracy to commit genocide, incitement to genocide, and complicity are all major crimes like genocide per se, not minor offences. They also enjoyed the moral and financial support of the Security Council of the UN. In 2004 the UN Assistant Secretary-General for Legal Affairs shocked his colleagues when he publicly expressed doubts about the ICTR and ICTY. Ralph Zacklin, who helped create the tribunals, wrote in the most disparaging terms about them (2004: 545): 'the ad hoc tribunals have been too costly, too inefficient and too ineffective. As mechanisms for dealing with justice in post-conflict societies, they exemplify an approach that is no longer politically or financially viable.' Wittmann and Pendas said the fault lay with the 1871 German law. By contrast, Zacklin claimed it was the institutional success of the tribunals that had appropriated a world to themselves disconnected from both the realities of finance, and responsibility to the victims in whose name the proceedings were convened. The accomplishments, in terms of convictions, were modest, their progress was glacial, and their contribution to the restoration of social peace was questionable.

What has changed since 2004? Adam Smith (2009) examined the performance of the tribunals. His report reinforces Zacklin's earlier misgivings.

The courts have been monumentally expensive. The yearly ICTY budget from 1993 to 2007 expanded a thousand-fold, from $276,000 to $276 million; at various times in its tenure, the ICTY alone has accounted for 10 percent of the UN's entire annual operating budget. In all, from 1993 through 2007 the ICTY cost $1.2 billion, and is on pace to cost as much as $2 billion by the time it completes its mandate...Judicial productivity, however, has seemingly not matched the expense. The average cost per conviction at the tribunal has been estimated at nearly $30 million, more than fourteen times the average cost per capital conviction in the United States...The Rwandan tribunal is somewhat less costly, though it is projected to also have spent more than $1.4 billion by the time it finishes operations...In 2004, the Rwanda and Yugoslavia tribunals together constituted 15 percent of the total UN budget (Smith 2009: 182–3).

The ICTR budget for 2010–11 was $245 246 500. The ICTY budget for 2010–11 was $301 895 900. Both failed to meet their original 2010 'completion strategies'. The hybrid courts in Sierra Leone, Cambodia, East Timor, and Lebanon were created in part as a result of cost escalation at the ad hoc courts. How have they fared in comparison? Again, we turn to Smith. In the case of the Special Court for Sierra Leone, he reports as follows: 'The original budget was very ambitious and called for only $54 million over three years; since the special court's opening in 2002, that amount has more than tripled' and the three-year mandate has morphed into eight (Smith 2009:183). That was for ten cases, but the most important case, the indictment of Charles Taylor, was moved for security reasons to The Hague, duplicating much of the costs already invested in Freetown.

The Khmer Rouge atrocities were mentioned earlier. The costs of their genocide trials at the Extraordinary Chambers in the Courts of Cambodia were reported by Rebecca Gidley (2010: 14). 'In terms of its finances, the budget for the court from 2005 until 2010 is US$142.6 million.' Gidley comments that this is a lot less than either the ICTR or the ICTY, but she fails to mention that there were only five accused in the docket. Also, the UN News Service (UN News 2010) at the time pointed out that 'for 2011, the total budget of $46.8 million is unfunded'. This suggests that the projected costs were nearly $189 000 000 if one includes 2011, or about $38 000 000 per case (RNW 2010). The hybrid courts do not appear to be less costly than the ad hoc courts on a *per capita* basis. But they raised more than financial questions.

As of mid-2012, there had been only one conviction at the Extraordinary Chambers in the Courts of Cambodia (ECCC), that of Kaing Guek Eav (aka 'Duch') who was commandant of the Tuol Sleng prison during the Khmer Rouge rule (1975–79). At least 14 000 people were tortured, and sent to their deaths there. Virtually no one survived. Throughout the trial, Duch cooperated with prosecutors. He said he was deeply remorseful for all the suffering he had created, and apologized to the dead, to their families and to all Cambodians (Mydans 2009). However, on the last day of his nine-month-long trial in November 2009, he petitioned the court to ignore all the evidence of murder and torture carried out by him or under his supervision, and asked that he be released without any further penalty. The public was shaken. On appeal of his thirty-five-year sentence on 30 March 2011, he reiterated his request to the Supreme Court Chamber, and asked them to acquit him and set him free. The court noted that this was equivalent to rejecting his culpability for his crimes. His behaviour raised grave questions about the sincerity of his remorse, a point related to the peculiar subjectivity of guilt raised earlier in this chapter. One is reminded of Hans Frank's very limited acceptance of responsibility at Nuremberg for Nazi crimes in Poland, which was mentioned earlier. The Rwandan genocide? Same story. Cruvellier (2010: 14) writes of Froduald Karamira, one of the ringleaders of the Rwandan genocide, who was convicted of genocide before the criminal courts in Rwanda: 'Froduald Karamira never showed the slightest hint of remorse. He always maintained an air of defiance before his judges in Rwanda.' He was publicly executed in Kigali in 1998.

There are two sets of reasons that the UN ad hoc and hybrid courts have been so costly, made such slow progress, and have so little to show for the investment. The first has to do with paradoxes of genocide outlined earlier. The vast majority of the perpetrators are not psychopaths with obvious criminal tendencies, but ordinary people who do not exhibit the usual symptoms of shame and remorse when confronted with evidence of their crimes. In addition, the crimes with which they are charged have become conventionalized. i.e. treated as above the law, or prosecuted only in the case of those on the political margins of power. The task of the courts is also different in terms of the scale of atrocities. Unless the courts focus exclusively on the most senior leaders in politics, and the military, the docket will have more cases than it can comfortably handle. The second set of problems concerns the very weak capacity of the courts to induce guilty pleas. In the common law countries, the vast majority of criminal matters are disposed of through guilty pleas, primarily negotiated guilty pleas (Brannigan and Levy 1983). These are the exception at the ad hoc tribunals. If crime were tried in the domestic courts without plea negotiations, this would slow their progress considerably. But more to the point, many of the high-level white-collar crime charges can only be established by testimony from co-accused working in the same operation against the more senior actors, a process that may lead to sentencing differentials associated with pleading, and appearing as a prosecution witness against future co-accused (Hagan, Nagel and Albonetti 1980). The ad hoc tribunals have been reluctant to do this because of the perception that the gravest international crimes would be discounted by plea-bargaining. We see evidence for this in the case of Jean Kambanda.

Kambanda was made prime minister of Rwanda after the coup d'état on 6–7 April that occurred with the murder of the president and the prime minister. The military junta installed a new government within days, and appointed Kambanda as prime minister. He was apprehended in Kenya in 1997, and returned to Arusha to face genocide, conspiracy to commit genocide, incitement to commit genocide, complicity in genocide, and crimes against humanity. He cooperated extensively with the prosecutor and provided days of interviews outlining how the junta had organized the mass murders, who did what, when, and where, and voluntarily submitted a plea of guilty to all charges. At the time, he declined court-appointed representation, and was kept isolated in custody from other offenders. He did not enter into a quid pro quo agreement to testify against other suspects, and was sentenced to life imprisonment without any possibility of release. At that point, he attempted to recant his confession on the grounds that his open cooperation ought to have resulted in some diminution of penalty, given his remorse, his confession, and his cooperation with the office of the prosecutor. The court found the crime so grave that these mitigating factors were unworthy of any weight, a view advanced by Madam Prosecutor, Carla Del Ponte. This sent a signal to every other accused who may have considered cooperating with the tribunal to bring the more recalcitrant offenders to justice through their evidence against them. Of the thirty-two completed cases at the ICTR, seven were convicted as a result of guilty pleas. At the ICTY, twenty of the 161 cases have been similarly resolved. These trends are the opposite of what is found in the common law national courts. In my view, the tribunals have already discounted the gravity of 'the crime of crimes' by eliminating the death penalty. The progress of the tribunals would have been greatly expedited by negotiating guilty pleas. The cost might be a reduction in sentence by several years—but a much greater capacity to register convictions, and to promote a culture of remorse. In fact, it might be argued that the inability of the courts to expedite guilty pleas contributes to the maintenance of the culture of impunity where no one is expected to admit guilt.

Justice on the cheap in East Timor

As I have stressed, the hybrid courts as well as the ad hoc tribunals have been very costly, and experienced appalling delays. On the other hand, the Special Panels for Serious Crimes (SPSC) in East Timor was starved of funding, receiving about $6 million annually from the UN in 2001, rising to $7–8 million by 2005. It conducted fifty-five trials involving eighty-seven accused. Eighty-four persons were eventually convicted for serious crimes arising from the mayhem of Indonesian-sponsored militias operating in East Timor in 1999 that were designed to enforce Indonesian dominance and to suppress the island's aspirations to political independence (Cohen 2006a). Some 1 400 murders were recorded during the September 1999 referendum. When the UN shut down the courts, almost 600 other murders were under investigation. Conviction of over eighty accused in four years was a higher figure than any other tribunal at the time. Despite this, the SPSC was shut down by Security Council Resolution 1543. The vast majority of the offenders were illiterate farmers who had been enrolled in pro-Jakarta militias. There were grave questions about the competence of the tribunal. All this was documented by David Cohen (2006b). For example, during the first fourteen cases, no court reporter, stenographer, or audio recording was utilized. As a result, all the appeals were conducted without benefit of trial transcripts, except for notes recorded by one of the judges. There was no experienced defence bar; it was essentially unfunded. Not surprisingly, the defence failed to call any witnesses at all in the first fourteen trials. Cohen (2006b: 93ff) also points out that a UN programme designed to create judicial infrastructure ended badly. Some twenty-five legal workers were schooled for several years in the basic principles of law. When they were evaluated in 2005, every single candidate was judged to be legally incompetent, including four native persons who had served as judges in the earlier trials, and whose judgments had contributed to the convictions. In spite of the relatively large number of convictions, the UN withdrew funding and the chief judge sealed all the case files, preventing future scrutiny.

The SPSC was plagued with under-funding, lack of access to competent translators, inability to apprehend senior Indonesian military and political suspects, and a hostile Portuguese-speaking government that was more interested in peace with Indonesia through diplomatic reconciliation than through criminal trials. From my perspective, what made these trials important was that the vast majority of those who were convicted pleaded guilty. Linton and Reiger (2002: 2) note that 'one of the most interesting and unique features of these cases is the fact that almost every accused person admits to being involved in some aspect of the crime with which he is charged, for example, that he killed'. This may have been because there was no access to experienced defence counsel, or because of 'the desire of many of them to acknowledge their involvement in crimes and be reconciled with their communities'. The evidence against them was presented at trial nonetheless. The courts resisted acknowledgement of the fact that the accused wanted to plead guilty. Like the Auschwitz accused, they had little remorse. Because they were peasants, they felt little autonomy in their actions, but unlike the Auschwitz accused, they wanted to repair the breach of the peace by acknowledging their guilt. 'In Timorese culture, the expected practice for the accused was to confess his crimes…In order to promote the culture of the not guilty plea required by the Western court systems, the UN experts had to train the Timorese to lie' (UN diplomat Shashi Tharoor, quoted in Moghalu 2008: 14).

If common law experience is any guide, guilty pleas can expedite the legal process. However, it may be that a diplomatic process and/or a national court process may be a better outcome than what is offered at the international level. Adam Smith makes this case in his analysis of the conflict in the Balkans. These are two lessons based on his research in this region. Specifically, the first is that the cessation of hostilities following the Dayton Peace Accords led many to call for the cancellation of the Hague prosecutions, and the release of persons apprehended by the ICTY. Since the Serbs had been persuaded to put down their arms, and President Milošević had helped broker the deal, further prosecution appeared to be perverse, since the initial call for the tribunal was designed to halt aggression. Smith argues that the objectives of justice, and those of peace, sometimes operate at cross-purposes. Moghalu stresses the same point in his analysis of the competing agendas of security and diplomacy. Diplomats can often negotiate the end to conflicts without bringing anyone to trial; frequently, it is easier to de-escalate the tension between combatants when aggressors effectively receive immunity, or pardons, as a guarantee of the establishment of security. One reason that Serbs developed such an aversion to the ICTY was that many thought it was made redundant by the Dayton Accords. The same issue has led former Bosnian Serb President Karadžić to refuse to plea, claiming that his participation in the Dayton Peace Accords was negotiated to leave him free of subsequent prosecution (MacDonald 2009).

Smith's second point is that nation states should prosecute breaches of international humanitarian law internally. He points out that before Milošević was surrendered to the ICTY, he 'was arrested, indicted, and set for trial in Serbia' (2009: 326). Croat prosecutors were already prosecuting Croats for crimes against Serbian populations and Bosnians were likewise prosecuting their own citizens for war crimes against Serbs and Croats. Smith rejects the idea that domestic prosecution for these sort of inter-ethnic atrocities is impossible.

Larger Legal Problems: Fact-Finding Without Facts

The questions about trials and tribunals raised by Wittmann, Pendas, Smith, Zacklin, and other critics raise issues that probe whether the courts contribute to an accurate history of atrocity, and whether they are efficient and effective in restoring peace. Nancy Combs (2010) raises a more fundamental question: are the tribunals effective as courts? Her book, *Fact-Finding Without Facts* raises the uncertain evidentiary foundations of international criminal convictions. Her critique is based on a detailed investigation of how the chambers actually acquire information from witnesses. She focuses on the ICTR, and all the hybrid courts except Lebanon. Although her sampling frame is exploratory, her position is convincingly argued.

If one reviews the *viva voce* evidence at the ICTR, the EECC, the Special Courts for Sierra Leone, and the SPSC in East Timor, one finds that the witnesses are by and large illiterate peasants who are unable to provide basic reliable information required by the prosecution to establish the *actus reus* of the crimes. These deficiencies include the following basic points: inability of witnesses to report the dates (specific months or weeks) when the crimes were observed; inability to describe the duration of the events associated with massacres, and/or the distances travelled by survivors during the events. In addition, the witnesses repeatedly fail to provide estimates of the number of victims or perpetrators involved, and the witnesses are often unable to understand two-dimensional representations of crime scenes, such as maps or drawings. They cannot recall important details such as the make of a vehicle used by paramilitaries, or whether they were using some type of gun or 'bows and arrows' (Combs 2010: 39).

In addition, the witnesses are unable to appreciate such adversarial procedures as cross-examination, and appear insulted when questioned about their evidence. They struggle to answer simple questions such as 'what happened next?' or 'what else did you see?' Even more disturbing, in important cases as much as half the oral testimony led by the prosecutor departs significantly from pretrial interview statements made available to the defence.

Combs attributes the causes of these weaknesses in evidence to several factors. The level of illiteracy among witnesses frequently exceeds 50 per cent. Support for effective multilingual translations is frequently unavailable or inadequate, so repeatedly the bench is uncertain what exactly the witness is reporting. Linguistic differences and the life experiences of peasants undermine their ability to function effectively in Western-style trial courts; in many oral cultures, direct accusation is considered rude, and people are constrained to formulate accusations in indirect language. In adversarial proceedings, this evidence appears to be evasive and inconclusive. In addition, pre-existing animosities between the groups in conflict make perjury common, since witnesses naturally favour their own side in ethnic or racial conflicts.

Combs outlines the consequences. Trial judges, typically from industrialized nations, adopt what she describes as a 'lackadaisical attitude toward testimonial deficiencies' and admit evidence to the record that would raise serious concerns about witness credibility in Europe and America. Furthermore, the vagueness of the factual evidence makes it difficult for the accused to offer alibi evidence about their alleged involvement in crimes, since the case they must rebut, due to the ambiguity of testimony, frequently is inherently imprecise. More worrisome is that the criterion for conviction is effectively lowered from 'beyond a reasonable doubt' to 'preponderance of evidence'. In addition, the high levels of perjury suspected, particularly at the ICTR, are virtually never investigated. Combs notes, in an aside, that all the current ICC cases deal with central African conflicts whose testimonial deficiencies likely reflect the same problems Combs documents in all the current non-European tribunals.

Combs explains the lackadaisical approach of the judges as follows. Since the judges are elected by the Security Council based on their commitment to international courts, they are reluctant to rule out evidence that would be inadmissible in Europe or America since this would doom the courts. According to Combs, they admit such evidence particularly where the accused's official position is evidence of his or her *probable* involvement in atrocities. Politicians, military personnel, and militia commanders are assumed by the trial chambers to be culpable, even if the evidence is vague or contradictory. The result is a very high conviction rate, based largely on testimony that would be ruled inadmissible by domestic courts.

Critics of the international courts would condemn the enterprise on these grounds alone since the criterion of guilt is the preponderance of evidence. Combs offers three basic solutions to this situation. First, the courts could explore modest procedural reforms to improve fact-finding to raise the reliability of evidence. Second, the courts could undertake major procedural reforms in how evidence is presented, and could formally adopt doctrines of collective culpability to bring them in line with the existing practice. And finally, the international community could revisit the ability of domestic courts to prosecute what have become defined as transnational crimes.

The first remedy consists of modest procedural reforms to improve translations. 'Many of the colossal interpretation failures that I have recounted stemmed not from intractable linguistic and cultural divergences but from resource restraints' (2010: 276). Remedy: better translation services and more funds. In addition, the office of the prosecutor has to improve the competence of investigators, and ensure the continuity of the evidence, so that discrepancies between statements and testimony cannot be dismissed as investigator incompetence. This might require audio recording of statements. Combs also stresses the value of on-site visits by the judges to the crime sites to better appreciate the conditions under which the witnesses gathered information. And finally, the courts have to be more aggressive in labelling and punishing perjury.

Combs is not optimistic that modest reforms would have much impact. More serious procedural reforms might replace the adversarial nature of the evidence presentation with the inquisitorial methods under which the judges have a central role in establishing the case against the accused, and come to trial briefed on the evidence, and better prepared to direct the questioning of the witnesses themselves. In principle, the courts draw from both common law and continental procedures; this change would follow more closely the continental approach. In addition, Combs explores how the courts could reduce the impact of testimonial deficiencies by aligning the stated and the actual conviction justifications through more explicit adoption of 'associational doctrines' (2010: 321). For example, in the case of Duško Tadić, the court of appeal at the ICTY ignored the fact that there was no direct evidence against the accused that he had killed five captives. It was enough that he was known to have kidnapped them in an illegal operation of ethnic cleansing. Since it was said to be common knowledge that such captives were often killed, it was said that Tadić knew *or ought to have known* that the captives might be endangered. The court of appeal dealt with the absence of direct evidence 'by constructing an expansive legal doctrine that permits the imposition of criminal liability on defendants who did not themselves personally commit the crimes in question or intend that such crimes be committed' (2010: 324). This is the doctrine of joint criminal enterprise. By entering into a criminal collaboration, defendants can be linked to atrocities in which they played no personal role, but which formed part of the common purpose of the enterprise, and which were foreseeable as potential outcomes (2010: 328). While this doctrine has been criticized as a theory of guilt by association, and while it expressly obviates the accused's specific intention, Combs argues that the tribunals have already tacitly adopted the doctrine, even when they do not refer to it explicitly.

Combs also argues more broadly that the international tribunals should be prepared to lower the threshold for conviction—ultimately leading to a higher incidence of mistaken or false convictions than would be acceptable in a domestic prosecution. This is because the international cases are more likely to falter 'as a consequence of investigatory failures than as a consequence of true evidentiary insufficiency' (2010: 352). Also,

there is a greater likelihood that he (as opposed to a domestic defendant) committed the same crime but in a different way...[and/or]...there is a greater likelihood than in the domestic context that he committed some other crime...Finally, even if the international defendant committed no crime during the genocide, he may bear some moral culpability for acquiescing in it (2010: 355).

Combs's last remedy is offered in an uncharacteristically perfunctory way in the conclusion. It examines the possibility of replacing the international tribunals with domestic trials based on the international jurisprudence (2010: 367). These courts would not have the same translation problems, perjury would be more easily detected, and the local judges would have a better sense of the local context of the conflicts. However, as Combs points out, many countries rocked by atrocities do not have functioning judicial institutions. In addition, such trials might be open to political interference. Combs concludes that 'there is little reason to believe that recourse to domestic mechanisms will substantially enhance fact-finding accuracy' (2010: 372). But surely that depends on the jurisdiction.

On the issue of domestic courts, Combs's view contradicts Smith's evidence from the Balkans. He reports a far higher level of success where there exists an effective judiciary with a modicum of independence. Smith also reports on the successes in Latin American countries whose dictators departed office after legislating amnesties for themselves. Smith notes how governments in Chile and Argentina subsequently have reopened these cases and brought the authors of atrocities before the court, without UN legal services. Smith makes a compelling case for re-examining the role of domestic courts in establishing cosmopolitan justice.

Although Combs is chilly on the prospects of the domestic option, ironically, she does not appear to be convinced of the value of the international alternative. 'My normative assessment of the tribunals' fact-finding deficiencies assumes that international criminal trials are valuable endeavors. But just how valuable and for what purposes are questions that I believe to be unanswerable at present' (2010: 372). This might have been Fritz Bauer's reaction after the Auschwitz trial. But after decades of transnational justice from across the globe, it is a very pessimistic conclusion.

This conclusion suggests another view. I think Combs's work puts the nail in the coffin for transnational tribunals, particularly as they apply to largely illiterate societies. Although they may have been conceived in cosmopolitan society, the UN has exported these hybrid institutions to non-European venues where they are largely dysfunctional, where the witnesses are baffled by the role they are expected to fulfil as actors with stronger alliances to the court than to their own communities; where they are stymied by the perverse attention to minutia about dates, times, and duration that they do not ordinarily heed; and where they are assumed to accept complex understandings of the relationship between guilt and individual autonomy, whether or not this reflects the mentality of their own communities. Where the societies are relatively cosmopolitan (Sarejevo; Belgrade), the domestic courts already appear to have a capacity to function without the UN courts.

Combs's scepticism about the courts is shared by Zahar (2010) who believes that witness memories at the tribunals are typically far removed in time from the original events, and frequently questionable and influenced by suggestions of investigators and prosecutors. 'Nowhere does international justice feel more experimental and insecure than at the evidentiary coal face of the witness hearing. The observations...go to the larger question of how convincing international fact-finding really is.' Based on his observations of hundreds of witnesses at ad hoc tribunals, he goes on to say that

the truth about the trials I have experienced, which include cases of all sizes and complexity, is that the evidence can be written up in one direction (guilt), or in a radically different direction (acquittal), depending on the final preferences of the judges...Most of the time the evidence can be led with equal ease in either direction...The factual findings with which I am familiar, and which I have no reason to believe are exceptional, are not findings 'beyond a reasonable doubt' but rather 'reasonable findings in the circumstances.'

Nice (2001) also identifies many of the imperfections of the ad hoc tribunals but expresses more optimism for their capacity to overcome them.

Court of Remorse

Another recent critical account from the courts is provided by Thierry Cruvellier who reported on the Arusha courts for five years.

In *Court of Remorse*, Cruvellier (2010) captures the disorganization and incompetence that marked the creation of the Arusha court in its early years. When Canadian Louise Arbour replaced Goldstone, she found that the office of the prosecutors 'lacked strategy, discipline, and coherence' (2010: 15). The registrar and the deputy prosecutor were forced to resign. Arbour succeeded in bringing a series of indictments against twenty-eight defendants associated with Colonel Bagosora, considered at the time the architect of the genocide, but the court refused to permit such a massive joint trial. Bagosora was always treated as the mastermind behind the genocide, the head of the 1991 army committee that supposedly started planning the massacres, the individual who left the Arusha accords in 1993 promising to 'unleash the apocalypse', and who ignored the murder of the ten Belgian peacekeepers working under Romeo Dallaire. Bagosora was a retired general and chief of staff. When his superior left on a trip in April, he assumed command of the army for three days. The court dismissed his culpability for all events associated with the genocide, save for these three days. The 1991 army committee did not plan the genocide, and was staffed by several generals who openly opposed it, including Leonidas Rusatira. The witnesses who reported the 'apocalypse' quote were discredited. Although he was sentenced to life imprisonment, on appeal (December 2011) Bagosora's penalty was reduced to thirty-five years and the question of who implemented the genocide is still an open question. The mountains of material gathered by investigators over seventeen years were largely irrelevant. Cruvellier (2010) calls this 'the brainless genocide' and suggests that it is indicative of the incompetence that has marked the court from the start.

Cruvellier's book is a searing condemnation of the tribunal, which documents failures of disclosure, inconsistent sentencing philosophies, inept investigations and prosecutions, and an unwholesome over-reliance on questionable eyewitness evidence, often given anonymously or *in camera*, and often accepted naively. He reports how senior military figures who appear as witnesses in the defence of other military figures are threatened themselves with indictments. He is critical of the under-reporting of the procedures by major news agencies as well as the legal harassment of journalists sceptical of the courts who have been threatened with contempt. Cruvellier leads one to conclude that the standards of legal practice are not *higher* at the international level than in the common law courts, but significantly lower.

Conclusion

Are current judicial responses to mass murder 'cosmopolitan'? It does not appear so. The international community may have begun the process effectively at Nuremberg in 1945. But the effectiveness of the courts (tribunals, hybrids, and the ICC) has become increasingly questionable the more they proliferate. Cost is relevant, but Combs's evidence is more worrisome, because she establishes that justice provided by the tribunals outside of Europe proceeds with lower standards of evidence than would be acceptable in most Western jurisdictions. In contrast, in the hybrid courts, the UN is imposing legal traditions that are foreign to the indigenous populations. The unstated implication is that these tribunals will accelerate the 'modernization' of peasant societies in terms of a legal code and procedure that are euro-centric. The West is imposing law based on Western conceptions of fairness, culpability, and procedure, irrespective of the level of development of such societies. Ironically, the West makes these changes by directing financial support into The Hague, not Kigali, Belgrade, or Sarajevo—cities that could use the investment to develop indigenous legal solutions. The sovereign impunity for crime at the domestic level has migrated from the national context to the level of superpowers. Now the superpowers can hold the sovereigns of minor nations accountable for their crimes, while escaping control themselves. This is epitomized by the failure of the superpowers to join the Rome Treaty in support of the ICC. This is not the world of Kant as much as the world of Nietzsche. The genealogy of good and evil is power.

The interests of victims of mass atrocities might be better served by prosecution of perpetrators under national criminal law, by internal truth and reconciliation commissions, by diplomacy and pardons, and by inter-state acts of compensation such as those arranged at the International Court of Justice (ICJ). I shall explore some of the possibilities of these alternatives in the next chapters.

8

The Civil Remedy for Genocide

Introduction: Crime Control Versus the Justice Model

Contemporary criminologists are sceptical about the extent to which criminal law inhibits criminal behaviour. That is to say, trends in crime are only weakly responsive to initiatives associated with the criminal justice system. This does not mean that formal institutions of justice are dispensable. On the contrary, they are essential to ensure that there is an appropriate response to crime. Specifically, police and prisons are essential for removing harmful elements from society. That is true of the role of the ad hoc and hybrid courts, and the permanent ICC. However, if one were looking to eradicate social misconduct in a free and democratic society, these formal judicial institutions would have a much weaker effect than such institutions of *informal* social control associated with families, schools, and communities (Sampson and Laub 1993). The genocide courts invite a similar analysis. What role can they play in restraining sovereigns from making war, and endangering their subjects and neighbours?

The history of criminal justice over the past half century has shown that the leading penal philosophies are a poor investment if the object of intervention is 'crime control', i.e. policies designed specifically to suppress the rate of crime. In the 1950s, in the age of Skinner, it was believed that tendencies to commit offences among crime-prone populations could be reversed by *rehabilitation*, that is, by systematically rewarding desired outcomes and shaping more pro-social responses. This was succeeded by *deterrence* theory, based more or less on the same underlying understanding of human nature, but emphasizing the value of negative reinforcements or 'costs'. This approach was favoured widely among economists, based on their assumption that people generally respond to incentives, particularly penalties. Despite significant investments in both types of interventions, the evidence based on patterns of recidivism suggests that outcomes measured by recidivism show little positive evidence of either kind of treatment. Both approaches tend to over-look the individual differences in self-control that make some persons resistant to change, particularly as they mature. The latest trend in penology has involved incapacitation, particularly of that section of the offending population that commits crimes at a high rate, relative to their composition of the population. If these could be selectively removed from society by behavioural classification early in their careers, public security would increase proportionally. Unfortunately, this would require their detention *before* they had made a nuisance of themselves, something reprehensible under the rule of law. In addition, the ability of scientists to diagnose future behaviour from past behaviour is rife with estimation problems due to the individual differences among those who break the law. As a result, *selective incapacitation* would remove too many offenders who would be of little subsequent risk to society, and would miss many who would merit incapacitation according to the theory.

The frustration with attempts to develop an approach to penology based on scientific expertise that would give greater ability to manage offender populations than policies based on common sense led to a sentencing reform movement based almost exclusively on 'the justice model' and offender culpability. One of the proponents of this approach, Andrew von Hirsch (1976), advocated the abandonment of sentencing rationales based on the offender's supposed need for treatment, his alleged underlying dangerousness, and/or the need for future deterrence. Von Hirsch argued for several things. The likelihood that the offender might repeat the crimes should be irrelevant to the length of sentence. Indeterminate sentences based on the expectation of maturational reform should be abolished. Discretion in sentence type, and length, should be sharply curtailed, and penalties should be based exclusively on seriousness of the offence and applied equitably. Imprisonment would be confined to the most serious crimes, and the widespread use of lengthy penalties would be curtailed, as would policies such as parole, which often make the length of sentences arbitrary and unpredictable. As an aside, I would suggest that von Hirsch's 'hard-nosed' approach never contemplated life sentences or determinate incarceration for thirty years, a penalty common at the ICTR, and the gacaca courts. The severity seems to reflect the UN courts' need to register the magnitude of the harm. However, a penalty of determinate lifetime incarceration without possibility of release may be more cruel than capital punishment itself.

The current sentencing practices in the common law countries are a mix of crime control strategies and the justice model. Over the career of individual offenders, they amount to post hoc selective incapacitation through the use of increasingly severe penalties arising from repeated offences because repeated convictions raise the tariffs on future crimes. The effectiveness of this form of sentencing as crime control, or retributive justice, is critically hobbled by the deep chasm between the individual criminal act and the ability of the society to observe it, to apprehend the offender, to meet the test of evidence required to establish guilt, and to provide a penalty sufficient to provide an aversion to crime. This is the problem of attrition in the crime funnel. The link between any one criminal act, including serious crimes, and subsequent incarceration for that act is remarkably small (Gavin and Polk 1983; Polk 1985).

If national justice cannot provide a tight alignment between the commission of crime, and the certainty, celerity, and severity of punishment (Beccaria 2003), what chance has the scheme of international justice, particularly as the latter operates, for all intents and purposes, without a dedicated police force? In addition, it operates at a snail's pace, often in territory hostile to its existence, and open to charges of political bias, particularly in respect of the indictment of the most politically senior accused. Increasingly, it operates with uncertain funding that is responsive to the charity of donor states, and in a vacuum of political accountability divorced from any specific political constituency that could reform it effectively and efficiently. It also operates without the requisite expertise at the start of its mandate and loses the latter prematurely as the courts approach their completion dates and personnel relocate to more permanent opportunities.

At this point, an obvious question presents itself. What are the objectives or what are the aims of the international criminal justice process? As noted, in the national contexts, sentencing philosophies based on an interest in crime control or crime reduction derive from doctrines that provide a myriad of contradictory rationales for sentencing. I have mentioned rehabilitation, deterrence, and incapacitation. A penalty may be awarded with the intention of therapeutic intervention designed to reform the specific offender, thereby contributing to future crime prevention. Or the judge may be an advocate of deterrence, and must determine how her penalty will apply to the individual accused (*specific* deterrence), or future persons who might learn a lesson from the penalty given to the latter (*general* deterrence). In addition, she might want to distinguish, for example, the benefits of a punitive fine from a period of incarceration (*marginal* deterrence). Again, the expectation is that deterrence of one kind or another will contribute to future crime prevention. Alternatively, the penalty might be designed to create *compensation* for the victims of crime through a monetary award, or a *community service* order to promote security through public service. Here the emphasis is repairing a breach of the social order in the past, and fostering social cohesion in the future. Other rationales emphasize *denunciation* of the crime, and a call for *retribution* against the offender to register society's revulsion at the offence. These are indifferent to controlling the future, and more consistent with the justice approach advocated by von Hirsch. Yet other penalties seek *reconciliation* of the victims and the offenders, and seek to replace retributive justice with restorative justice. The single most divisive issue in sentencing policies in criminal matters in common law jurisdictions is the disparity in sentences handed down by different judges for similar offences according to inconsistent sentencing philosophies. These issues have been debated extensively in the context of national jurisdictions, but sentencing philosophies in the international courts have yet to undergo a thorough evaluation in terms of their objectives, and how and whether they achieve them (D'Ascoli 2011). This is a point made in Thierry Cruvellier's study of the Arusha court where he contrasts the views of Judge Gabriel MacDonald with those of Judge Lennart Aspegren. The former claimed that the tribunal was trying to contribute to 'peace and reconciliation' in the Great Lakes region of Central Africa, while the latter claimed that 'the entire staff is there solely to assist the judges in the trials and with the judgments. And not for any other reason. Not for peace. Not so that Hutus and Tutsis get along. Not for any of that' (quoted in Cruvellier 2010: 168).

The leading rationale at Nuremberg appears to have been retribution: those who made aggressive war against other countries were forced to answer for their crimes and risk capital punishment. This rationale evolved essentially from a strict application of the rule of law. The summary execution of leading Nazis was attractive to some, but ultimately was replaced with the decision to submit their enemies to the rule of law, 'one of the most significant tributes that Power has ever paid to Reason'. In addition, there was a pedagogical or ideological intention: to discredit the political legitimacy of National Socialism, and Japanese imperialism. The rationales of the ICTR and ICTY appear similarly motivated by retribution, but they also pay lip service to the goals of social reconciliation between the groups in conflict, presumably achieved through denunciation of the offenders, and retribution for their heinous misconduct. Like the Rwandan gacaca court, they appear to hold a philosophical position under which reconciliation can only follow 'justice'. This appears to presume ironically that people are brought together by what divides them, i.e. that security between groups in conflict is based on retributions against one side. There is a related interest in ending the perceived impunity for crimes undertaken by sovereigns and their delegates. The doctrine of retribution and ending impunity appears to receive most support among those observers in Western Europe and America who are furthest removed from the conflicts. The legal processes in The Hague and in Arusha have not enjoyed the popular assent its advocates had hoped for among members of the communities in conflict, since the leading offenders typically deny any personal culpability for crime and, like Milošević, Karadžić, and Mladić, enjoy tremendous social support in their native communities (Ivkovic and Hagan 2011). As for the Tutsi genocide, the Arusha courts are off the radar for ordinary Rwandans, but it is well known that the vast majority of accused are from the Hutu community, and that the current Tutsi military elite enjoy immunity from prosecution, not only for crimes committed during the invasion of Rwanda in 1994, but for excesses that occurred during the subsequent invasions of Zaire and the Democratic Republic of Congo (DRC). These observations reinforce my scepticism about the utility of a primarily retributive remedy for mass murder, particularly when the legal process appears incapable of encouraging repentance and regret among the perpetrators. This is a point shared with Mark Drumbl (1997: 635). If it were possible to disinvest in the current judicial approach, what are the alternatives, and specifically, is there a civil law remedy? Prior to Norman law (Sellar and Yeatman 1930), Anglo-Saxon law provided for compensation and reparation for all manner of crime (Jeffrey 1957). Why not human rights crimes? Are these any more grave than the aggressions that marked the Great War? And for which the Allies sought reparations against Germany? Although these amounted to a kind of collective punishment, and created hardships detrimental to German's recovery, they demonstrated that civil remedies are not foreign to international law in even the gravest offences.

Compensation and Reparation

There have been several social movements over the last century or
two to seek reparations for groups of people who have suffered
collective violations of their freedoms, particularly at the hands of
the sovereign state. Probably the most famous contemporary case
has been the US debate over the reparations for slavery that existed
from 1620 in colonial America up to 1865 when it was abolished
at the end of the US Civil War. The question of reparations came up
in the 2008 US presidential election. Are the current descendants of
slavery entitled to any symbolic and/or material compensation for
the privations experienced by their ancestors? What would that
consist of, who would pay, and who would benefit from this act?
The consensus of opinion, particularly among the European
descendants, seems to be that whatever changes that occurred following the civil rights movement were sufficient to repay that debt
to history. Nonetheless, there were various attempts following the
civil war to expedite the settlement of the freed slaves in the 19th
century, to recognize the predations of slavery, as well as the failure
of governments to curb lynching in the 20th century. But no individual compensation has ever been seriously contemplated (Brophy
2006).

The question of compensation was raised more recently in
Canada in respect of Natives and their marginalization in Canadian history. Were the survivors of the residential schools in Canada
entitled to any consideration in view of the traumatic experiences
that arose when the European settlers and their descendants created institutions designed to expunge Native customs and languages? This was a process that created intergenerational loss of
both identity and security, and resulted in epidemics of dysfunctional behaviours among survivors. In 2008 Stephen Harper, the
Canadian prime minister, formally apologized in Parliament for the
residential schools and announced a $2 billion compensation pack-
age available without litigation to Native survivors. The Native
children not only were forcibly removed from their families
throughout their key formative years to expedite their assimilation
into European cultures, but suffered frightful levels of physical and
sexual abuse at the hands of the religious orders who operated the
schools, and experienced levels of fatalities from illness and disease,
primarily tuberculosis, that reached 40–50 per cent of the student
bodies in some schools in the first decades of the twentieth century,

a condition described at the time as 'a national crime' (Bryce 1922). This is a situation that Powell (2011) aptly describes as 'barbaric civilization', a process in which colonial pacification created untold grief and suffering among Natives in the name of the settler's 'social improvements', including assimilation and cultural genocide (Moses 2008). Former Canadian Prime Minister Paul Martin, testifying in April 2013 at the Canadian Truth and Reconciliation Commission said that the Canadian residential schools engaged in 'cultural genocide'.

The treatment of US and Canadian citizens of Japanese origins who were detained by their governments during the Second World War raised other questions about the culpability of government vis-à-vis their minority populations. Within months of the attack on Pearl Harbor by the Japanese imperial navy, some 120 000 Japanese Americans and 23 000 Japanese Canadians were stripped of their private property with minimal compensation and relocated from the Pacific coast to crowded rural detention centres where they were recruited for agricultural work and road construction. They were fingerprinted and detained like convicted criminals. In 1988 Prime Minister Mulroney and President Reagan offered their apologies for this wholesale suspension of liberties, and their respective governments paid compensation to individual survivors in the amount of $20 000 and provided funds to create centres to commemorate the detentions.

These cases—African slavery, Native residential segregation, and Japanese detention—entailed privations of minority populations of various levels of gravity, and for different periods of time, but they were not explicitly recognized in terms of genocide.

However, even in cases of genocide, there has been an exploration of compensation as a remedy for the evils perpetrated on victims (Zweig 1987). Holocaust survivors sought recognition from German governments and the Swiss banks for losses incurred by their actions during the Second World War. In 1952, the Conference on Jewish Material Claims Against Germany negotiated a settlement with the Federal Republic of Germany that obtained compensation for injuries inflicted upon individual Jewish victims of Nazi persecution. The committee negotiated for the return of, and restitution for, Jewish-owned properties and assets confiscated or destroyed by the Nazis; obtained funds for assistance in the resettlement of Jewish victims of Nazi persecution, many of whom had become stateless displaced persons; administered individual compensation programmes for genocide survivors; and helped reclaim East German Jewish-owned property, and allocated the proceeds from its sale to institutions that provided social services to elderly, and needy victims of the Nazis (Taylor, Schneider, and Kagan 2009: 104). The German government contributed about $60 billion in satisfaction of settlements negotiated under this agreement. It also supported a series of further pensions and adjustment funds that post-dated the initial deadline set to establish claims (Taylor et al: 105). These settlements were designed to repair *material* losses. They were in no way seen as establishing 'moral atonement' (Authers 2006: 424).

In the late 1990s, a series of class action lawsuits were initiated against Swiss banks by plaintiffs in US courts who argued that they, and/or their relatives, had been illegally deprived of their wealth. A settlement was negotiated by the parties that resulted in the creation of a $1.25 billion 'Settlement Fund' to compensate persons who were deprived materially as a result of financial misconduct on the part of the banks. The fund also provided compensation for persons who had been forced to work under SS control. The settlement was based on evidence that the banks had surreptitiously retained, and concealed, the savings of persons assumed to be deceased as a result of the war. It was also based on the finding that the banks had profited from the laundering of money created by illegal labour operations in the Third Reich (Gribetz and Reig 2009: 115). Private German companies also contributed to the fund as a result of their profiteering from forced and slave labour. During the war, the SS had created an enormous work force of as many as 7.7 million people, including Russians, Poles, and Ukrainians, who were 'recruited' to work in German war industries without compensation, adequate food, clothing, or shelter (Allen 2005). In addition to these 'forced' labourers, the SS created 'slave' labour industries based on the work of Jews detained in concentration camps. The fund paid $7,500 to surviving slave labourers and about $2,500 for forced labourers, the difference reflecting the dramatically different conditions under which they worked. In this settlement, it was expressly noted that the size of the compensation was trivial in view of the suffering of the victims, and hence that it was symbolic. Unlike the earlier material claims settlement, these payments were accompanied by an explicit apology (Authers 2006: 427), combining recognition of moral culpability with symbolic material reparation.

One of the longest-standing claims for compensation is the struggle by contemporary Armenians for the hardships and murder of the Turkish Armenians in 1915. It is a matter of public record that the Turkish state seized Armenian schools, churches, personal property, bank accounts, and other personal wealth, and converted them to state property. Where the survivors of the Holocaust were able to put considerable pressure on post-war Germany to acknowledge that state's liability, and to negotiate civil remedies with it, the Armenians have never succeeded in advancing their claims with governments of Turkey. In the German case, there was considerable pressure on Germany from the Allies to accept liability, particularly in light of the Marshall Plan, and America's initiative in rebuilding Germany. The Armenians have recently had more success in advancing the case with companies that sold insurance to their deceased relatives in Anatolia. Within the last decade, French and American insurance companies have agreed, in principle, to pay out claims to several thousand families amounting to over $50 million. Part of their ability to do so arose from laws, such as that in California, that permitted claimants to prosecute claims in that state after the period in which they should have been filed (i.e. the Armenian Genocide Insurance Act of 2004). Ironically, the government of the Young Turks responsible for the Armenian 'Golgotha' (Balakian 2009) had tried to collect on the policies of those whose properties they had seized, and who were murdered at their hands. At the time the insurance companies refused to pay, but never had to settle accounts with the dead, the dispossessed, or their heirs until recently.

What the literature on compensation suggests is that there is a developing international civil law parallel to criminal law that provides remedies to victims of human rights abuses. However, the basis of compensation varies from case to case. Sometimes, a financial payment is justified in terms of restitution for material losses, arbitrary confiscation of property, or forced labour; sometimes it is a reparation based on recognition of suffering or privation. A settlement may have a purely material foundation, but frequently, it has a symbolic and/or moral dimension based on recognition of guilt, and amounts to an expression of remorse. Sometimes the relief is available to all members of a class (the Japanese detained and interned post-Pearl Harbor) or only victims in certain defined statuses (slave labourers). Sometimes the payment is compellable under international law. For example, the UN Compensation

Commission was created by the Security Council in 1991 to force Iraq to pay damages for victims of the illegal occupation of Kuwait in 1990. By 2005, over $52 billion in claims had been awarded, and over $19 billion had actually been paid (Houtte, Das, and Delmartino 2006: 378). Other times, the compensation is negotiated politically and is driven by what Robert Drinan (2001) called the 'politics of shaming' and amounts to a contract entered into voluntarily by parties who wish to resolve conflicts. Nonetheless, one thing is clear: the civil remedy does not appear to be an *alternative* to the criminal remedy. Indeed, when we look at recent developments at the UN ad hoc tribunals, the utilization of compensation and reparation appears to be poised to grow and appears to be *in addition* to retribution.

Development of the right of remedies and reparation at the UN

The case for compensation was made on two occasions by Judge Patrick L. Robinson, President of the Chambers of the ICTY, in speeches at the United Nations. In 2009 he told the General Assembly that

as President of the Tribunal, I have met on a number of occasions with victims' groups who have expressed their anguish at the failure of the international community to provide any kind of compensation for their suffering. In many respects, these victims feel that they have been forgotten by the international community and that their rights have been disregarded (Robinson 2009).

Without compensation, he feared there could be no guarantee of a lasting peace in the region. In other words, the considerable investments already made in the court, and the retributive process, would appear in his mind to be only the first step in securing peace. But, in addition to that, he implied that the UN has created positive rights under international law by which victims of human rights violations are entitled to a remedy. He referred first to the UN Assembly's 1985 *Declaration of Basic Principles for Victims of Crime and Abuse of Power*, and second to the Assembly's 2005 *Basic Principles and Guidelines on the Right to a Remedy and Reparation for Victims of Violations of International Human Rights and Humanitarian Law*. According to Robinson, these measures were adopted because the objective of the law is not only to punish offenders, but also to restore dignity to victims by providing them some material means to help them rebuild their lives. And while the costs of such measures ought to be borne by the offender and national funds from the offender's state, in cases where the states are indigent, 'other sources of funds' should be sought. In 2011 Judge Robinson returned to these themes when he stated to the Security Counsel that 'the Tribunal cannot, through the rendering of its Judgements alone, bring peace and reconciliation to the region. Other remedies should complement the criminal trials if lasting peace is to be achieved, and one such remedy should be adequate reparations to the victims for their suffering' (Robinson 2011). Moreover, in this second address he referred to the need for the proposed fund to cover both victims *and witnesses*. 'More than 6,900 witnesses and accompanying persons from all over the world have been called to appear before the Tribunal. Without the courage of these witnesses to step forward and give evidence, there would be no trials, and impunity would reign.' Following this logic, reparation ought to be made available to persons directly victimized, in order to restore their dignity and recognize their suffering. This is a population of hundreds of thousands, if not millions in the Balkan states and/or Rwanda; and this should be *extended* to another circle of people in recognition both of their courage as witnesses, and of their cooperation with the tribunals.

Judge Robinson's 2009 address to the UN stressed the disappointment of the victim groups with the failure of 'the international community' to provide any compensation for their suffering. The 1985 document to which he first refers notes that victims should be treated with compassion and respect for their dignity, and that they are entitled to seek redress for harms through access to mechanisms 'as provided for by national legislation' (OHCHR 1985, para 4). The document goes on to say that where 'compensation is not fully available from the offender or other sources, *States should endeavour* to provide financial compensation' (para 11, emphasis added)— not the international community. Likewise, in the second document adopted by the General Assembly in 2005, under the section on reparation for harm suffered, paragraph 16 reads: 'States should endeavour to establish national programmes for reparation and other assistance to victims in the event that the parties liable for the harm suffered are unable or unwilling to meet their obligations.' These programmes are domestic obligations. Judge Robinson's financial requests at the UN are based on shifting a national burden to other member states who were not party to the atrocities, creating a new kind of international welfare.

The document adopted by the General Assembly in 2005 provided a detailed description of what would be required for full and effective reparation. The resolution reflects the conflicting and overlapping rationales associated with compensation discussed earlier in this chapter by simply folding them all in. The provision of reparations would include 'restitution, compensation, rehabilitation, satisfaction and guarantees of non-repetition' (OHCHR 2005 para 18).

- Restitution would restore the victim to the original situation that existed before the gross violations of international human rights law occurred. It would include restoration of liberty, enjoyment of human rights, identity, family life and citizenship, return to one's place of residence, and return of employment and property.
- Compensation would be provided for any economically assessable damage, proportional to the gravity of the violation of human rights law, and would cover physical or mental harm, lost opportunities, including employment, education and social benefits, material damages, loss of earnings, 'moral damage', and costs required due to legal or medical assistance.
- Rehabilitation would include medical and psychological care as well as legal and social services in order to ensure recovery of health and mental health, and access to legal aid and welfare counselling.
- As for 'satisfaction', this item included a host of provisions including: effective measures to curb continuing violations; verification of the facts of the violation, and full and public disclosure of the truth of violations; identification of missing human remains, if necessary, and appropriate disposal of them; an official recognition of the violation designed to restore the dignity and reputation of the victims; public apologies and acceptance of responsibility by the perpetrators; restoring the dignity and reputation of the victims; judicial and administrative sanctions against persons liable for the violations; commemorations and tributes to the victims; international humanitarian law training at all levels.
- Finally, guarantees of 'non-repetition' suggest that victims are entitled to assurances that steps are taken to dismantle the

organization undertaking the violation of human rights, and are taken to neutralize the persons responsible for them.

As a policy document, the scope of reparations is visionary. It attempts to tap the many contradictory issues that compensation raises. But surely many of the remedies are alternatives. If one considers briefly the section on 'satisfaction', it calls for the authorities to prosecute those suspected of violations through 'judicial and administrative sanctions', and also to have them make public apologies and accept responsibility. This is comparable to operating a criminal trial at the same time as a truth and reconciliation commission (Schabas and Darcy 2004). The one is based on a frank and open disclosure of inculpatory admissions; the other is premised on the right to remain silent. The objective of the one is retributive justice, while the other seeks community healing and reconciliation. Criminal convictions seek retribution; apology seeks reconciliation. Public policies should have clear objectives and a rationale for choosing between them. In the case of retributive justice and compensation, Judge Robinson argued that both are required, but for different reasons. In principle, I think he may be correct, but I believe he is mistaken in regard to the parties responsible for reparation. This is not the responsibility of the ad hoc tribunals, or of the international community. In addition, motions adopted by the General Assembly, such as the ones to which he refers, are not binding on member nations. This aspect of international justice is more poetry than law. There are two further points to establish in respect of reparations, to bring this part of the analysis to a conclusion. The first concerns the World Court's decision regarding the dispute between Serbia and its neighbours. The second concerns the current ICC.

The World Court Mediates Charges of Genocide

The ICJ or 'the World Court' is the official permanent legal organ of the United Nations. It adjudicates conflicts between member states over such things as territorial disputes or access to marine transportation according to international law. It also sits in an advisory capacity to answer questions put to it by organs of the UN. For example, in 1996 the General Assembly asked the court to determine if the use of nuclear weapons in warfare was lawful. As of 2012, there had been 151 cases before the court since it began operations in 1947. In 1993 the court received a complaint from Bosnia and Herzegovina against the Federal Republic of Yugoslavia (Serbia and Montenegro). It alleged that a massive invasion by Yugoslavian military forces had resulted in widespread violations of human rights, including genocide against the non-Serb population in violation of the Genocide Convention. Croatia had seceded from the Yugoslav federation in June 1991, followed by Macedonia in September. Bosnia and Herzegovina declared independence in March 1992. And Serbia and Montenegro dissolved the Socialist Federation of the Republic of Yugoslavia, and declared the Federal Republic in April 1992. Serbs invaded Croatia and Bosnia-Herzegovina in an attempt to create a larger Serbia. The Bosnia-Herzegovina applicants asked the court to order preliminary measures to reverse the injuries of the Serb invasion. They asked specifically that the Serbs be required to desist from ethnic cleansing, from murdering, kidnapping, and raping citizens of Bosnia-Herzegovina, from destroying villages and towns, from bombarding civilian targets, from laying siege to urban areas causing starvation, and from otherwise interfering with the security and autonomy of the new republic. Article IX of the Genocide Convention provided a mechanism by which any party to the convention that had a dispute with another party about its interpretation, application, or fulfilment could refer this to the ICJ. When Yugoslavia signed the convention, it committed itself to desist from genocide, and actively to prevent its occurrence. In 1992 the army of the Federal Republic of Yugoslavia (FRY) seemed to be doing just the opposite. The 1993 application pre-dated the slaughter at Srebrenica, and much evidence of horrific killings, but the wholesale destruction of villages was already apparent. When they brought the application to the ICJ in March 1993, the applicants called for reparations. They argued that Yugoslavia had 'an obligation to pay Bosnia and Herzegovina, in its own right and as *parens patriae* for its citizens, reparations for damages to persons and property as well as to the Bosnian economy and environment caused by the violations of international law in a sum to be determined by the Court' (Bosnia 1993 para r). In 1999 Croatia brought a similar complaint against Yugoslavia for violations of the Genocide Convention, and also sought reparations (Croatia 1999).

The court did not resolve the Bosnia-Herzegovina proceedings against Serbia-Montenegro until 2007 (fourteen years after the application and twelve years post-Srebrenica); the Croatian case is still in progress. The court determined that there was a legal dispute between the applicant (Bosnia-Herzegovina) and the respondent (Serbia-Montenegro) arising from their common obligations within the framework of the 1948 Convention. The court concluded that though neither party had signed the initial agreement, they were nonetheless obligated to it as a result of 'state succession', i.e. both states had morphed out of a prior state that had joined the convention. As to the question of whether Serbia was responsible for genocide, or any of the derivative offences (i.e. conspiracy to commit genocide, incitement to genocide, complicity in genocide), they concluded in the negative. Their judgment turned on the *dolus specialis* requirement in the convention. The law requires that the perpetrators are attempting to destroy in whole or in part members of the targeted group *as such*. They contrasted genocide with 'ethnic cleansing' which, on the facts, was pursued with ferocity, but without the special mental element (to destroy the group *as such*). If the mistreatment of civilians amounted to war crimes or crimes against humanity, the court did not have jurisdiction. However, the court did determine as a factual matter that genocide had occurred at Srebrenica, and that 'the Main Staff of the VRS (the army of the Republika Srpska) had the necessary specific intent to destroy in part the group of Bosnian Muslims' (Bosnia 2007). However, the perpetrators were from Bosnia, the applicant's own state. The court then considered whether the respondent—Serbia—was legally responsible for the Srebrenica massacres committed by Bosnian Serbs. 'In light of the information available to it, the Court finds that the acts of those who committed genocide at Srebrenica cannot be attributed to the respondent under the rules of international law of State responsibility.' The VRS was not a formal organ of the army of the FRY. There was no evidence that the VRS was acting under its orders, or that it exercised effective control over the VRS.

However, the case against the Serbs did not end there. The court found against the respondent in several other areas. Specifically, the court found that Yugoslavia had not taken general steps to prevent genocide, that it had supplied weapons to paramilitary organizations, including the VRS, with knowledge that violence was likely to occur given the nature of the animosities between the conflicting parties. In addition, it had violated the obligations in the provisional measures ordered in 1993 'to take all measures within its power to prevent commission of the crime of genocide and to ensure that any organizations and persons which may be subject to its influence do not commit any acts of genocide'. The court concluded that the respondent 'did nothing to prevent the Srebrenica massacres and it thus violated its obligation to prevent genocide'. In addition, it had failed to surrender General Mladić, who had been observed repeatedly moving freely in Serbia, despite the existence of a warrant for his arrest at the ICTY. Mladić, as VRS commander, supervised the Bosnian Serb occupation of Srebrenica. Under the convention, Yugoslavia was obligated to cooperate with any penal tribunal created by the convention under Article VI, such as the ICTY, and had failed to meet that obligation. The last part of the judgment was what amounted to a general order to comply with the convention, prosecute persons known to have breached it, and cooperate with the international tribunals designed to punish it. Yugoslavia was absolved of the commission of genocide per se but found culpable *for failure to prevent genocide*. That failure permitted the Bosnian Serbs to commit genocide, but the VRS were not respondents in this case.

The final aspect of the judgment was the court's consideration of the applicant's request for reparation. The basis for the decision appears quite narrow. While acknowledging Yugoslavia's violation of its obligation to prevent genocide,

the Court finds that, since it has not been shown that the genocide at Srebrenica would in fact have been averted if the Respondent had attempted to prevent it, financial compensation for the failure to prevent the genocide at Srebrenica is not the appropriate form of reparation. The Court considers that the most appropriate form of satisfaction would be a declaration in the operative clause of the judgment that the Respondent has failed to comply with the obligation to prevent the crime of genocide.

Likewise for the other main failures on Yugoslavia's part (e.g. failure to surrender Mladić), 'an operative clause' in the judgment that the respondent failed to do what the law required, would be the extent of the remedy that the court found appropriate.

This decision will strike some readers as perverse. There was significant evidence that the army of the FRY had equipped, and remained in communication with, the VRS and that both groups had engaged in ethnic cleansing against non-Serbs throughout the Balkans with brutal consequences. Since the court concluded that ethnic cleansing was not equivalent to genocide, all the FRY army's collateral behaviour in ethnic cleansing with the VRS, conspiracy, incitement, complicity etc., was outside the *actus reus* of the Genocide Convention, and beyond the jurisdiction of the court. The area of law that was relevant within the scope of the convention—genocide—did not yield evidence that Yugoslavia's failure to prevent genocide made it a party to genocide (although such bystander roles of sociological complicity are part of the sociogenesis of genocide). Would genocide have been averted if the army of the FRY had opposed it? Since it did not happen, it did not constitute admissible evidence. Arguably, the court requires proof that is impossible to produce: 'it has not been shown in fact that the genocide would have been averted . . .'. How can a conditional outcome be 'shown' (i.e. what *would* have been or occurred), and said to be 'in fact' an outcome, when the event never happened, and where its non-occurrence would likely be speculation and consequently have no weight as evidence? The court's logic is narrow. Even if we accept the court's 'doxa' about Yugoslavia's innocence in respect of Srebrenica, on what logic would the court reject any reparations on the positive finding of *failure to prevent genocide*? Why did this court, which has the capacity to award reparations, take such an indifferent view of the dignity of the victims of genocide whose case Judge Robinson championed from the perspective of the ICTY? The answer seems to be that there is no *legal* link between a failure to prevent genocide, and the consequences of that failure. The misconduct of the Serbs is not *causally* related to the victimization of the Bosnian Muslims. Hence, the court had no grounds to award reparations, except nominally.

Although reparations were denied in this case, the court took a more positive view of the claim by the DRC. In 1998 the DRC filed a notice that it had been illegally occupied by the armed forces of Uganda, Rwanda, and Burundi, and had experienced massive civil rights abuses and crimes against humanity in respect of mistreatment of unarmed civilians (DRC 1999). The claim was sustained, and the ICJ awarded reparations to the DRC from Uganda in an amount to be mutually negotiated by the parties, or, in the alternative, to be set by the court through further proceedings (DRC 2005). The cases before the ICJ are of interest to criminologists since they suggest that very serious breaches of human rights, and war crimes, *may* have a civil remedy independent of a criminal remedy. However, the cases in this court appear to drag on for decades, and the grounds for awarding or rejecting reparations, as in the Srebrenica case, are narrow. If the Genocide Convention had permitted the referral of crimes against humanity and war crimes to the ICJ, crimes associated with 'ethnic cleansing' would have a firmer legal foundation in that court, and might have permitted the development of a purely civil remedy for such privations.

Reparations at the International Criminal Court

The ICC was created by the Rome Statute, which was supported by 120 nations at a UN diplomatic conference in 1998, and was designed to create a permanent international criminal court. Seven states opposed the Rome Statute, and twenty-one abstained. It came into being in 2002, by which time over sixty countries had ratified the treaty. It is situated in The Hague. As of 2012, there were seven cases in various stages of progress, all from Africa (Uganda, Darfur, Central African Republic, DRC, Kenya, Côte d'Ivoire, and Libya). The cost of the court is managed by the Assembly of States Parties (ASP), and, like the ad hoc courts, has been steep—about half a billion euros from 2002 to 2009, or about 100 000 000 euros annually in recent years (Mettraux 2009). The ASP consists of states who are party to the treaty, and who support the court financially. As noted earlier, many of the key international powers have not ratified the treaty. Another major stumbling block for the court is the inability of the contracting parties to reach a consensus on the definition of aggression, the crime that was the centerpiece of the Nuremberg prosecutions. These problems may be overcome with time.

One of the innovative features of the ICC is its provision of reparations arising from violations of international humanitarian law, which cover genocide, war crimes, and crimes against humanity, a feature notably missing from the ad hoc tribunals. The provisions are embedded in a larger set of considerations meant to heighten victim participation at various stages of the proceedings, and to give them a voice more like that encouraged in restorative justice processes. Under the Victims and Witnesses Unit (VWU), the court is able to provide protective measures and security arrangements for the witnesses and victims, as well as providing counselling and other appropriate assistance. These services are available not only to direct victims, but to persons, such as family members and dependents, who have been indirectly affected by the human rights violations. The Victims' Participation and Reparation Section (VPRS) communicates with victims in a number of ways to advise them about case progress, how they can contribute testimony, file applications for reparations, and how to seek legal representation for their own interests. Both the VWU and the VPRS are operated under the court's registry branch.

In 2002 the ASP created a Trust Fund for Victims (TFV). This was designed to be supported through volunteer donations. The total TFV voluntary contributions by November 2010 were €5.8 million. Contributions in 2010 totalled €1.25 million, the highest level of annual contributions at that date. In 2011, the United Kingdom made a further donation of €500 000. The lion's share of the contributions has come from European countries (TFV 2010: 40). It is premature to draw conclusions about the effectiveness of the fund. The 2010 Progress Report indicates that programmes have reached tens of thousands of people in places like the DRC, pre-dating any criminal convictions at the ICC. The fund is able to recognize persons under ICC jurisdiction, independent of specific convictions. The programmes combine individual reparations with community-based programmes, and appear to invest relatively modest amounts of money. In the DRC, the TFV partnered with various international aid agencies to invest approximately $3 179 883 in 2008–2009 on thirteen active projects that had over 40 600 direct beneficiaries. These were victims of torture, mutilation, war orphans, rehabilitated child soldiers, and other victims of violence. The services consisted of psychological counselling, education, physical rehabilitation, and material support (TFV 2010: 15–16).

On the other hand, REDRESS reported in July 2011 that 470 victims were denied an opportunity to participate in a hearing to confirm charges against war crimes suspect Callixte Mbarushimana, due to insufficient resources at the ICC in the VPRS. Mbarushimana was an ex-FAR warlord charged with crimes against humanity, and war crimes in dominating the civilian population of North and South Kivu in the eastern DRC after the end of the Rwandan genocide. The Registry received requests from thousands of victims from various cases, and does not appear to have the resources to extend the legal support to permit their views to be represented at the ICC. When one compares the investment in the retributive side of the ICC—the investigations, prosecutions, witness assistance, appeals, and punishments of the accused—with the investment in the rehabilitative and reparative side of the ICC in terms of victim and survivor services, the differences are impressive: over ~$200 000 000 (~€100 000 000) annually for the former versus $5 or $10 million annually for the latter. What there does not seem to be at the international level is an economic rationality that would justify such an asymmetrical investment in the two approaches, and a cost-benefit analysis of each. The fact that this court has explicitly embraced both approaches to breaches of international humanitarian law may make it possible to estimate what each approach is capable of yielding. But this is a question for the future.

Last Word: A Civil Society Solution?

The consensus among criminologists is that *informal* patterns of social control associated with families, schools, and communities are essential to curb offending behaviour before careers in crime set in. What is it that corresponds to 'informal social control' when we shift from garden-variety crime to political crimes such as genocide? When we examine political crimes, such as massacres and genocides, the 'sovereign', on the contrary, is the primary actor. That is, the elites are assumed to be the prime movers of violence. In my view, this violence has its roots in the concept of 'political transcendence'—the use of war and domination to create Hitler's *Lebensraum* in 'the East' through the colonization of the Ukraine and Russia, and the biological elimination of inferior racial groups such as Jews, Slavs, and mental defectives. Pol Pot sought rejuvenation of the Khmers through a return to the simplicity of peasant life in collective agriculture. The Rwandan Akuza sought the preservation of Hutu ascendency by eliminating their Hamitic oppressors. Each elite group seized the voice of the collectivity to eliminate its rivals and enemies, thereby establishing their mastery over the reins of government. As a result, many people died. So what is the control theory solution?

In the last chapter we raised a number of problems that shake confidence in a purely criminal law solution of the kinds witnessed at the ad hoc tribunals and the hybrid courts. In this chapter we have raised the possibility of an alternative to the criminal law route through reparation in one or another forms of civil law. The recurring pattern that emerges is a proliferation of nested legal procedures that do not contribute convincingly to genocide prevention, that add expectations of reparation on top of retribution, and that widen the jurisdiction of the court from a few hundred offenders to countless victims without any prospect of devising social responses that are financially and politically sustainable. In *Informal Reckonings*, Woolford and Ratner (2008) reported a similar pattern: attempts to achieve conflict resolutions through informal proceedings such as mediation, restorative justice, or reparation rarely succeed in returning ownership of the problem totally to those who experience it in their communities, or prove effective in radically changing society. However, the search for such remedies requires much ingenuity. Mark Osiel (2005) proposed that where there is 'superior responsibility' in a bureaucracy, civil service, or army that is involved in atrocities, international states adopt practices that would impose 'collective monetary sanctions on the officer corps, who can readily monitor prospective wrongdoers and redistribute costs to individual members actually culpable'. This is a way of linking the 'small fry' who carry out atrocities and the 'big fry' who control the political process. Such an approach would form part of a wider strategy to use different legal remedies to avert and address mass atrocities.

The key to genocide management in the long run is genocide prevention. And the key to genocide prevention is the cultivation of social structures in which the sovereign's aspiration for political transcendence is restrained. This does not mean that people should abandon their aspirations. It means that we need populations of engaged citizens who will not permit their states to silence their voices, reduce their heterogeneity, and further their interests in disregard for the plurality of interests in society. This populist element is central to the third form of genocide response that has emerged in contemporary societies: the truth and reconciliation commission. That is the subject of our next chapter.

9

Truth and Reconciliation Commissions: The Third Option

Introduction: Telling the Truth

Nuremberg set the standard for 'recovering' societies in creating a legal foundation on which a future could be erected by bringing the enemies of society to face criminal prosecution. In addition to the prosecution of the leading surviving Nazis, the Nuremberg courts held twelve subsequent trials on a variety of cases. The 'Doctors' Trial' prosecuted sixteen defendants for experimenting on concentration camp prisoners to study the effects of everything from high altitude exposure to malaria and sterilization. The 'Einsatzgruppen case' prosecuted those who operated the mobile execution squads designed to eliminate the Jews and the Soviet officials trapped behind the advancing invasion of Eastern Europe in Operation Barbarossa. Two cases were prosecuted against the industrialists at I.G. Farben and at Krupp arms manufacturers for use of slave labour. The trials were all completed by 1949, and resulted in 133 convictions. The current ad hoc tribunals for genocide were created with similar expectations. They do not appear to enjoy the credibility of Nuremberg. Also, the prospect of remedying gross violations of human rights committed by one state against another through reparations at the World Court is real, but currently tenuous. In contrast to the scepticism associated with criminal and civil remedies for genocide, there is a 'sensibility' in contemporary society that holds that social justice, and a secure peace in communities marred by political violence, might be better served through a process in which people involved in the conflict confront their past by an open discussion of the atrocities that, on the one side, they have committed and, on the other side, they have experienced. The underlying assumption is that grave conflicts can be defused, and prior conflicts deprived of their ability to inflict grief, if the energies of violence can be 'talked through' and shared interpersonally, and that the violent impulses associated with the past can be neutralized or abated through frank and honest communication.

The gacaca courts in Rwanda were premised on this, but only in part. The perpetrators were encouraged to accept responsibility for their misconduct, to confess, and to seek redemption and forgiveness. No amnesty: offenders were expected to be punished accordingly. This point of departure differs from the criminal indictment that specifies who is a perpetrator, an accused, and who is a victim. Similarly, it differs from the civil law perspective in which the victim is an applicant and the perpetrator is a respondent. Nonetheless, these truth commissions have become numerous at the end of the last century, and the beginning of the new one. They have also escaped the widespread criticisms associated with the criminal litigation of war crimes and genocide in Arusha and at The Hague. If criminal indictment of individuals for genocide and other infractions of international humanitarian law through the ad hoc tribunals and the ICC is the first option, and if the ability of countries to sue one another for damages and reparations at the World Court is the second option, then truth and reconciliation commissions (TRCs) within nation states represent the third option.

The TRCs that have appeared in the aftermath of conflicts within nations in the late 20th century appear to have been created at the same time as the restorative justice projects emerged out of dissatisfaction with the more traditional processes of criminal indictment. Restorative justice, which has gained significant presence in North America, Australia, and New Zealand, is contrasted with retributive justice. Its advocates argue that it is premised on the need to return ownership of social conflicts to the stakeholders in the offence. Christie (1977), in particular, stressed how contemporary criminal trials marginalized the victims and their communities, relegated the resolution of conflicts to professionals, and silenced those with the greatest stake in the breach of the peace. He later identified how the preoccupation with punishment had taken on a life of its own in the sprawling gulags of Russia and the megaprisons of the US (Christie 2000). His scepticism regarding retributive justice resonated with the prison or penal abolition movement (Pepinsky 2006). Herman Bianchi (2010) advocated the use of sanctuaries as alternatives to carceral environments, and argued that these could be pursued to mediate conflicts in a forum that bypassed the retributive system and permitted persons in conflict to negotiate settlements on their own terms. The restorative justice literature tends to advocate the use of alternatives to the retributive system, but the actual implementations usually occur at a point in the proceedings in which the offenders have already been indicted and pled guilty. Such practices as sentencing circles and victim-offender reconciliation are alternatives to the normal sentencing practices in criminal courts, which traditionally have left determination of penalty up to the presiding magistrate. The sentencing circles elevate the voice of all the key stakeholders in the community, the families of the perpetrator and the victims, the neighbours and friends of the stakeholders, and in the case of aboriginal communities, the elders and spiritual leaders. The process, in some measure, restores the ownership of the offence to the community that is affected. Likewise, the process of victim offender reconciliation is designed to give voice to the victim, and to expose the perpetrator of the offence to the physical and emotional injuries he or she caused. It is noteworthy that criminal cases in jurisdictions that employ restorative justice measures do not assign cases automatically to such processes. Where an accused is recalcitrant, hostile, and/or incorrigible, the usual retributive course is normal. The search for restorative justice processes appears to be most intense in aboriginal communities whose populations experience levels of conflict with the law far surpassing their representation in the population, and for whom the English legal process is often seen as the ongoing postscript of colonialism. The irony of the restorative justice process is that, except for sentencing, it is sometimes not all that independent from the system that it hoped to replace (Pavlich 2005).

The Record of Tribunals and Commissions of Inquiry: Brazil and Argentina

The United States Institute of Peace has tracked the appearance of these commissions over time, and found that they varied significantly in their composition, focus, and 'success'. While these are not always directed at cases suggestive of genocide, they all reflect grave patterns of widespread human rights abuses typically associated with police and security forces. The US Institute of Peace records over forty such inquiries or commissions dating from 1974. These are identified in Table 9.1. What they appear to have in common is a fundamental shift in citizen security that signals a move from a state of crisis to a state marked by peace and cooperation (Hayner

1994). By way of illustration, I turn to two examples of such commissions, both drawn from South America: Brazil (1986) and Argentina (1984).

The earliest inquiry of interest in my view appeared in Brazil, and operated from 1979 to 1983. It resulted in a Portuguese-language report published in 1986, *Brasil: Nunca Mais*—no more—never again (Arns 1998). This report documented the systematic use of torture against criminals, and the political opponents of the Brazilian government during the period when the country was ruled by a military dictatorship (1964–85). I mention parenthetically that there had been an earlier commission in Uganda created in 1974 by dictator Idi Amin to mask the gross human rights violations owed to his own security forces. It failed to legitimate the regime. The South American inquiries were quite different. After the return to civilian rule in 1985, the self-appointed commission in Brazil was initiated by the archbishop of Sao Paulo, Cardinal Paulo Evaristo Arns, and Presbyterian Minister Jaime Wright. The inquiry employed the services of some thirty-five investigators, and received funding from the World Council of Churches in the amount of $350 000. Notably, government did not delegate the project, and the investigators worked surreptitiously. The report established the routine use of torture by security forces against enemies of the regime in over 17 000 cases. A 1979 law was passed to provide amnesty to security personnel who used abduction, torture, and extrajudicial execution under the pretext of national security. Those records were made available to stakeholders interested in the amnesty process at the Military Supreme Court where such parties could borrow files overnight to assist them in preparing their cases. This permitted Arns and Wright to document the misconduct of police and army officers by copying all the official records, and sending microfilms of the records to the World Council of Churches in Geneva. The amnesty law was never successfully challenged. None of the violators of human rights was ever prosecuted. Nonetheless, in the aftermath of *Nunca Mais*, compensation was paid to members of 135 families of the victims of torture. The report appears to have provided an atmosphere that accompanied the return of democracy, without the Nuremberg-style criminalization of the former military offenders, while holding them collectively accountable for massively abusive behaviour. The release of the report was delayed until the re-emergence of democratic government.

At approximately the same time, a report was produced in Argentina in 1984 with a remarkably similar title in Spanish: *Nunca Más* (Hayner 2011: 46). This was a truth commission created by a democratic government that replaced a series of military juntas who conducted the 'dirty war' against left-wing students, trade unionists, and politicians in the 1970s. It was formally called the National Commission on the Disappeared. Between 1976 and 1983, approximately 9000 individuals simply vanished from Argentine society, victims of kidnapping and murder by the state's security forces. The defeat of the Argentine military in the battle with Britain over the Falkland Islands brought the dictatorship into crisis, and facilitated a return to civilian rule. President Raul Alfonsin was elected in 1983. One of his first acts in office was to repeal the amnesty that the military had created to protect itself from prosecution, and to launch the truth commission. As of 2010, some 700 former security personnel were prosecuted, and more than fifty were convicted. However, the military destroyed many of the state records pointing to responsibility in the chain of command, and failed to produce the documentation of illegal detention required by victims for compensation.

These two remarkable reports had dramatic effects in their respective countries by reaffirming the rule of law, and questioning the impunity with which sovereigns and their representatives could override the rights, and security, of individuals. Neither held public hearings, as has become routine in the more recent TRCs, and their dramatic impacts followed the publication of their reports. *Nunca Mais* became a best-selling book in Brazil. Several common themes emerge. First, the levels of victimization in both cases were staggering. In each country, tens of thousands of victims were identified, cruelly tortured, and/or murdered. As noted in previous chapters, these crimes tend to have become conventionalized. They were made the subject of amnesties that relieved the perpetrators of any individual accountability for their aggression. They also arose in political jurisdictions marked by military dictatorships where individual rights were terminated by force, or the threat of force. Also, the levels of reparations were considerable. In Argentina, US$3 billion was provided to victims of illegal detention. In Brazil, the figure earmarked for victims was US$1.5 billion. Also, these are both national initiatives. By contrast, only a handful of the commissions reported in the US Institute of Peace database originated directly with an international organization, or with the UN.

For example, in 1993 a consortium of international NGOs conducted an investigation in Rwanda to examine the waves of murders of the Tutsi minority. It represented the International Federation of Human Rights, Africa Watch, Inter-African Union of Human Rights, and the International Center for Human Rights, and was led by, among others, Alison Des Forges and William Schabas. The UN Security Council mandated an investigation in Burundi to investigate the assassination of Hutu President Melchior Ndadaye in 1993, and the indiscriminate murders that occurred between Tutsis and Hutus thereafter. The UN also intervened in 1991 in the El Salvador civil war to mediate conflict between leftist guerillas and US-backed Salvadoran military forces. Virtually all the remaining commissions were national in character, typically initiated by new governments, although, as we shall see, the UN has subsequently become an important advocate of the 'third option'. In many cases, the new governments were constituted after a civil war, or after the removal of a dictatorial military government. In this respect, the groundbreaking Brazilian report was atypical in the sense that it was initiated by a non-governmental body, but it *did* follow the return to democracy after a period of military dictatorship. It ushered in a template for social renewal based on the principles of disclosure and accountability and was the first of many documents to establish that dictatorship could be politically discredited by historical analysis.

The commissions referred to in Table 9.1 are as variable as the countries from which they originate. This has important consequences in understanding the contributions that these commissions can make to social policies regarding infringements of humanitarian law: *Nunca Mais* was not an investigative body with legal traction. It had no right to subpoena witnesses. The 'commissioners' only disclosed themselves after the fact. Obviously, the legal power to question people under oath, and publically to identify those who are implicated in human rights violations are important. Also, there is the question of representation among the commissioners of those who were denied human rights. To what extent are such commissions socially responsible or representative? Consider a counter-example. Zimbabwe's Robert Mugabe experienced international pressure to explain the massacre of political dissidents in Matabeleland in 1983, where it is believed his ZANLA forces murdered 1 500 people, and where suppression of dissent is thought to have claimed another 20 000 lives. The Chihambakwe Commission was created to investigate such incidents. However, it had no representation of those who were victimized. No official report was published. The government claimed that it feared the report would spark further political violence. The Legal Foundations and the Catholic Commission for Justice and Peace detailed Zimbabwe's mass murders in *Breaking the Silence* (1997) based on a variety of evidence, including eyewitness accounts, and the discovery of human remains from graves and mine shafts, which established the repression imposed on the region by Mugabe's army (Hayner 2011: 242). Mugabe's suppression of Chihambakwe's report simply minimised his exposure to international ridicule for his mistreatment of his political opponents. This was a commission of amnesia that contributed neither to truth nor reconciliation.

The appearance of such commissions is a new legal phenomenon. They are all preoccupied with human rights, and are frequently based on evidence of massive violations of human rights, if not genocide per se. The majority of the commissions refer to 'truth' and/or 'reconciliation' in their mandates or titles, but not exclusively. They vary in their ability to identify perpetrators of crimes against human rights. Algeria and Morocco excluded such information. The questions of amnesty for perpetrators, and reparations for victims, are also common issues. Sometimes, such commissions operate in tandem with judicial processes that have the power to investigate, and prosecute, perpetrators of human rights violence, as in Sierra Leone. Frequently, they are associated with religious or faith-based institutions that present an alternative social authority to secular government. Archbishop Desmond Tutu is famously recalled as chair of the South African Truth and Reconciliation Commission (SATRC), in which he promoted a distinctive, faith-based idea of Christian reconciliation. Mentioned already was the role of Cardinal Arns in the Brazilian report. Archbishop Nicolas Cotungo chaired the Uruguayan Commission for Peace (2000), which investigated the campaign of disappearances, kidnappings, and assassination of leftists during the 1973–85 military dictatorships in that country. Bishop Sergio Valech chaired the 2003 inquiry into abuses associated with the military dictatorship of Augusto Pinochet in Chile. Religious leaders also played leadership roles in the 2004 Paraguay Truth and Justice Commission (Bishop Mario Medina), the 2007 Ecuador Truth Commission (Sister Elsie Monge), the 2003 Democratic Republic of Congo TRC (Bishop Jean-Luc Mulemera) and the 2002 Sierra Leone TRC (Bishop Joseph Humper). This does not appear to

Table 9.1 Record of truth and reconciliation commissions or inquiries*

Country and year	Title of commission	Focus
Brazil 1979	Nunca Mias. NGO report	Systematic use of torture to deal with political opponents of the military regime.
Bolivia 1982	National Commission for Investigation for Forced Disappearances	155 cases of forced disappearances were documented. No mandate to investigate other abuses.
Zimbabwe 1983	Zimbabwe Commission of Inquiry into the Matabeleland Disturbances	More than 20 000 civilians killed by military in political conflict with President Mugabe.
Argentina 1983	National Commission on the Disappeared (Nunca Mas)	Thousands disappeared under a military dictatorship.
Uganda (a) 1974 (b) 1986	Commission of Inquiry into (a) Disappearances of People, and (b) Violations of Human Rights	The disappearance of regime critics (1974) and the killing of hundreds of thousands of citizens during the dictatorship of Idi Amin (1986).
Peru 1986	Commission of Inquiry to Investigate the Massacre of Prisoners	Uprising of Shining Path prisoners led to widespread massacres in Peruvian prisons.
Nepal 1990	Committee of Inquiry to locate the Persons disappeared during the Panchayat period	Disappearances of opposition members during military dictatorship.
Chile 1990	National Commission for Truth and Reconciliation	Disappearance, killing, torture, and kidnapping during Pinochet's dictatorship.
Chad 1990	The Commission of Inquiry into the Crimes and Misappropriations Committed by Ex-President Habré	Civil war followed by dictatorship, assassinations, torture, illegal detentions, and disappearances.
Germany 1992 (1995 2nd report)	Study Committee for working through the History and the Consequences of the SED Dictatorship in Germany	Psychological legacy of dictatorship in East Germany.

(continued)

Table 9.1 (*Continued*)

Country and year	Title of commission	Focus
El Salvador 1992	Commission on the Truth for El Salvador	Civil war, and the use of government 'death squads'.
Ethiopia 1993	The Special Prosecution Process by the Office of the Special Prosecutor	Summary executions, disappearances, and torture by military government.
Rwanda 1993	International Commission of Investigation on Human Rights Violations in Rwanda since 1 October 1990	Massacres of Tutsis after the Ugandan invasion of 1990.
Sri Lanka 1995	Commissions of Inquiry into the Involuntary Removal or Disappearance of Persons	Disappearances and murders during the ethnic conflict between Tamils and Hindus.
Haiti 1995	National Truth and Justice Commission	Human rights abuses during the military coup in 1991.
Burundi 1995	International Commission of Inquiry for Burundi	Indiscriminate murder of Hutus by Tutsi security forces.
South Africa 1995	Commission of Truth and Reconciliation	Human rights abuses associated with apartheid.
Ecuador 1996	Truth and Justice Commission	Paramilitary attacks on traditional farmers.
Guatemala 1999	Commission for Historical Clarification	Genocide of 200 000 Mayan peasants.
Rwanda 1999	National Unity and Reconciliation Commission	Reconstruction after genocide and civil war.
Nigeria 1999	Human Rights Violations Investigation Commission	Political killings during successive military governments from 1984 to 1991.
Uruguay 2000	Commission for Peace	200 disappearances during military rule.
South Korea 2000	Presidential Truth Commission on Suspicious Deaths	Suspicious deaths of dozens of government critics.

Country and Year	Commission	Description
Côte D'Ivoire 2000	Mediation Commission for National Reconciliation	Hundreds of deaths during contested elections.
Panama 2001	Panama Truth Commission	Torture and disappearances of opposition members.
Peru 2001	Truth and Reconciliation Commission	Assassinations, torture, disappearances, and terrorism in the civil war.
Serbia and Montenegro 2002	Truth and Reconciliation Commission for Serbia and Montenegro	Ethnic cleansing in the Former Yugoslavia.
Timor Leste (East Timor) 2002	Commission for Reception, Truth and Reconciliation	Widespread murder of civilians by Indonesian-led militias.
Sierra Leone 2002	Truth and Reconciliation Commission	Forced displacements, abductions, mutilations, and killings.
Ghana 2003	National Reconciliation Commission	Killings, abductions, disappearances, and seizure of property.
Democratic Republic of Congo 2003	Truth and Reconciliation Commission	Civil war and widespread sexual violence.
Chile 2003	National Commission on Political Imprisonment and Torture	Torture and arbitrary detention.
Algeria 2003	Ad Hoc Inquiry Commission in Charge of the Question of Disappearances	Political conflict and thousands of disappearances.
Paraguay 2004	Truth and Justice Commission	Torture and disappearances in Operation Condor.
Morocco 2004	Equity and Reconciliation Committee	Forced disappearances and arbitrary detentions.
Liberia 2006	Truth and Reconciliation Commission	War crimes and crimes against humanity.

(continued)

Table 9.1 (*Continued*)

Country and year	Title of commission	Focus
Ecuador 2007	Truth Commission to Impede Impunity	Arbitrary detentions, torture, and disappearances.
Solomon Islands 2009	Truth and Reconciliation Commission	Ethnic conflict between settlers and indigenous people led by rival gangs.
Kenya 2009	Truth, Justice, and Reconciliation	Political violence after elections.
Canada 2011	Indian Residential Schools Truth and Reconciliation Commission	Abuse of native children, destruction of traditional culture, and systematic destruction of intergenerational ties.

*Titles of commissions are translated into English.

Source: United States Institute of Peace 2012 (<http://www.usip.org> Truth Commissions by country.

be accidental. Someone with religious credentials appears to add greater credibility to the search for truth and accountability than someone with a purely legalistic or secular orientation. If we examine these forty commissions, can we perceive the circumstances that appear to have preceded and precipitated them? While no one pattern is common throughout, the role of social conflict, civil war, and dictatorial rule, and recovery from such circumstances, are recurrent themes. In the following section, I describe five processes that appear to create the conditions that have called into existence the wave of commissions observed from the mid-1970s.

Five Major Conditions Resulting in National TRCs

(1) Political repression giving rise to armed insurgencies: conflicts of natives vs settlers

We find evidence for this pattern in Peru, Guatemala, and El Salvador. In Peru, the Shining Path and the Túpac Amaru Revolutionary Movement arose in the 1980s to protest the social and economic inequalities of Peruvian society. The armed confrontation resulted in an estimated 70 000 deaths concentrated in the Ayacucho Province of Peru among the indigenous Andean population. In Guatemala, there was a thirty-six-year conflict between the indigenous Mayans and the Spanish settlers that resulted in an estimated 200 000 deaths, the majority of which were Mayan. The Commission for Historical Clarification (1991) labelled this conflict as genocide. In El Salvador, opposition to a series of military juntas coalesced in the Farabundi Marti National Liberation Front (FMLN), which brought together a number of communist-inspired movements opposed to the concentration of ownership of land in the hands of a small number of elite families. The FMLN led a fierce guerilla war against the Salvadoran army from 1980 to 1991. The truth commission was part of the UN-brokered peace agreement that saw the FMLN become a legitimate political party in El Salvador. There were two commissions in Peru, one after the massacres of prisoners in Peruvian jails (1986), and a second (2001) after the defeat of the Shining Path movement by arrest of its leaders in 1992, and the subsequent removal of President Fujimoro in 2000. Fujimoro had conducted the war of aggression against the movement. The Guatemala Truth Commission (1999) was created as part of the UN negotiated peace agreement between the state and the Revolutionary National Unity of Guatemala (URNG) in 1994. In each case, a state confronted armed insurrections that reflected the gross inequalities of life between indigenous people and the colonizers who dominated the economy and society. Although all these were national truth commissions, the UN appears to have taken a role in fostering such processes as part of a peace-making strategy.

One cannot fail to notice that fifteen of the forty cases presented here are from South America, and eighteen from Africa, continents whose development, particularly during the Cold War, was characterized by strong military leadership. However, the issue of repressive leadership associated with armed insurgencies is not limited to these regions. The commissions in Sri Lanka and Nepal followed from minority insurgencies against strong and repressive governments. The Tamil Tigers conducted a twenty-five-year guerilla war against the Hindu majority in Sri Lanka with an estimated 100 000 conflict-related deaths, tens of thousands of 'disappearances', and countless acts of terrorism in the Tamil struggle for social equality. In Nepal, an autocratic kingdom suspended representative government from 1961 to 1990. Maoist insurgents undertook a campaign against the government from 1996 to 2006. A peace agreement led to the creation of a commission to investigate the disappearance of state critics during the period of conflict.

Some of the truth commissions are based on the recognition of private militias or 'death squads' that were created to bolster oppressive regimes. This was established in Ecuador and Leste Timor. Ecuador established a Truth and Justice Commission in 1996. Democratic rule returned to Ecuador in 1979, replacing a military dictatorship. However, the political situation was volatile. The country went through six presidents between 1979 and 1996. Pressure on settlers to redistribute land among indigenous populations led to the funding of paramilitary groups to assassinate critics of the state who were calling for land reform. These death squads were thought to be funded by the large landowners. The Ecuador Truth and Justice Commission (1996) never finished its report, but documented 300 murders carried out by groups allied with the political elite to suppress dissent. In Timor Leste, the Indonesian government recruited and paid peasant militias to attack those advocating independence from Indonesia. In both cases, the major players employed 'designates' to further their conflict with insurgents without getting blood on their own hands. These cases of political conflict based on suppression of opportunities differ from opportunistic attempts to seize state power that are described next.

(2) Militias and warlords challenging failing governments

Four commissions arose from conditions under which dissident political groups attempted to overthrow weak, failing, or ineffective governments. This occurred in Liberia, Sierra Leone, the DRC, and Haiti. In Liberia, during President Samuel Doe's regime (1980–89), the constitution was suspended. Doe seized power in a military coup in 1980, assassinated the president, and massacred the cabinet. His elections in 1985 were widely viewed as fraudulent. Former ministers Charles Taylor and Prince Johnson broke with Doe and fled the country. Both returned with armed militias to overthrow Doe. A group affiliated with Johnson seized and killed Doe in 1989. The first civil war (1989–96) arose from fighting between Taylor, Doe, and Johnson for control of Monrovia. There was indiscriminate killing on all sides. A second civil war (1999–2003) occurred after Taylor's election as president. The Economic Community of West Africa (ECOWAS), led by Nigeria, intervened to restore peace. Some 200 000 people were killed in the fighting between the militias, and a million people were displaced. The UN Mission to Liberia created the truth commission as part of the peace process negotiated through the Accra Peace Accord. A decade later in neighbouring Sierra Leone, the Revolutionary United Front (RUF) opposed the government's move to create multiparty elections, and fought for control of the state and the country's diamond industry. An alphabet soup of militia groups (RUF, AFRC, NPLF, SLA, CDF) fought one another for dominance. The UN brokered a peace agreement between the RUF and the government of Sierra Leone, part of which provided for the creation of a truth commission. In the DRC, a series of dictatorships was replaced with the country's first democratic elections in 2006. The levels of preventable deaths throughout Congo's transition to responsible government have been staggering. As part of the Comprehensive Peace Agreement signed in 2002, the UN provided for a commission to establish the truth among the conflicting versions of history, and to promote peace, reparation, and reconciliation.

Haiti's commission was created after the return to power of Jean Bertrand Ariside in 1994. He had been ousted by a military coup in 1991 led by General Raoul Cedras. He was returned to power as the legitimate head of state through the intervention of the UN, and 20 000 US troops. The commission was intended to expose the abuse of human rights during the period of the military dictatorship. These four cases represent states in trauma with little ability to provide the security associated with modern governance. I also mention here the 2002 Serbia and Montenegro Commission, which called for truth and reconciliation in the former Yugoslavia. The central power of the Yugoslav state unravelled with the demise of communism. The commission disbanded without making a final report, a fact attributed to the Serbian bias of the commission. The truth commissions make a record of their tragic histories, and arguably foster preconditions for the creation of more effective future governments. Their priorities are primarily peace building and, secondarily, 'justice', i.e. retribution.

However, sometimes the descent into violence is not a function of *under*-control where the state fails, but quite the opposite: dictatorships.

(3) Corrupt military interference in democratic politics: material corruption

This occurred in both Panama and South Korea. Panama's elected president, Arnulfo Madrid, was ousted by a military coup in 1968 by General Omar Torrijos. Torrijos negotiated full authority over the Panama canal with the US in 1999. The project was a source of enormous fees for the country's elites, and corruption was a hallmark of his government. After his death in 1981, Torrijos was succeeded by Manuel Noriega, another corrupt general implicated in the international narcotics trade. Elections in 1989 undermined Noriega's rule, but were annulled in the face of widespread rioting. This threw the country into chaos. US troops invaded, and apprehended Noriega for narcotics offences. Exhumations on a military base in 2000 uncovered the human remains of persons abducted and murdered by previous military officials. Mireya Moscoso, widow of Arnulfo Madrid, was elected president, and created the truth commission to expose human rights abuses during the periods of military rule.

In Korea, the elected government was overthrown by a military coup led by Major General Park Chung-Hee in 1961. After his assassination in 1979, he was replaced by another military dictator, Lieutenant General Chun Doo Hwan. Backlashes against the military dictatorships in the late 1980s led to a reintroduction of responsible government. Long-time human rights activist Kim Dae-Jung was elected president in 1987. He called for investigations of the disappearances of political critics during the period of military rule. The return to democracy requires an accounting of history and the naming of atrocities that went unmentioned when free speech was suspended.

(4) Wholesale abuse of human rights as ideological subversion

The coup d'état in Chile that led to the removal of democratically elected President Salvador Allende by General Augusto Pinochet in 1973 differed from the situation in Panama; the latter appears to have been motivated by careerism, and personal financial advancement. Pinochet's coup was ideological, and it led to the active suppression of socialists for geopolitical reasons. Persons suspected of socialist ties were abducted, disappeared, tortured, and murdered, particularly in the year of the coup, 1973. Pinochet lost the presidential national election to Patricio Aylwin in 1989 by a narrow margin. Aylwin called for a National Commission for Truth and Reconciliation to investigate political violence under the Pinochet regime. The 'Rettig Commission' established that 2 279 persons were killed for political reasons, including 957 people who disappeared. A second Chilean inquiry in 2003 extended its focus to the use of torture and illegal detention as a tool of social control by military authorities. The 'Valech Commission' discovered several thousand more cases of abuse, and implemented reparations of victims of arbitrary detention and torture. In 2010 Chile opened the Museum of Memory and Human Rights in Santiago to mark this period of political suppression. Other reports from South America suggest that 'forced disappearances', torture, and murder were not uncommon in Argentina, Bolivia, Uruguay, Paraguay, and Ecuador during the period of the suppression of left-wing elements in South America. Similar patterns of forced disappearances, torture, and extrajudicial executions were reported in a number of military dictatorships elsewhere: Algeria, Chad, Ghana, Ethiopia, and Morocco.

(5) Dictatorial suppression of all political opposition via military government

The leading cases here are Zimbabwe, Uganda, and Paraguay. I have already referred to Mugabe's repression of political opponents in Zimbabwe. The report was never published. A similar process was evident in Uganda. Hundreds of thousands of persons disappeared during the dictatorship of President Idi Amin in Uganda (1971–79). Yoweri Museveni ousted dictator Milton Obote in 1986, and established a form of responsible government. The Commission of Inquiry into Violations of Human Rights, Uganda's second look at the Amin regime, was designed to document the displacements, disappearances, extrajudicial executions, and other violations of human rights during Amin's rule. The 1974 Uganda commission report was never published. The three commissioners who heard evidence that the disappearances were due to the actions of Amin's own security forces were subsequently subject to repression themselves.

The Paraguayan Truth and Justice Commission investigated Alfredo Stroessner's thirty-four-year domination of domestic politics (1955–89) in which political dissent, indigenous rights, and left-wing thinking were ruthlessly suppressed. Unlike other Latin American strongmen, Stroessner was re-elected as president repeatedly, but reigned through control of the military. The issue of Stroessner's one-man rule was galvanized by Martin Almada's discovery of the 'Archive of Terror' in a police station in Asunción, Paraguay in 1992. This was the documentation of Operation Condor, a joint initiative of various dictatorships in South America to suppress left-leaning political causes across South America. Among the three tons of documents discovered, there was evidence of 50 000 persons killed, 30 000 persons disappeared, and 400 000 imprisoned during the 1970s and 80s to suppress Marxism, socialism, and communism. Operation Condor was implemented in 1975, and received financial and logistical support from the US. The security forces coordinated the monitoring of specific individuals believed to be associated with subversive causes, including students, professors, trade unionists, radical priests, and lawyers. A number of assassinations of prominent public figures have been traced directly to Operation Condor. The US coordinated much of this activity through the infamous 'School of the Americas', a training centre for Latin American and Caribbean security forces, located at the military base at Fort Benning, near Columbus, Georgia.

Some lessons?

The five processes sketched above capture some of the major social events that were investigated by truth commissions following periods of grave social conflicts and/or privations that traumatized whole communities, and suggest the diverse issues they tackled. However, the account given here is not exhaustive. There is no mention of the two German commissions created after German reunification. Neither ever dealt with the extreme depravities found in many of the leading commissions; nor have I referred to the Canadian inquiry into the abuse of Natives in residential schools. TRCs are emerging as a legal format to mediate groups in various levels of conflict that do not always entail mass murder. Nor are the five categories necessarily mutually exclusive. Opportunistic warlords, armed insurgencies, and liberation movements often have the capacity to act as brutally and as dictatorially as the forces they oppose. It is equally true that dictatorial leaders often enjoy the confidence of the populations they govern. Neither situation *automatically* invites an *ex post facto* truth commission based on a confident judgment about which party was the offender, and which the victim. An extreme example is the case of Liberia, where both the established governments and their opponents showed gross disregard for the lives of the general population in their conflict for state control. Choosing between the government and the insurgents on the basis of their moral superiority would be arbitrary. Having noted this, it is also true that the commission histories tend to be written by the 'official' victims. Indeed, 'victor's justice' may be just as live an issue at TRCs as at the criminal trial alternatives.

Finally, the five categories may not be independent; a repressive dictator may call into life an insurgent movement that did not exist previously, with the result that societies are brought into conflict and change. The societies are also in flux; neither democratic nor dictatorial rule is immutable. Weak democracies may invite the stability of a strong leader; and the excesses of strong leaders may drive civil society into the arms of the career democrat. The commissions combine both memory and amnesia to various degrees. In the next section, I explore this paradox further by examining several of the key parameters associated with truth, justice, and reconciliation in two leading commissions. They pertain to the argument regarding the cathartic effects of truth-telling processes that have become the quasi-judicial attraction of the TRC option.

Two Views on Catharsis at the TRCs: South Africa Versus Sierra Leone

South Africa produced the most famous TRC, the SATRC. It has received more international and academic scrutiny than any other. How does it compare with the TRC in Sierra Leone? The SATRC was negotiated in 1995 almost as an afterthought in the constitutional negotiations between the insurgent African National Congress (ANC), and the government of F. W. de Klerk, the last apartheid government in South Africa. The legalization of the liberation parties brought the end to exclusive white rule. ANC negotiators were interested in holding accountable those legally responsible for repression in South Africa during apartheid. As part of their devolution of power, the apartheid leaders wanted blanket amnesty. A post-amble to the draft constitution chose a truth commission as a compromise, and as a way of documenting past political repression, while at the same time creating a framework for the future development of the multiracial state. The commission was a quasi-judicial body that engaged in fact-finding about abuses associated with the apartheid state, including the Sharpeville massacre, the assassination of liberation workers, the disappearance of over 1 500 persons opposed to the regime, and the confiscation of land and forced displacement of native Africans. The mandate also covered crimes committed by members of the ANC, as well as the Inkata Freedom Party (IFP). The commission was organized around three committees: the Human Rights Violation Committee, which investigated abuses occurring between 1960 and 1994; the Reparation and Rehabilitation Committee, which developed proposals to recognize the losses, both material and moral, associated with apartheid; and the Amnesty Committee, which evaluated requests for amnesty from those willing to make a full confession to their part in human rights crimes. This latter feature of the commission was probably its most controversial, since it appeared to indemnify serious offenders against liability for criminal prosecutions in exchange for revealing the truth about their crimes. There were 7 112 petitioners. The committee refused amnesty in 5 392 cases, and granted it in 849 cases. The balance of applications appears to have been withdrawn. Actually, the conditions for amnesty were quite stringent. The crimes had to be directly related to the political struggle, not ordinary criminal offences. The confession had to be full, made in public, and published. Persons who offered claims of self-defence were excluded. And the crimes had to be *proportional* to the political objective.

The commission held fifty public meetings in a number of centres throughout the country over 244 days. It received some 20 000 statements from victims, witnesses, and their families. However, participation was far from universal: 'Even Archbishop Tutu's most eloquent pleas could not persuade whites to come forward to testify in significant numbers' (Hunter-Gault 2000: vii). Media coverage was intensive with live radio reporting of the proceedings, and weekly in-depth television reviews. Much of this is described in Krog's *Country of My Skull* (2000). The most riveting evidence came from survivors of abuse at the hands of state security police who engaged in murder, kidnapping, and forced disappearances as well as torture, beatings, and arbitrary detentions of suspected opponents of apartheid. Sometimes the corpses were 'braaed' (barbequed) to dispose of them. The security forces assassinated critics not only in South Africa, but overseas and elsewhere in Africa. It also attempted to provoke conflict between indigenous African parties (the ANC and IFP) to divide opposition to apartheid. 'Much of what had transpired in the past was shrouded in secrecy. The truth had been concealed and was not easily accessible' (Borer 2004: 22). In addition, victims of violence at the time were singularly unsuccessful in having their cases reviewed politically or judicially. They suffered in silence. Hence, one of the functions of the commissions was to put the recollections of atrocities on the public record. Those who had been intimidated and silenced were given a voice. Surely, justice would follow.

But there were two problems here. The first concerns whether the statements given in public were full and accurate reports. A related question was whether an effective identification could be made of the suspected perpetrators implicated in the evidence. These reports may have contributed vivid, wrenching, and emotional evidence, but this does not ensure that they got at 'the truth, the whole truth and nothing but the truth' in terms of helping investigators to bring criminal charges against anyone. This is a recurrent problem in legal matters: differentiating what appears to have occurred versus what can actually been proven on the evidence admitted. The matter was compounded by the lapse of time between the events and their reporting, the trauma of the individuals making the report, and their impartiality. Many of the events occurred decades before they were recounted, and would be difficult to corroborate, either through documentary evidence, or other eyewitnesses. Under such circumstances, the prospect of a criminal conviction of a specific offender would be remote. Indeed, Magnus Malan (Minister of Defence) and nineteen senior officers implicated in the murder of thirteen persons in KwaZulu-Natal were all acquitted at trial in 1996. Part of the memory deficit could be addressed 'by encouraging a public unburdening of grief to discover what in truth had happened' (Borer 2004: 22). Families of victims and survivors could share their recollections, but this could reveal only specific victimizations known to the witnesses, and general patterns of repression, detached from any specific knowledge of who was responsible. In addition, testimony was voluntary, and the issue of its representativeness is compromised by the stories that were *not* volunteered. What is the implication? Graybill and Lanegran (2004: 7): 'out of a population of 43 million people, only about one thousand individuals acknowledged their responsibility for apartheid's crimes, receiving amnesty and re-integration back into society'. This suggests that the standards of truth telling (sincerity, credibility, and honesty) were different from the standards of justice (reliable evidence, direct knowledge, reliable identification, corroboration etc.) In other words, truth and justice operated somewhat independently, and arguably have different objectives.

The second problem is that there seems to be an assumption that the exposure of these general truths through recollections leads naturally to reconciliation, and that the sharing of such memories is cathartic. As a general proposition, there is no reason to believe a priori that social reconciliation requires truth (Allen 1999: 317), or that truth telling will result in it. This connection appears to derive from either a medical model, or a religious one. In the medical model, the supposition is that trauma has to be confronted by reliving the events that caused it, so that the individual can 'let go' of it. The religious model suggests a process of conversion in which the offender makes a confession, expresses repentance, and seeks forgiveness. 'Proponents of reconciliation often turn the discourse of justice into the language of therapy and healing, or the moral and religious discourse of forgiveness' (Avruch and Vejarano 2002: 41). This was a theme advocated by Archbishop Tutu and other commissioners. However, to speak of a country-wide reconciliation is misleading. A country is not an individual with the capacity to forgive. Or as Hamber and Wilson put it (2002: 36): 'Nations do not have collective psyches which can be healed.' A statesman like

President Mandela can express remorse on behalf of a government, but this act is symbolic, and its impact on a population is difficult to assess. Rosalind Shaw argues similarly (2004a): 'the language of national healing anthropomorphizes the nation as a feeling and suffering entity'. All this suggests that there are gaps between *memory* (truth telling through recollection), *justice* (establishing culpability of specific individuals according to stringent legal standards based on such revelations), and *reconciliation* (the subsequent 'healing' of previously divided communities). The process is further hobbled when the commission has fewer powers than a criminal court to investigate and corroborate, not so much 'truth', as what passes for 'facts'. This process is bound to raise far more accusations than convictions, a situation that describes the SATRC quite well.

The Sierra Leone commission takes this argument one step further: truth telling may not actually serve the objectives of either justice *or* reconciliation. The Sierra Leone conflict was a civil war (1990–96) fought by the RUF against the government of President Joseph Momoh. The RUF conducted a war marked by terrorism, and was known for its 'signature' mutilations of arms and feet, for its widespread practice of rape, and its recruitment of children into its militia. A peace was negotiated in 1996. A civilian president was elected, Ahmad Kabbah, only to be ousted almost immediately by the Armed Forces Revolutionary Council. The UN stepped in to restore order in 1998. Part of the peace process was the creation of a TRC that began its public hearings in April 2003 with funding from the UN's Office of the High Commissioner for Human Rights. The UN conducted workshops across Sierra Leone to create interest in the TRC, and to encourage the population to testify in public meetings to establish the history of what the country had gone through in the previous decade. As of 2008, over 29 000 victims had registered for reparations, including amputees, war wounded, child soldiers, and victims of sexual violence—following recommendations from the commission. Rosalind Shaw, an anthropologist who had conducted ethnographic research in five provinces, indicates that in reality there was little popular support for the TRC. The TRC was created in tandem with the hybrid criminal court—the Special Court for Sierra Leone (2002)—designed to prosecute the leaders of the militias behind the civil war.

As a result of her work at the community level in Sierra Leone, Shaw (2004a; 2004b) calls into doubt the conventional wisdom about the relationship between remembering, healing, and reconciliation. While it is true that such commissions are designed to permit ordinary individuals to register their own recollections of history, the report of a TRC tends to synthesize these selectively in order to create an official memory. Conjuring up the past in a particular way fashions how civil society will adopt a future-oriented politics, will tip the balance towards particular parties, and may make the population governable through control of their memory. Shaw argues, on the contrary, that memory is a *process*, 'and always a contested one'. Her work challenges the usual presumptions about TRCs. First, she argues that the presumption of catharsis through dwelling on past trauma is simply inconsistent with the social instincts of the people she studied in Sierra Leone. Rather than dwelling on the past, the most prominent instinct among her respondents was to 'forgive and forget' (2004a). Second, while some people do experience relief and satisfaction from naming past abuses, this may only make sense when the prior conduct of terror was secretive, and unacknowledged. In Sierra Leone, the abuses were always in plain view. The militias acted with impunity because they were well armed and openly dismissive of legal restraints. In a society with thousands of amputees, and legions of rape-survivors, there was no particular advantage of public truth telling for what was already common knowledge. In the case of the SATRC, some 60 per cent of those who testified about their abuse felt *worse* after testifying (Hayner 2011: 184). Public acknowledgement of abuse may not be cathartic, even at the individual level. Shaw's third point is that there are extensive non-discursive practices of confronting traumatic memories through rituals, and visions, found among the Sierra Leonans (Shaw 2004b). The TRC emphasis on reopening old wounds through verbal testimony may in fact have inhibited reintegration and reconciliation. In her field study, she found entire villages that agreed to refuse to testify because this competed with their own memory management practices. In addition, virtually no ex-militiamen appeared at the TRCs, because they feared that anything they said would invite reprisal from other ex-militiamen, in spite of the fact that, as part of the peace agreement, low-level militia members were given immunity from prosecution at the Special Court for Sierra Leone (SCSL). They nonetheless feared that anything disclosed at the TRC might implicate them in criminal proceedings at the SCSL.

In Shaw's view, healing occurred through processes of 'social forgetting'. This did not mean that everyone experienced clinical amnesia. On the contrary, there was a studious refusal to acknowledge past violence in public speech, and to resurrect it among strangers. Individuals 'exorcized' their memories through prayer, Bible reading, and baptism rites that included washing the body ritually to remove the blemish of past misconduct. This was particularly relevant in the rehabilitation of child soldiers. Giving the child a 'cool heart' through these practices helped to remake them as persons without returning to the trauma that they had survived. The UN's promotion of the TRC format threatened grassroots practices of the management of memory, trauma, and reconciliation.

Shaw's view is reinforced by Tim Kelsall's ethnographic study of TRCs in Sierra Leone. He makes several points based on his observations in Tonkolili in northern Sierra Leone. In the Sierra Leone Truth Commission hearings, 'the truth is seldom told', i.e. the perpetrators were extremely reluctant to fully report their actions, with the effect that the observers became increasingly agitated. Although there were several reasons for this, the primary reason was that 'public truth-telling lacks deep roots in the local cultures of Sierra Leone'. On the contrary, 'a staged ceremony of repentance and forgiveness, a multicultural concoction that drew on Christian, Islamic, and traditional religious forms, struck deeply resonant chords with the participants and forged a reconciliatory moment, even in the absence of truth' (Kelsall 2005: 363). By implication, the formal truth and reconciliation process competes with indigenous practices by which people manage their own past traumas, in Shaw's view 'non-discursively' and in Kelsall's view 'ritually'.

Helena Cobban makes some comparable points about the reconstruction in Mozambique after a seventeen-year civil war that ended in 1992. Her analysis challenges the leading Western supposition that in such recovering states, it is essential to find as many individuals accountable as possible through 'a rising global tide of Western-style prosecutorialism' (2007: 16, 236). She also challenges the idea that extensive public processes of truth establishment and truth telling are prerequisites to healing. The peace accord negotiated between RENAMO rebels and the Frelimo government did not provide for either legal response. A general amnesty was declared. No distinction was made between victims and perpetrators. Instead, there was an agreement that a common designation applied to all survivors of the conflict who were designated as 'affetados', or persons affected by violence. There were numerous healing ceremonies based on traditional medicine, including purification rites, as in Sierra Leone. There was agreement that the political process was to be forward-thinking, egalitarian, and democratic, and not to be preoccupied with past trauma, since this was viewed as an impediment to a grass-roots healing process. This is a not a remedy which could apply in every case, but Cobban's point is that we should neither presume there is a one-size-fits-all remedy, nor that the affected communities are without endogenous cultural resources to rebuild their societies.

Conclusions

I suggested that the emergence of TRCs since the mid-1970s presented a 'third option' as a remedy to grave breaches of international humanitarian law—separate from a purely retributive approach in the criminal courts, and a reparative approach through the ICJ. It might be more accurate to argue that the TRCs combine and complement the functions found in the earlier options. Virtually every TRC develops a strategy to compensate victims of abuse. However, when these take the form of monetary payments, they are typically modest. For example, reparation under the SATRC amounted to a one-off payment of about US$3 800. In Chile, victims were awarded about $200 a month. Also, the existence of the TRC does not preclude criminal prosecutions. In Sierra Leone, these legal processes occurred simultaneously, although this design probably made former militia members reluctant to contribute to 'truth telling' at the TRC meetings. In Argentina, the civilian government first had to repeal amnesty laws that barred prosecution of former junta members. This was done in 2003. In 2011 sixteen former officers at the infamous naval academy, ESMA, were convicted of crimes against humanity, and received long prison sentences (IJT 2011: 4). In 2012 another eight were tried for the kidnapping of new-borns from illegally detained women. Hundreds of babies were taken from their mothers, and given to families of the military officers and friends of the junta, before the mothers were murdered. Many of the children (now adults) have subsequently been reunited with their biological families as a result of DNA matches. In 2012 the government of Brazil created a truth commission to investigate human rights abuses that were exposed in *Nunca Mais* (RNW 2012a). However, the 1979 amnesty law was upheld by the Supreme Court in 2010, blocking criminal prosecutions of military criminals in that country.

Although the TRCs have many weak and contradictory elements, working at the periphery of contemporary criminal law, they also have a great capacity to redefine the future potential of criminal justice. What are the features of the TRCs that make them attractive as legal or quasi-legal responses to grave breaches of human rights? The first and foremost is that they provide the survivors and their families with a forum to publicly share their experiences. Many of the political atrocities discussed here were carried out clandestinely, so that there was no comprehension of the scope and nature of the repression. However, participation is voluntary, and the resulting 'history' may not be reliable, particularly if the perpetrators boycott the process. In principle, this could be remedied by giving the commissions the power to compel witnesses, but that would transform the truth commissions back into criminal courts, defeating the attraction of the TRCs as an alternative model. A second important achievement is the development of strategies to make reparations to victims and survivors. The effectiveness here is more symbolic than substantive. In South Africa, a fund of US$74 000 000 was created by the government. This was about US$300 000 000 less than what the commission recommended. However, there are other symbolic methods that need to be considered: creation of holidays to commemorate the political struggles, turning former detention centres into museums, and devising other ways to honour the privations suffered in the past. The third achievement is that the commissions, as community events, help to build ties between people by emphasizing their common experiences of repression, so that they may contribute to community and national cohesiveness.

As for their effectiveness in creating reconciliation among former enemies, the jury is out on this question. The same applies to the question as to whether truth telling has positive cathartic consequences, and contributes to healing at an individual and/or collective level. These claims are more an article of faith, than conclusions based on objective changes in the participants and their communities.

The last point is that TRCs as devices for peace making in post-conflict societies will continue to enjoy popularity as nations take responsibility for human rights abuses at the national level, and as the viability of the international criminal option, and the hybrid option, become increasingly less attractive. The fly in the ointment is that the power of the new ICC may seize jurisdiction of cases from particular states, and institute criminal prosecutions under the powers conferred by the Rome Statute, thereby trumping the national support for a TRC alternative (Schabas 2004). Whether this results in synergy, or acrimony, remains to be seen.

10

Conclusion: Beyond the Banality of Evil

Introduction: The Banality of Evil

The fiftieth anniversary of the trial of Adolph Eichmann in Jerusalem was 2011. The fifty-first anniversary of his execution was 2012. We continue to wrestle with his significance. The trial of Eichmann, more than the Nuremberg trials, put a human face on the Holocaust that had never been aired so publicly. Survivors had always reported to their families and friends privately what they, and their families, had experienced personally at the hands of the Nazis, but Gideon Hausner's prosecution of Eichmann gave a coherence to the cacophony of voices of survivors from across Europe that brought the enormity of the Final Solution into vivid relief, and captured the scope of the Nazi plan to annihilate every Jewish community in Europe. It gave the survivors a common voice that had never been uttered at the previous war crime trials in Nuremberg, and helped forge a sense of solidarity among the founders of the new state of Israel. However, the predominant understanding about the Holocaust, and those who authored it, was reflected in the term coined by the philosopher, Hannah Arendt—'the banality of evil'. The architects of genocide were portrayed as dull, uninspired 'desk murderers' who simply followed superior orders, who probably did not fully understand the overall process, and who had no personal or direct knowledge of the mass killings. Eichmann was portrayed not so much as a monster as a clown. In contrast to Arendt, this book has been a criminological odyssey to go beyond this level of understanding. It builds in part on the recent biography of Eichmann by Cesarani (2006) and his trial by Lipstadt (2011).

The trial of Eichmann attracted enormous interest both inside Israel as well as internationally. More reporters covered this trial than Nuremberg. Eichmann had entered Argentina with false documents and a new identity in 1950, where his family joined him in

1952. Information of his presence was conveyed by a German-Jewish immigrant to Fritz Bauer (who later prosecuted the Auschwitz trial). Bauer contacted the Israeli authorities, and Eichmann was kidnapped under the nose of Argentinian police authorities who were apparently shadowing him. He was transported secretly to Israel for trial. The dramatic apprehension, and the fact that the accused would be prosecuted by a court representing his victims made the proceedings especially poignant. Lipstadt outlines many of the procedural difficulties of the trial—the fact that the state of Israel post-dated the period of crimes, that the crimes occurred in Europe, that the Israeli law was *ex post facto*, that the impartiality of an Israeli court could not be gainsaid, that the retention of Israeli lawyers for the defence of a Nazi might prove difficult, etc. A German defence lawyer, Robert Servatius, who had experience at Nuremberg, was retained. His fee of $30 000 was paid by the state of Israel, eager to demonstrate its fairness, after the federal government of Germany declined to cover his costs.

Eichmann was interrogated at length prior to trial by police investigator, Captain Avner Less. He acted initially as though he would cooperate fully. According to Lipstadt (2011: 43) 'he spoke freely', but Captain Less also noted that he was capable of cold sophistication and cunning, and that he would 'lie until defeated by documentary proof' (2011: 44). Then, instead of accepting responsibility, he would invoke the necessity of following state or superior orders. This pattern of denial recurred throughout the proceedings. Prior to the war, Eichmann was assigned the task of researching Zionism, and produced an SS orientation booklet on the subject. He made a clandestine trip to Palestine to attempt negotiations with Zionist groups to expedite the resettlement of German and Austrian Jews, but was apprehended in Haifa, and deported by the British authorities to Egypt. After returning to Germany, Eichmann lectured the SD (the intelligence unit of the SS) in a day-long seminar outlining what he claimed were numerous secret conspiracies among international Jewish associations to assassinate Nazi leaders.

When Gideon Hausner began to draft the case against Eichmann, investigators confined attention to crimes with which Eichmann was directly involved. After consulting with Rachel Auerbach at Yad Yashem Holocaust memorial, Hausner radically broadened the approach. He created a list of witnesses, many of whom were survivors, to put into the record every important phase of the mass killings of European Jews in order to capture the extent and complexity of the Final Solution. The indictment charged Eichmann with implementing the Final Solution, mass murder of Jews at Polish death camps, murdering Russian Jews with the mobile killing squads, forced sterilization of concentration camp inmates, plundering property, and causing the deaths of untold thousands in forced-labour camps, transit camps, and ghettos, etc. The list of crimes went on and on. There were credible eyewitnesses with personal memories of these atrocities, but frequently Eichmann had nothing to do with the events led in evidence. This fact was not lost on the defence, nor on the panel of three judges. This was probably prejudicial to the accused but 'it would give a voice to the victims they had not had before', even if it often amounted to hearsay and bordered on gossip (Lipstadt 2011: 55). In this sense, the trial came to function in part as what would later be recognized as a truth commission.

Nonetheless, the court heard chilling evidence that suggested that Eichmann was no simpleton. In fact, the Third Reich was somewhat of an amorphous organization where, according to Lipstadt, 'subordinates often took the lead' (2011: 64). A fact that should not be overlooked is that Eichmann supervised the last great transports of the Holocaust that originated from Hungary *in person*. When Himmler ordered the delay of the transport of the Hungarian Jews until the military situation in the East was more favourable to the Reich, Eichmann pressed on. He met with Jewish leaders, lied to them about peaceful resettlement of Jewish workers in German industries, and eventually conned them out of their wealth. He attempted to get the Hungarians to raise money and trucks for the Reich war effort in exchange for Jewish prisoners. The scheme failed when Joel Brand, a Hungarian Jewish leader, was arrested on suspicion of spying after making contact with British agents in Istanbul. Beginning in April 1944, Eichmann deported 440 000 Hungarian Jews to Auschwitz on some 145 transports in less than two months. The figure of 440 000 beggars the imagination. He also organized forced marches of Jews overland to the west without adequate food, water, or medical support. This resulted in further massive casualties. Eichmann became more committed to the Final Solution than his superiors. When various countries agreed to resettle Hungarian Jews, he went to great lengths to obstruct their departure, and to ensure that they would not survive. This was at a point in the war when everyone knew that the Reich's days were numbered, short of a miracle from the V-weapon programme at Nordhausen. The top brass knew this. There was an unsuccessful assassination of Hitler in July 1944 as senior Nazis attempted to forestall the inevitable military defeat. In the course of sixty-seven audio tapes recorded by a Dutch SS officer, Willem Sassen, in Argentina in the late 1950s, Eichmann 'bemoaned the fact that the regime had not killed more Jews and expressed great satisfaction about how smoothly the deportation process had run' (Lipstadt 2011: 67). In a speech to his men in the spring of 1945, Eichmann estimated that the war had cost the lives of five million Jews, and that 'he would jump into his grave fulfilled at having been part of this effort' (Lipstadt 2011: 132). During his cross-examination, Hausner had Eichmann read a transcript from the Sassen tapes in which he admitted not only that he carried out orders to murder the Jews but he added that he carried out the orders 'with the degree of fanaticism one expected of oneself as a National Socialist of long-standing' (Lipstadt 2011: 137). Again, in the Sassen tapes he indicated, according to Lipstadt, 'the joy he had felt at moving Hungarian Jews to their death at an unprecedented clip and the pleasure of having the death of millions of Jews on his record' (2011: 169–70). In view of these admissions, the banality thesis does not survive scrutiny. In addition, in direct examination by Judge Halevi before deliberation of the verdict, Eichmann indicated that, while he had given an oath of allegiance to the Nazi regime that required him to follow orders unconditionally, in several cases he had turned a blind eye, and helped a number of Jews escape, including a relative. In other words, compliance with orders was *at his discretion*, not absolute obedience, as he had argued incessantly.

From Obedience to Duty

We started this study with a re-analysis of the experimental studies of Milgram that were inspired by the picture of Eichmann that had been created by Arendt's reports. This has been the paradigmatic approach to understanding genocide for two generations. The experiments depicted the compliance of persons operating under pressure from a superior power. The obedience paradigm suggested that persons occupying subordinate positions in bureaucracies enter a natural 'agentic state' that curtails their control of choices, and that this depicts the situation in which Eichmann found himself. On closer inspection, this neither captures the original events, nor does it accurately depict what was occurring in Milgram's experiments. In fact, when subjects formed the impression that the experimenter's commands were producing injury, they resisted commands to obey. Burger's replications of Milgram similarly recommended that direct commands to the subjects to obey were the ones that were least likely to result in subject compliance. This rehabilitation of the issue of agency in our critique of the banality of evil dovetails remarkably with the first paradox examined in Chapter 2: the ordinary nature of the men recruited to carry out the mass murders, and the voluntary character of their compliance. Browning's evidence from Police Battalion 101 reinforces the idea that compliance sprang more from a sense of 'duty' than duress. In fact, Eichmann reported at trial that he had tried to act in compliance with Kant's categorical imperative from the *Critique of Practical Reason*, by which he meant he always acted within the requirements of the law, which in Nazi Germany derived from the head of state. In Eichmann's words from the trial: 'The Kantian categorical imperative was disposed of shortly as follows: "True to the law, obedient, a proper personal life, not to come into conflict with the law." This, I would say, was the categorical imperative for a small man's domestic use' (Session 105(4), District Court of Jerusalem, Nizkor 2011). He was troubled, on the one side, that the head of state could request such drastic actions as mass murder, and admitted, on the other side, that he did not understand the categorical imperative completely. 'I only took from these writings what I could understand, and what my imagination could somehow grasp.'

Jonathan Littell explored the mentality of the Nazi senior commanders and their philosophical outlook in his acclaimed novel, *The Kindly Ones* (2009). Littell's protagonist, Dr Maximilien Aue, becomes a member of the *Einsatzgruppen* during the eastern campaign. In the course of this fictional career in Poland, Russia, Ukraine, and the Caucasus, he meets Eichmann, Himmler, Göring, Speer, Heydrich, Höss, and Hitler himself. Littell depicts a conversation between Eichmann and Sturmbannführer Aue in which the subject of duty and obedience are explored in the context of Kantian philosophy, particularly the *Critique of Practical Reason*. Eichmann argues that people, like him, are not slaves to authority, but carry out their duties in accord with the Führer Principle—*Führerprinzip*—anticipating the leader's thinking, and acting in a way in which he would approve, even without explicit instruction. But, in Littell's imaginary rendition, the Führer himself is acting in response to the authority conveyed on him by the Volk. 'You have to live out your National Socialism by living your own will as if it were the Führer's, and so, to use Kant's terms, as a foundation of the *Volksrecht*' (2009: 567). The fictional Eichmann proclaims, 'we are not serving the Führer as such, but as representative of the *Volk*, we serve the *Volk* and must serve it as the Führer serves it, with total abnegation. That's why, confronted with painful tasks, we have to bow down, master our feelings, and carry them out with firmness' (2009: 567). In my view, Littell captures persuasively the primacy of duty—although Eichmann actually preferred the term 'fanaticism' to Aue's 'firmness'.

The paradox of the compliance of ordinary men was related to two further phenomena discussed in Chapter 2: the tendency for such mass atrocities to escape criminal definition, to be 'conventionalized', and the subsequent enlargement of the scale of atrocities. Having rejected the obedience paradigm, in subsequent chapters, I explored both the issue of how events become labelled as genocide (or escape that label), and the circumstances that help us explain the events. In terms of explanation, I explored Elias's account of the rise of self-control in European civilization, and his analysis of the dynamics of public life after national unification in *The Germans*. Rather than concluding that the Nazi state represented a widespread reversion to 'barbarism', the evidence is more consistent with the idea that certain states, as a function of their historical development, produce an over-control of the citizenry. This is not a function of obedience to bureaucratic authority, but an over-identification with the political leadership that cultivates a powerful sense of duty characterized by both pathological altruism and a sense of fatalism. This again is reflected in Eichmann's testimony. He acknowledged the joy with which he undertook atrocities, but also reported with resignation: 'I saw that I was unable to change anything and unable to do anything' (Session 105(4)). This combination of emotions, pathological altruism, and fatalism seems to account for the lack of guilt, or remorse, among *génocidaires* identified repeatedly throughout the study.

The Legal Responses

The final section of this study reported on the three major forms of legal (or quasi-legal) responses to genocide, and the crimes against international humanitarian law: international criminal trials, international reparations, and national TRCs. After reviewing the evidence in each approach, one is left with the conclusion that there is no single effective remedy to genocide. The international criminal approach is neither effective, efficient, nor financially sustainable. This is true whether one considers the ad hoc tribunals or the hybrid courts. The new ICC enjoys the support of many of the middle powers, but none of the superpowers, and to date has confined its attention to the continent of Africa. The creation of such a permanent institution does not, regrettably, resolve the issues of funding, political bias, or delay, but, on a more positive note, it seems to have made a priority out of support for the victim communities. Even if we are correct in identifying limitations of the current courts, they cannot be abandoned entirely, since failure to respond would cultivate further the culture of criminal impunity. In terms of reparations, there is a glimmer of hope in decisions from the World Court charged with settling disputes between Bosnia-Herzegovina and Serbia; and the DRC and Uganda. In both cases, the court discussed reparations, and opened the door for potentially non-criminal, inter-state remedies for crimes against international humanitarian law. Again, this institution moves extremely slowly, but, as a solution to inter-state conflicts, it is underutilized. The TRCs meet yet another need: the recovery of national memory, the pursuit of historical truth, and the creation of conditions of community and effective governance, if not reconciliation. We are entering an age where such commissions are becoming increasingly prevalent, and where the methodology and structure of such institutions are becoming more uniform as knowledge of their work is more widely communicated (Hayner 2011: 236). The world is on a path where all three options present tools, however imperfect, to deal with the aftermath of genocide, and other mass atrocities.

Mark Drumbl comes to a similar conclusion in his analysis of post-genocidal Rwanda, but I think that his suggestions have relevance elsewhere. He describes his approach as 'cosmopolitan pluralism' in which the world recognizes that there are different social geographies of atrocities, which may require variable options in terms of remedies (2007: 186). His working list of solutions includes: first, 'trials for notorious murderers and leaders'; second, 'community-based integrative shaming for all other offenders'; third, a truth commission to obtain testimony from citizens and international officials in order to make the past more transparent; and fourth, the creation of an international fund for compensation of genocide victims (Drumbl 2000: 1235). This provides a 'polyc-entric' agenda that may or may not be feasible in all respects in every situation. Nonetheless, it is a commendable start at recogniz-ing that the options that we explored in the last three chapters are not necessary alternatives, nor mutually exclusive. In the next sec-tion, I want to explore some of the pre-emptive policies that might build on this polycentric agenda in advance of the atrocities while rethinking sovereignty.

Restraining the Sovereign

In *Leviathan* (1651) Thomas Hobbes advanced the thesis that orderly societies emerge from a contract between an all-powerful sovereign and the citizens of the realm, under whose terms the lat-ter surrender some of their individual freedom in order to benefit from the security provided by the former. The contract was to avoid the condition of nature in which life would be solitary, poor, nasty, brutish, and short. The sovereign, imbued with reason, would make the laws that would be strictly binding on the population. The sov-ereign would also have a duty to educate the population by instill-ing reason in them, so that they consented mindfully to the contract that was the precondition for the creation of a prosperous com-monwealth. A century later in 1764, Cesare Beccaria revisited the prerequisite of the laws to create the conditions for 'the greatest happiness shared by the greatest number' of people. According to Beccaria, very few persons before him had undertaken to demolish the ill-founded beliefs that had resulted in the 'unbounded course of ill-directed power which has continually produced a long and authorized example of the most cold-blooded barbarity' i.e. execu-tion by garroting, torture, burning at the stake, and massacre of prisoners of conflict. This critique was the objective of *On Crimes and Punishments* (Beccaria 2003). According to Beccaria, no one ever sacrificed a portion of his liberty on behalf of the common good:

Laws are the conditions under which independent and isolated men united to form a society. Weary of living in a continual state of war, and of enjoy-ing a liberty rendered useless by the uncertainty of preserving it, they sac-rificed a part so that they might enjoy the rest of it in peace and safety.

Beccaria outlines the consequences. Only laws can decree punish-ments for crimes, and authority for their creation 'can reside only with the legislator who represents the entire society united by a social contract' (2003: 17). He then lays out the implications regarding the necessary characteristics of laws: clarity, division of powers, celerity, proportionality, etc. All this is well known. Both Hobbes and Beccaria focus on how laws bind the people to the sovereign, but neither deals with the issue of why the sovereign would be bound to the populace, and/or restrained by them, through contracts and law. The sorts of atrocities addressed in this study tend to be political in origin, and originate with the sovereign. Hobbes and Beccaria are writing at a point in time when relatively enlightened absolute monarchs had already appeared, and restraint was taken for granted.

Norbert Elias deals with this question of restraint in his analysis of the sociogenesis of the state (2000: 257). He identifies a number of transformative processes that led from feudal anarchy to the modern European democracies with their restrained rulers. Elias's account is quite detailed but some of the key processes can be outlined here. As Europe came out of the 'dark ages' the population was largely sedentary, and organized around clans and extended households in which the economic, political, and military functions were coextensive with domestic life and grounded in specific 'real estate', i.e. specific land holdings. As the population increased, families were under pressure to expand their holdings, to monopolize control of their territory, and to compete with rival families experiencing the same pressures. The ongoing competition between rivals over generations created 'elimination contests' in which certain clans were either wiped out entirely, or consolidated through intermarriage. The small land holdings gradually expanded into larger estates, i.e. larger monopolies. As the elimination contests created enhanced holdings, and as the leading families acquired the monopoly on the legitimate use of force, and the legitimate right of taxation, the number of dependents on the emerging noble families began to increase exponentially. The effect was ironic. 'The more people are made dependent by the monopoly mechanism, the greater becomes the power of the dependent, not only individually but collectively' (2000: 270). How so? The complexity of the expanding courts requires tax collectors, mercenaries hired from the expanding towns, architects and planners, diplomats, judges, teachers, entertainers, and armies of farm labourers—all of which makes the emergent monarchs dependent on their own dependents. The monopoly eventually escapes control of any single individual, and what was a *private* monopoly of a dwindling number of rising aristocratic families emerges as a *public* monopoly known as the 'nation' under a single monarch. Simultaneously, the rise of the bourgeoisie passes power from land-based wealth to the money economy, and prosperity through trade. This necessitates standardization of the monetary system, the protection of ever widening zones of trade, protection of peaceful industry and agriculture, regulation of markets, and coordination of the interests of the competing nobility, the towns, and the clergy. This results in a tipping point: 'the hour of the strong central authority within a highly differentiated society strikes when the ambivalence of interests of the important functional groups grows so large, and power is distributed so evenly between them, that there can be neither a decisive compromise nor a decisive conflict between them' (2000: 320). From this constellation of forces, there arises what Elias calls 'the royal mechanism'. This was the absolute monarch who acquires supremacy by balancing the competing interests of all the stakeholders in the kingdom. The process was somewhat different in England, France, and Germany. The time frame was measured in centuries. But the result was the same: the sovereigns attained a pinnacle in the power hierarchy to the extent that they played a decisive integrative function. They became the mechanism that linked the increasingly complex division of labour known as the state, but their ability to loot the population and transcend the rule of law ended. The relative stability of European states appeared hand in hand with the retreat of the distinction between the ruler and the ruled (2000: 315).

The modern Elisian state restrains the sovereign in a number of ways. The populace is ruled not by force but by their consent. Their various interests are represented through political parties. The parties negotiate their common interests through representative governments. The sovereign becomes a symbolic head of state. The rights of the populace are enshrined in law. Conflicts between individual stakeholders, and groups, are mediated by a strong and independent judiciary. Political actions are scrutinized in the open by a free and independent press. And individuals are free to pursue their aspirations for change, faith, and happiness through private organizations. When we examine the cases of societies that have been the subject of gross human rights violations, many, most, or all of these features are missing, and as a result, their sovereigns are warlords, dictators and/or occupying forces, none of which reflect 'the royal mechanism'. In fact, the conditions of life in places such as eastern Congo and Darfur are reminiscent of the European feudal landscape where the elimination contests have not produced a consolidated territory under a single, dominant clan. The warlords have not united the population, nor have they evolved to the point where they can mediate the competing interests in the regions. Power resides with brutal military force. Exploitation of natural wealth (minerals and timber) by the warlords allows them to maintain power without integrating the state, a situation sometimes described as the natural resource trap (Collier 2007).

In South America, the cult of The General is arguably the legacy of Simon Bolivar, the enlightened hero who drove the Spanish colonial armies out of the continent, severing the power of the Spanish crown, and precluding the emergence of a 'royal mechanism'. The senior military man—The General—assumed the function of the monarch without any restraints of the sort that evolved in Europe through the royal mechanism. When we reflect on societies that have been the sites of genocide and other gross human rights violations, none are characterized by the rule of law, an independent judiciary, universal suffrage and free elections, a system of rights enshrined in law, a free press, or democratic governments. Where they exist, these institutions are underdeveloped, or in suspension. Nonetheless, these social developments are important for longer-term restraints on the sovereign (i.e. the political elite), and such restraints are critical to prevent genocide and other gross violations of human rights. However, we must remember that the picture that Elias provides for the emergence of the state is based on the European cases. No claim can be made that these mechanisms of restraint are universal, or that they are foolproof even for Europe.

Rethinking Sovereignty

The arsenal of mechanisms for preventing genocide is not limited to Eliasian elements of state formation that characterize the internal economic, legal, and political developments of a nation. In fact, we see that the strict autonomy of states in the Westphalian legacy is increasingly being eroded by greater global integration (Barbour and Pavlich 2010). The emergence of new norms with respect to the interaction between states may alter how future outrages may be prevented. Several tools are emerging to combat genocide in the new global village. I begin with a discussion of the concept of

'Responsibility to Protect'. First, it is necessary to contrast this concept with that of 'humanitarian intervention'. In 1999 NATO led an aggressive war against Serb forces in the province of Kosovo on the assumption that Serbian armed forces were murdering Albanian Kosovars. This mission was not supported by the UN Security Council. Indeed, it was opposed by the Russian Federation, and would have been vetoed by Russia, a Serbian ally. NATO justified its aggression as essentially humanitarian. This created a crisis at the UN. In response to this, in 2000 the government of Canada sponsored an international conference to address the tension between the rights of sovereign states to be free from external interference in respect of their internal affairs, and the humanitarian imperative to intervene globally in cases of mass atrocities. This was the International Commission on Intervention and State Sovereignty (ICISS 2001). The conference was concerned not only with the Kosovo situation, but the UN's failure to act in Rwanda, and its ineffective actions in Bosnia, Somalia, and Kosovo. Bernard Koucher, co-founder of *Médicins sans Frontières*, and French foreign minister from 2007 to 2010, had long advocated 'le droit d'ingérence'—the right to interfere—in foreign nations that were impeding the delivery of international humanitarian assistance. The ICISS was more broadly based. It sought to move the debate from the question of 'national security' to 'human security'. It argued two basic principles: (a) that the primary responsibility for the protection of people lies within the state itself, (b) but where the state is unwilling, or unable to avert serious harm due to internal war, insurgency, repression, or state failure, 'the principle of non-intervention yields to the international responsibility to protect' (R2P) (ICISS 2001: xi), including military intervention. The ICISS also stressed that the action had to meet a number of conditions: (a) a 'just cause' threshold—it had to prevent large-scale loss of life or ethnic cleansing; (b) it had to be undertaken with the 'right intention' i.e. to halt or avert human suffering; (c) military intervention had to be the 'last resort' after every non-military option had been exhausted; (d) the intervention had to employ 'proportional' means, i.e. the minimal steps necessary to secure the objective; and (e) the intervention had to have a reasonable prospect of success.

The ICISS was an attempt, on the one hand, to create a new norm (Luck 2010) with respect to sovereignty by acknowledging the Westphalian independence of states, while, on the other, trying to broaden the meaning of sovereignty by adding new obligations necessitated by changing international conditions (Axworthy 2012). Sovereignty was being redefined as a 'conditional right' (Sewall 2010: 161). In addition, the advocates of R2P needed a concept that was a game-changer and that was separate from the concept of 'humanitarian intervention'. According to Garth Evans, who chaired the ICISS, 'the very core of the traditional meaning of humanitarian intervention is coercive military intervention for humanitarian purposes—nothing more or less' (Evans 2012: 377). And humanitarian intervention had already become discredited at the UN in the aftermath of NATO's unilateral action against Serbia.

The report was taken up at the 2005 UN World Summit meetings. Paragraphs 138 and 139 of the resolution were adopted by the General Assembly under the title of 'Responsibility to protect populations from genocide, war crimes, ethnic cleansing and crimes against humanity'. The first paragraph simply read that each member state has the responsibility to protect its populations from the crimes identified. The second paragraph did not refer to the broad conditions of application of the ICISS. Instead, it said the international community also has the responsibility to use diplomatic, humanitarian, and other peaceful means to help to protect populations from such crimes. It added that should national authorities fail to protect their populations, the UN was prepared to take collective action through the Security Council, in accord with the peace-making powers provided for in Chapter VII of the UN Charter (UNWSO 2005). This was the first step in recognizing the more limited conceptualization of sovereignty proposed by the ICISS.

The next step was the discussion of the Secretary-General's document 'Implementing the Responsibility to Protect', which was brought to the General Assembly in 2009. It laid out three principles for the application of the R2P policy: (a) the protection responsibilities of the state; (b) the need to provide international assistance, and capacity building, to assist each state to meet its responsibilities; and (c) a timely and decisive response to resolve the problems. The response to the document was generally favourable. The vast majority were supportive of the initiative, and at least some of the pillars laid out in the document (Burke-White 2012: 32). Delegates from Cuba, Nicaragua, Sudan, and Venezuela wanted to reopen the whole debate. The General Assembly voted instead to endorse the Secretary-General's report, but in face of resistance from several states, changed the wording to tone down the statement 'to continue to consider the responsibility to protect doctrine'. Part of the concern for many who had reservations was the possibility that the 1993 US invasion of Iraq and the 2008 Russian invasion of Georgia could be justified as R2P. In other words, superpowers could use the doctrine to mask their geopolitical interests. Rotberg (2010: 12) reports pessimistically that 'the power to govern well or badly has continued to trump the protection of individuals or groups at risk within the state'. However, R2P is an ongoing project. Chalk, Dallaire, Matthews, Barqueiro, and Doyle (2010) have developed strategies to move the agenda forward by mobilizing the will to intervene, as have Albright and Cohen (2008). As Evans (2012: 380) advises, patience is imperative: 'it is important that RtoP advocates fully internalize and act in accordance with a lesson we should by now all have learned: that this is all going to be a long haul, with progress slow and often disappointing'. What is important is that this doctrine has begun to redefine sovereignty, and provides a new tool in the repertoire of weapons to combat genocide and gross human rights violations (Genser and Cottler 2012). It was invoked in NATO's assistance in the overthrow of the Gaddafi regime in Libya in 2011, and may have a further role in removing other dictatorships in the region. There are several other tools.

National trials of foreign génocidaires

After the conflicts in the former Yugoslavia and Rwanda, many *génocidaires* emigrated to the safety of other countries in Europe, North America, and Australia. The 1948 UN Genocide Convention (Article V) required the nations who joined the convention to enact legislation that permitted them to provide effective penalties for persons guilty of genocide in their domestic courts. Canada introduced legislation against hate propaganda and the advocacy of genocide in 1985. In 2000 it passed a broader bill, the Crimes Against Humanity and War Crimes Act. In 2009 a Canadian court convicted a Rwandan national, Désiré Munyaneza, of seven counts of war crimes, crimes against humanity, and genocide, for leading a gang of Hutu murderers and rapists against Tutsi civilians in 1994. Munyaneza had applied for refugee status unsuccessfully. Evidence at his trial showed that the store at which he worked in Rwanda had ordered 2 300 machetes before the massacres, and that he distributed these to initiate the slaughter in Butare. The judge heard testimony from sixty-six witnesses, and the court travelled to Rwanda, France, and Tanzania to hear evidence. The judge was convinced that Munyaneza acted as a ringleader of an ad hoc militia responsible for numerous atrocities in Butare and the surrounding area, distributed weapons to the provisional militia, looted Tutsi houses and businesses, commanded roadblocks for the identification and slaughter of Tutsis, and used his vehicle for the transport of victims to places where they were raped and killed. Munyaneza was convicted on all counts, and was sentenced to life imprisonment, a sentence equivalent to first-degree murder. He will be eligible to seek parole after twenty-five years' imprisonment. The trial was extraordinary due to travel requirements to gather evidence, but the $4 000 000 costs were modest by UN tribunal standards (Perreaux 2009). The trial of a second suspected *génocidaire* is pending.

In Germany, the Supreme Court of Düsseldorf convicted Nikola Jorgic, a Bosnian Serb, of eleven counts of genocide and thirty counts of murder for his part in ethnic cleansing of Bosnian Muslims in 1992. Jorgic had lived in Germany from 1969 to 1992, but returned to Bosnia after the beginning of hostilities, where he led a paramilitary group that murdered twenty-two citizens of Grabska, and forced fifty residents from another community out of their homes, murdering three of them. His conviction of genocide under German law was upheld on appeal based on section 16, article 220a of the German Penal Code, which conferred on the German courts the power to prosecute genocide. In addition, the Geneva Convention, to which Germany was a party, had declared genocide as a crime that all nations had a duty to punish. Jorgic's appeal to the European Court of Human Rights upheld Jorgic's conviction under German law. These provisions provided that German criminal law was applicable and that, consequently, German courts had jurisdiction to try persons charged with genocide committed abroad, regardless of the defendant's, and the victims', nationalities. Similar trials have been held in Finland, France, Austria, the Netherlands, and Belgium.

The decisions in these various jurisdictions are not based on the principle of universal jurisdiction. Universal jurisdiction is a legal concept that permits any country to prosecute offenders where so ever and when so ever a crime occurs, and is justified on the presumption that the crime is such a threat to international security that it requires the maximum latitude of the legal institutions of the world's nations. Piracy has been recognized as one of these offences. The jurisprudence is less clear on the question of slavery, trafficking in women for prostitution, or international narcotics trafficking. The national trials are an important arsenal in the suppression of genocide because they are permanent institutions with reliable funding, competent staffing, and decided jurisprudence. They complement the current ad hoc tribunals and the ICC. In addition, in countries such as the USA and the Russian Federation, they *may* provide a venue for genocide prosecutions for jurisdictions that have not joined the Rome Convention. However, they require national legislation that is consistent with the UN Convention, and the current jurisprudence that has evolved from the UN tribunals and hybrid courts. They are another resource in the toolbox for genocide suppression. In a reciprocal development, as of 2012, the ICTR had transferred four cases for prosecution in France and Rwanda. At the ICTY a total of eight cases involving thirteen persons indicted by the ICTY were referred to courts in the former Yugoslavia, mostly to Bosnia and Herzegovina. On the basis of the ICTY indictments and the supporting evidence provided by the Tribunal's prosecutor, these cases will be tried under domestic criminal laws.

International legal assistance: reinforcing the rule of law in mobile courts in Congo

Another legal innovation has emerged in the eastern Congo under the aegis of the DRC's Kinshasa government, working with the America Bar Foundation: the Mobile Gender Justice Courts (OSISA 2012). Sexual violence has been rife in the eastern Congo since the occupation of the country by elements of the former national army of Rwanda that evacuated after their defeat in 1994. For example, on New Year's Day 2011, there was a mass rape of over fifty women and girls in the town of Fizi, DRC. The American Bar Foundation worked with military prosecutors from the government of the DRC to prosecute those responsible. A mobile court was stationed in Baraka, and seized and prosecuted senior officers for their responsibility for these crimes. Four high-level officers were sentenced to jail terms of fifteen–twenty years each. All told, eleven soldiers were brought to justice within six weeks of the incident. The mobile court was funded by a private US NGO, the Open Society Justice Initiative. It was in operation for two years starting in 2010, and travelled to remote regions of the DRC to deal with gender-based violence, and was designed to hold assailants responsible for sexual abuse of women and children. The court is complementary to the ICC, and is able to deal with military and civilian cases. In 2010 it established three civilian and six military trials, adjudicating 186 cases, 115 of which were for rape crimes (Askin 2011). The DRC 'gender justice courts' are reminiscent of the circuit courts established by the Normans to govern rural England. A similar system of circuit courts has been established in northern Canada to adjudicate legal cases in remote settlements in the eastern Arctic. In the DRC, the courts consisted of a panel of five military judges, the military prosecutor general, five defence lawyers, and civil party lawyers. The trials were held in makeshift outdoor courtrooms—tents—in towns that typically had no electricity or running water. The proceedings attracted the attention of hundreds of local people who had never witnessed a trial beforehand, but who had experienced unimaginable levels of trauma and capricious violence from local warlords. The decision to investigate, arrest, prosecute, and convict the perpetrators in the Fizi incident resulted from international pressure from the UN and the US, particularly the UN Secretary-General's Special Representative on Sexual Violence in Conflict, and the US Secretary of State. In fact, the UN has become increasingly aware of the use of sexual violence as a strategy in war, as reflected in the 1998 report on sexual violence in armed conflict (UN 1998). The subsequent Security Council motion 1325, adopted in 2000, recognized for the first time the vulnerability of women and children in armed conflicts. Though rape has perennially been viewed as a part of the 'spoils of war', there was no recognition of this at Nuremberg or the International Military Tribunal for the Far East (IMTFE). The statute creating the ICTY included rape as a crime against humanity. The ICTR included rape as both a war crime and as a crime against humanity. Rape committed during armed conflict is sometimes intended to terrorize the population, to destroy families and communities, and to change the ethnic make-up of the next generation. The mobile courts were highly sensitive to this form of victimization.

Judge Mary McGowan Davis, an acting Justice of the Supreme Court of New York, travelled to eastern Congo to observe the courts in action. There is no effective government in the eastern Congo. The American Bar Association paid the salaries of the lawyers representing both the victims and the accused, as well as providing a daily supplement to the judges and the police hired for security. The itinerary of the court depended on the number of dossiers prepared in advance in any one location, as well as the number of accused apprehended. The gender justice mobile courts were wholly local: the judges, prosecutors, police, and lawyers were all Congolese, and all worked together to bring a semblance of governance back to an area in which it was sorely lacking. Furthermore, the fact that the court convened in remote areas where the violence had occurred, and that the judges, lawyers, and court personnel lived under the same conditions as the local residents, created enormous credibility for the efforts to re-establish the rule of law in eastern Congo. The region lacks accessible roads. Many destinations can only be reached by air. Congolese justice officials lack computers, printers, and basic office supplies. The government cannot provide secure means of transportation for judges and court personnel. Where penalties and reparations are ordered against convicted individuals, these are never paid. 'There is no procedure for the forced seizure of goods from convicted defendants, nor do court authorities or the police evince any interest in assisting parties, who have been awarded financial recompense, to collect the payments they are owed' (OSISA 2012: 30). The government has no effective enforcement mechanisms. Not only that, much of the population lacks basic civilian records such as birth and death certificates. The arrival of the gender justice courts under military authority has been a game-changer in lawless eastern Congo. This is not a mechanism that prevents genocide. Nor is it a permanent legal institution. It is sponsored by a foreign NGO, on a trial basis, with funding that is short term. Legally speaking, the quality of justice is sometimes questionable with defence counsel receiving the indictment documents '20 minutes before the trial begins' (2012: 33). Also, the partnership of the American Bar Foundation with the Congolese military has resulted in a large number of military cases that are of more relevance for the governance of the army than civilian life (cases of desertion, refusal to obey an order, waste of ammunition, loss of a rifle, etc.). The Congo is not a failed state. It simply is a state that has not developed institutional completion of the sort found in urban Europe. It has trained a significant number of judges and lawyers who are capable of instituting the rule of law, but it does not have the infrastructure required to make it work. The American Bar Foundation has provided another resource in the toolbox of genocide remedies that we can employ to further the objective of Nunca Mias.

Five last points

If one were to design a world in which genocide did not occur, or in which it would be repressed, the primary objective would be to design a society in which there was responsible government. Responsible government restrains the sovereign, distributes authority of governance across all the stakeholders in society, and honours the rule of law. However, it has taken centuries for this form of government to emerge in Europe and the Americas. Democratic governments cannot implant democracy at will in developing countries, but can play a role on the world stage by supporting democracies where nations choose that course of development. But there also has to be a position in government that alerts the lawmakers to the development of genocide or crimes against humanity among its neighbours. Currently, this role is played by the press (Gutman et al 2007), but frequently the press is absent in remote regions such as Darfur, Tibet, and the Caucasus. The Secretary-General of the UN has an assistant specifically charged with alerting him to the prospect of mass atrocities across the world. This would seem to be an obligatory function of every foreign minister in a democratic country. Chalk et al (2010: 13ff) argue that the failure of democratic governments to have a capacity to respond to atrocities in foreign countries is palpable in terms of national security risks as a result of potential terrorism, pandemics of infectious disease spread among populations displaced by conflict, indigenous unrest in the national diaspora community, and huge bills in terms of overseas peacekeeping missions.

My second point is that the ICJ requires wider powers. In the case of Bosnia and Serbia reviewed earlier, the court should have had the power to investigate allegations of war crimes, and crimes against humanity. The 1948 UN Convention on Genocide indicated that disputes between the contracting parties relating to the convention 'shall be submitted to the International Court of Justice at the request of any of the parties of the dispute'. In Bosnia in 1992 there was a civil war. The Serbian faction in Bosnia was opposed by the Muslim faction. The former Yugoslavian national army controlled by Milošević in Belgrade was creating mayhem in Bosnia and Croatia. The court could only speak to state versus state conflicts, and exempted the Belgrade Serbs while providing no remedy against the Sarajevo Serbs. Nor was there any remedy available outside the Genocide Convention. This situation is too narrow on two points. The nation of Bosnia should have a right to prosecute a claim against a divisionist sector of its own society—the Bosnian Serbs. And the terms of reference should not be limited to genocide. Ethnic cleansing is just as detrimental to community survival as genocide. This court must play a more active role in mediating group conflicts. Following in the Westphalian tradition, the court is premised on the idea that the only actors with competence to appear are nation states, which are assumed to be integral units. The future success of the court will depend on recognizing that oftentimes the conflicts on which the courts will be asked to evaluate are divided, or incoherent states—pre-Westphalian entities, that do not fit the mould. And the conflicts do not always fit the legal definition of genocide. The court must adjust the jurisprudence to reflect these realities.

My third point concerns the international trade in arms. The world is awash with AK-47s, hand grenades, land mines, and even more destructive weapons. Few nations have a clean record on this extremely lucrative international trade. If we can agree to an embargo on the slaughter of whales, why is the restriction of the trade of weapons of mass slaughter that wreaked such devastation in Sierra Leone and Liberia so improbable? Curtailing such business would put a premium on non-violent methods of dispute resolution. In 2012 US courts sentenced Victor Bout to twenty-five years' imprisonment for his international arms dealing. The Russian 'merchant of death' provided weapons for some of the globe's bloodiest conflicts, including Rwanda, Angola, and the Congo. Bout was prosecuted because some of his materials were used against US military personnel. His imprisonment retards the ability of rogue states to acquire the ordinance to suppress their own populations. In April 2013 the UN General Assembly took the first steps to approve such an international treaty (CBC 2013). This convention would not suppress the trade, but would make it more transparent. In 2008 a Chinese ship with weapons destined for Zimbabwe was turned away in South Africa ports. The weapons were thought to be destined for the suppression of Mugabe's political opponents. This was an unusual circumstance and reflected the political action of South Africa's churches and unions. The international treaty is expected to make all such weapon transfers more accountable.

My fourth point is that the leading countries of 'The West' are long overdue for their own truth commissions. There are two points here. First, during the war on communism in South and Central America in the 1970s, the US conspired with fascist elements in the governments of Chile, El Salvador, Guatemala, Argentina, and other dictatorships that led to the torture and disappearance of hundreds of thousands of nationals from these countries. Second, in 2003 a joint mission, the US and the UK, invaded Iraq on the supposition that Saddam Hussein was making weapons of mass destruction. The free press failed to alert the public that such allegations were groundless. US casualties in the Iraq war amounted to over 35 000. Iraqi deaths are estimated to be over 1 000 000. Costs are measured in the *trillions* of dollars. Both periods of time have slipped from consciousness. These acts of aggression have become the Great Amnesia. No one remembers. No one is called to account. No retribution is offered. No estimate of the harm done is noted on the public record. But if Argentina, Brazil, Chile, and the other Latin states are required to enter a confrontation with their past, what lets the leading Western powers off the hook?

My final point is more problematic. As Marchak (2008) noted in her last book, there is 'no easy fix' for crimes against humanity. I do not plan to offer one here. But, if the world wants to cultivate effective social responses to violations of international humanitarian law, the remedies cannot be confined to the tools of criminal law. Incarceration of leading offenders does not repair the breaches to society that atrocities produce. Success in Europe after the Second World War was associated with massive reconstruction of the political and economic structures there and by fostering responsible government. Trials by themselves would have led nowhere. In addition, the remedies cannot always be *post hoc*. In my view the way forward is to renegotiate the supremacy of the sovereign state and to lay the foundations for future cosmopolitan governance, nationally and transnationally, that makes politically motivated mass murder ideologically indefensible and strategically impossible. This will take decades, but globalization makes this course of action not only feasible, but also unavoidable.

Bibliography

Abse, D. (1973). *The Dogs of Pavlov*, London: Valentine, Mitchel and Co.

Aderet, Ofer (2011). 'In newly released tape, Eichmann heard boasting about his role in Holocaust', 3 April, Tel Aviv: <Haartez.com>.

Adler, Reva, Cyanne Loyle, and Judith Globerman (2007). 'A Calamity in the Neighborhood: Women's Participation in the Rwanda Genocide', *Genocide Studies and Prevention* 2(3): 209–34.

Adorno, T.W., E. Frankel-Brunswick, D.J. Levinson, and R.N. Sanford (1950). *The Authoritarian Personality*, New York: Harper.

African Rights (2000). *Confessing to Genocide: Responses to Rwanda's Genocide Law*, June, Publication of African Rights: Kigali, Rwanda.

African Rights (2003a). *The History of the Genocide in Sector Gishamvu: A Collective Account*, January, Publication of African Rights: Kigali, Rwanda.

African Rights (2003b). *The History of the Genocide in Nyarugunga Sector: A Collective Account*, April, Publication of African Rights: Kigali, Rwanda.

African Rights (2003c). *The History of the Genocide in Nyange Sector*, August, Publication of African Rights: Kigali, Rwanda.

African Rights (2003d). *The History of the Genocide in Kindama Sector: A Collective Account*, November, Publication of African Rights: Kigali, Rwanda.

African Rights (2003e). *A History of the Genocide in Nkemero Sector: A Collective Account*, November, Publication of African Rights: Kigali, Rwanda.

African Rights (2003f). *Tribute to Courage*, December, Publication of African Rights: Kigali, Rwanda.

African Rights (2005). *The History of the Genocide in Gahini Sector: A Collective Account*, March, Publication of African Rights: Kigali, Rwanda.

Akhavan, Payam (2012). *Reducing Genocide to Law: Definition, Meaning, and the Ultimate Crime*, Cambridge: Cambridge University Press.

Albright, Madeline and William S. Cohen (2008). *Preventing Genocide*, Washington DC: United States Holocaust Memorial Museum.

Allen, Jonathan (1999). 'Balancing Justice and Social Unity: Political Theory and the Idea of a Truth and Reconciliation Commission', *University of Toronto Law Journal* 49(3): 315–53.

Allen, Michael Thad (2005). *The Business of Genocide: The SS, Slave Labor, and the Concentration Camps*, Chapel Hill, NC: University of North Carolina Press.

Allen, Tim (2011). 'Is "genocide" such a good idea?' *British Journal of Sociology* 62(1): 26–36.

Alvarez, José E. (1999). 'Crimes of States/Crimes of Hate: Lessons from Rwanda', *Yale Journal of International Law* 24: 365–483.

Arendt, Hannah (1963). *Eichmann in Jerusalem: A Report on the Banality of Evil*, New York: Viking. Revised 1964 and Introduction by Amos Elon 2006.

Arendt, Hannah (1992). 'Letters to Karl Jaspers', in *Hannah Arendt/Karl Jaspers Correspondence 1926–1969*, edited by Lotte Kohler and Hans Saner, translated by Robert Kimber and Rita Kimber, New York: Harcourt Brace Javanovich.

Arns, Paulo E. (1998). *Torture in Brazil: a Shocking Report on the Pervasive Use of Torture by Brazilian Military Governments, 1964–1979*, Original in Portuguese: *Brazil: Nunca Mais* (1986), Austin: University of Texas Institute of Latin American Studies.

Askin, Kelly (2011). 'Fizi Mobile Court: Rape Verdicts', 2 March, *International Justice Tribune*, 123; Netherlands: Radio Netherlands International. <http://www.rnw.nl/international-justice/article/international-justice-tribune-123> accessed 15 March 2011.

Authers, John (2006). 'Making Good Again: German Compensation for Forced and Slave Laborers', pp. 420–48 in Pablo de Greiff (ed.), *The Handbook of Reparations*, Oxford and New York: Oxford University Press.

Avruch, Kevin and Beatriz Vejarano (2002). 'Truth and Reconciliation Commissions: A Review Essay and Annotated Bibliography', *The Online Journal of Peace and Conflict Resolution* 4(2): 37–76.

Axworthy, Lloyd (2012). 'RtoP and the Evolution of State Sovereignty', pp. 3–16 in Jared Genser and Irwin Cotler (eds), *The Responsibility to Protect: The Promise of Stopping Mass Atrocities in our Time*, New York: Oxford University Press.

Balakian, Grigoris (2009). *Armenian Golgotha: A Memoir of the Armenian Genocide 1915–1918*, translated by Peter Balakian, New York: Alfred A. Knopf.

Ball, Howard (1999). *Prosecuting War Crimes and Genocide: The Twentieth-Century Experience*. Lawrence: University Press of Kansas.

Barbour, Charles and George Pavlich (2010). *After Sovereignty: On the Question of Political Beginnings*, London: Routledge.

Bass, Gary J. (2000). *Stay the Hand of Vengeance: The Politics of War Crimes Tribunals*, Princeton NJ: Princeton University Press.

Bassiouni, M. Cherif (2011). *Crimes Against Humanity: Historical Evolution and Contemporary Application*, Cambridge: Cambridge University Press.

Bauman, Zygmunt (1989). *Modernity and the Holocaust,* New material added in 1991 and 2000. Ithaca NY: Cornell University Press.

Baumrind, Diana (1964). 'Some Thoughts on Ethics of Research: After Reading Milgram's "Behavioral Study of Obedience"', *American Psychologist* 19(2): 421–3.

Baumrind, Diana (1985). 'Research Using Intentional Deception: Ethical Issues Re-visited', *American Psychologist* 40(2): 165–74.

Beccaria, Cesare (2003). 'On Crimes and Punishments' [1764] pp. 15–24 in Eugene McLaughlin, John Muncie, and Gordon Hughes (eds), *Criminological Perspectives: Essential Readings,* 2nd edn, London: Sage.

Becker, Howard (1963). *Outsiders,* New York: Free Press.

Belgium (1994). Kibat: Kigali Battalion of Belgium Peace-keepers, Calendar of Events: 6 April–19 April 1994, ICTR Exhibit.

Bianchi, Herman (2010). *Justice as Sanctuary: Toward a New System of Crime Control,* Eugene OR: Wipf and Stock.

Black, Edwin (2001). *IBM and the Holocaust: The Strategic Alliance between Nazi Germany and America's Most Powerful Corporation,* New York: Crown Publishers.

Blass, Thomas (2004). *The Man who Shocked the World: The Life and Legacy of Stanley Milgram,* New York: Basic Books.

Bloxham, Donald (2005). *The Great Game of Genocide: Imperialism, Nationalism and the Destruction of the Ottoman Armenians.* Oxford: Oxford University Press.

Borer, Tristan Anne (2004). 'Reconciling South Africa or South Africans? Cautionary Notes from the TRC', *African Studies Quarterly* 8(1): 19–38.

Bosnia (1993). 'Bosnia and Herzegovina brings a case against Yugoslavia (Serbia and Montenegro)', *Press Release,* 22 March, The Hague: International Court of Justice.

Bosnia (2007). 'Application of the Convention on the Prevention and Punishment of the Crime of Genocide (Bosnia and Herzegovina v Serbia and Montenegro), *Judgment,* 26 February, The Hague: International Court of Justice.

Boyle, Francis A. (2012). *United Ireland, Human Rights and International Law,* Atlanta GA: Clarity Press.

Brannigan, Augustine (2004). *The Rise and Fall of Social Psychology: The Use and Misuse of Experimental Method,* New Brunswick NJ: Aldine Transaction.

Brannigan, Augustine and J. Christopher Levy (1983). 'The Legal Context of Plea Bargaining', *Canadian Journal of Criminology* 24(4): 399–420.

Brannigan, Augustine and Nicholas Jones (2009). 'Genocide and the Legal Process in Rwanda: From Genocide Amnesty to the New Rule of Law', *International Criminal Justice Review* 19(2): 192–207.

Brophy, Alfred L. (2006). *Reparations Pro and Con,* New York: Oxford University Press.

Browning, Christopher (1992). *Ordinary Men: Reserve Police Battalion 101 and the Final Solution in Poland*, New York: Harper Collins. Afterword 1998.

Browning, Christopher (2000). *Nazi Policy, Jewish Workers, German Killers*, Cambridge: Cambridge University Press.

Bryce, Peter H. (1922). *The Story of A National Crime*, Ottawa: James Hope and Sons.

Buckingham, Stephen (2006). 'The French Tell Lies in Broad Day Light', *The New Times* (Kigali) 27 November, <http://www.ocnus.net/cgi-bin/exec/view.cgi?archive=105&num=26935&printer=1> accessed on 5 December 2006.

Bull, Hedley (2012). *The Anarchical Society: A Study of Order in World Politics*, 4th edn., New York: Columbia University Press.

Bullock, Alan (1962). *Hitler: A Study in Tyranny*, New York: Harper and Row.

Burger, Jerry (2009). 'Replicating Milgram: Would People Still Obey Today?' *American Psychologist* 64(1): 1–11.

Burger, Jerry, Z.M. Girgis, and C.C. Manning (2011). 'In their Own Words: Explaining Obedience to Authority through an Examination of Participants' Comments', *Social Psychological and Personality Science* 2: 460–6.

Burke-White, William W. (2012). 'Adoption of the Responsibility to Protect', pp. 17–36 in Jared Genser and Irwin Cotler (eds), *The Responsibility to Protect: The Promise of Stopping Mass Atrocities in our Time*, New York: Oxford University Press.

Cameron, Hazel (2011). *Complicity: The Hidden Role of Britain and France in Rwanda's Genocide*, Abingdon: Routledge.

Caplan, Gerald (2008). *The Betrayal of Africa*, Toronto: The House of Anansi.

Caplan, Gerald (2010). 'The Politics of Denialism: The Strange Case of Rwanda', Review of Herman and Peterson (Politics of Genocide), *Pambazuka News*, Issue 496. <http://pambazuka.org/en/category/features/65265>

Carson, W.G. (1979). 'The Conventionalization of Early Factory Crime', *International Journal for the Sociology of Law* 7: 37–60.

Carson, W.G. (1982). *The Other Price of Britain's Oil: Safety and Control in the North Sea*, London: Martin Robertson.

CBC (2013). 'UN adopts landmark treaty regulating global arms trade', Canadian Broadcasting Corporation World News, 2 April, <http://www.cbc.ca/news/world/story/2013/04/02/un-general-assembly-arms-treaty.html>.

Cesarani, David (2006). *Becoming Eichmann: The Life, Times and Trial of a 'Desk Murderer'*, New York: Capo Press.

Chalk, Frank, Roméo Dallaire, Kyle Matthews, Carla Barqueiro, and Simon Doyle (2010). *Mobilizing the Will to Intervene: Leadership to*

Prevent Mass Atrocities, Montreal and Kingston: McGill-Queen's University Press.

Chalk, Frank and Kurt Jonassohn (eds) (1990). *The History and Sociology of Genocide: Analyses and Case Studies*, New Haven: Yale University Press.

Chang, Iris (1997). *The Rape of Nanking: The Forgotten Holocaust of World War Two*, New York: Perseus.

Chang, Jung and Jon Halliday (2005). *Mao: The Unknown Story*, New York: Alfred A. Knopf.

Christie, Nils (1977). 'Conflict as Property', *British Journal of Sociology* 17: 1–5.

Christie, Nils (2000). *Crime Control as Industry: Towards Gulags, Western Style*, New York: Routledge.

Civikov, Germania (2010). *The Star Witness*, translated by John Laughland, Belgrade: Srebrenica Historical Project. <http://www.srebrenica-project.com/DOWNLOAD/books/Star_witness.pdf>.

Cohen, David (2006a). 'Justice on the Cheap Revisited: The Failures of the Serious Crimes Trials in East Timor', *Asia Pacific Issues* No. 80: May, Honolulu: East-West Center.

Cohen, David (2006b). *Indifference and Accountability: The United Nations and the Politics of Justice in East Timor*. Honolulu: East West Center.

Cohen, Stanley (2001). *States of Denial: Knowing About Atrocities and Suffering*, Cambridge: Polity Press.

Collier, Paul (2007). *The Bottom Billion: Why the Poorest Countries are Failing and What Can Be Done About It*, Oxford: Oxford University Press.

Combs, Nancy A. (2010). *Fact-finding without Facts: The Uncertain Evidentiary Foundations of International Criminal Convictions*, Cambridge: Cambridge University Press.

Coogan, Tim Pat (2012). *The Famine Plot: England's Role in Ireland's Greatest Tragedy*, London: Palgrave Macmillan.

Courtois, Stéphane, Nicholas Werth, Jean-Louis Panné, Andrzej Paczkowski, Karel Bartosek, and Jean-Louis Margolin (1999). *The Black Book of Communism*, Cambridge MA: Harvard University Press.

Croatia (1999). 'Croatia Institutes Proceedings against Yugoslavia for Violations of the Genocide Convention', *Press Release*, The Hague: International Court of Justice.

Cruvellier, Thierry (2010). *Court of Remorse: Inside the International Criminal Tribunal for Rwanda*, Madison WI: University of Wisconsin Press.

Dadrian, Vahakn (1996). *German Responsibility in the Armenian Genocide: A Review of the Historical Record of German Complicity*. Watertown MA: Blue Crane.

Dallaire, Romeo with Brent Beardsley (2003). *Shake Hands with the Devil, The Failure of Humanity in Rwanda*. Toronto: Random House.

Darley, John (1995). 'Constructive and destructive obedience: A taxonomy of principal-agent relationships', *Journal of Social Issues* 51 (3): 125–154.

D'Ascoli, Silvia (2011). *Sentencing in International Criminal Law: The Approach of the Two Ad Hoc Tribunals and Future Perspectives for the International Criminal Court*, Oxford: Hart Publishing.

Davenport, Christian and Allan C. Stam (2009). 'What Really Happened in Rwanda?' *Pacific Standard Magazine*, 6 October 2009 <http://www.psmag.com/politics/what-really-happened-in-rwanda-3432>.

De Waal, Alex (2004). 'Tragedy in Darfur: On Understanding and Ending the Horror, *Boston Review*, October/November <http://bostonreview.net/BR29.5/dewaal.php>.

Del Ponte, Carla (2008). *Madame Prosecutor: Confrontations with Humanity's Worst Criminals and the Culture of Impunity* (in collaboration with Chuck Sudetic), New York: Other Press.

Des Forges, Alison (1999). *Leave None to Tell the Story*, New York: Human Rights Watch.

Dorsey, D. (1994). *Historical Dictionary of Rwanda*, Lanham, MD: Scarecrow Press.

DRC (1999). 'Armed Activities on the Territory of the Congo' (*Democratic Republic of the Congo v. Uganda*) *Press Release*, 23 June, The Hague: World Court of Justice.

DRC (2005). 'Armed Activities on the Territory of the Congo' (*Democratic Republic of the Congo v. Uganda*) *Press Release*, 19 December, The Hague: World Court of Justice.

Drechsler, Horst (1980). *'Let us Die Fighting': The Struggle of the Herero and the Nama against German Imperialism (1884–1915)* translated by Bernd Zoller from original German edition 1963. London: Zed Books.

Drinan, Robert F. (2001). *The Mobilization of Shame: A World View of Human Rights*, New Haven CT: Yale University Press.

Drumbl, Mark A. (1997–1998). 'Rule of Law Amid Lawlessness: Counseling the Accused in Rwanda's Domestic Genocide Trials', *Columbia Human Rights Law Review* 29: 590–639.

Drumbl, Mark A. (2000). 'Punishment, Postgenocide: From Guilt to Shame to *Civis* in Rwanda', *New York University Law Review* 75: 1221–326.

Drumbl, Mark A. (2007). *Atrocity, Punishment, and International Law*, Cambridge: Cambridge University Press.

Durkheim, Emile (1893). *The Division of Labour in Society*, translated by W.D. Halls, Introduction by Lewis Coser, 1984, New York: Macmillan.

Durkheim, Emile (1985). *Readings from Emile Durkheim*, Kenneth Thompson (ed.), London and New York: Routledge.

Durkheim, Emile (1997). *Suicide*, translated by Jonathan A. Spaulding, edited by George Simpson, first published in 1897, New York: Free Press.

Ehrenburg, Ilya and Vasily Grossman (2002). *The Complete Black Book of Russian Jewry*. (Written 1941–1945). Translated by David Pattern, Foreword by I.L. Horowitz and Introduction by Helen Segall. New Brunswick NJ: Transaction Publishers.

Eisner, M. (2003). 'Long-Term Historical Trends in Violent Crime', *Crime and Justice; A Review of Research*, 30: 83–142.

Elias, Norbert (1996). *The Germans: Power Struggles and the Development of Habitus in the Nineteenth and Twentieth Centuries*, Translated from the German (1989) and edited by Eric Dunning and Stephen Mennell, New York: Columbia University Press.

Elias, Norbert (2000). *The Civilizing Process: Sociogenetic and Psychogenetic Investigations*, translated from the German (1939) and edited by Eric Dunning and Stephen Mennell, revised, London: Wiley-Blackwell.

Ellis, Lee and Anthony Walsh (1999). 'Criminologists' Opinions about the Causes and Theories of Crime and Delinquency', *The Criminologist* 24(4): 1–4.

Elon, Amos (2006). 'Introduction' to *Eichmann in Jerusalem: A Report on the Banality of Evil*, by Hannah Arendt, New York: Viking.

Engels, Frederick (1892). *The Condition of the Working Class in England in 1844*, translated by F. Kelley Wischnewetzky, New York: Cambridge University Press.

Erber, Ralph (2002). 'Perpetrators with a Clear Conscience', pp. 285–300 in Leonard S. Newnan and Ralph Erber (eds), *Understanding Genocide: The Social Psychology of the Holocaust*, New York: Oxford University Press.

Evans, Garth (2012). 'Lessons and Challenges', pp. 375–92 in Jared Genser and Irwin Cotler (eds), *The Responsibility to Protect: The Promise of Stopping Mass Atrocities in our Time*, New York: Oxford University Press.

Fein, Helen (1984). *Accounting for Genocide: National Responses and Jewish Victimization during the Holocaust*, Chicago, Ill: University of Chicago Press.

Fein, Helen (1993). *Genocide: A Sociological Perspective*. London: Sage. Originally published as Volume 38 of *Current Sociology*.

Foucault, Michel (1977). 'Nietzsche, Genealogy, History', pp. 139–165 in D.F. Bouchard (ed.), *Language, Counter-Memory, Practice: Selected Essays and Interviews*, Ithaca NY: Cornell University Press.

Foucault, Michel (1979). *Discipline and Punish*, translated by Alan Sheridan, New York: Random House.

Freud, Sigmund (1922). *Group Psychology and Analysis of the Ego*, translated by J. Strachey, London: Hogarth.

Friedrichs, David O. and Martin D. Schwartz (2008). 'Low Self-Control and High Organizational Control: The Paradoxes of White-Collar Crime' pp. 145–59 in Erich Goode (ed.), *Out of Control: Assessing the General Theory of Crime*, Stanford CA: Stanford University Press.

Fujii, Lee Ann (2009). *Killing Neighbors: Webs of Violence in Rwanda*, Ithaca NY: Cornell University Press.

Garland, David (1990). *Punishment and Society: A Study in Social Theory*, Chicago Ill: University of Chicago Press.

Gavin, Jim and Ken Polk (1983). 'NCCD Research Review: Attrition in Case Processing: Is Rape Unique?' *Journal of Research in Crime and Delinquency* 20(1): 126–54.

Genser, Jared and Irwin Cottler (eds) (2012). *The Responsibility to Protect: The Promise of Stopping Mass Atrocities in our Time*, New York: Oxford University Press.

Gewald, Jan Bart (1999). *Herero Heroes: A Socio-Political History of Namibia*, Oxford: James Currey.

Gibson, Stephen (2011). 'Milgram's Obedience Experiments: A Rhetorical Analysis', *British Journal of Social Psychology* 52:290–309.

Gidley, Rebecca (2010). *The Extraordinary Chambers in the Courts of Cambodia and the Responsibility to Protect*, St Lucia, Qld, Australia: Asia-Pacific Centre for the Responsibility to Protect.

Glueck, Sheldon (1946). *The Nuremberg Trial and Aggressive War*, Millwood NY: Klaus Reprint.

Glueck, Sheldon and Eleanor Glueck (1950). *Unraveling Juvenile Delinquency*. Cambridge MA: Harvard University Press.

Goldhagen, Daniel (1997). *Hitler's Willing Executioners: Ordinary Germans and the Holocaust*, New York: Knopf (with Afterword). Originally published in 1996.

Gottfredson, Michael and Travis Hirschi (1990). *A General Theory of Crime*, Stanford CA: Stanford University Press.

Gourevitch, Philip (1998). *We Wish to Inform You that Tomorrow we Will be Killed with Our Families*, New York: Farrar, Straus and Giroux.

Graybill, Lyn and Kimberley Lanegran (2004). 'Truth, Justice, and Reconciliation in Africa: Issues and Cases', *African Studies Quarterly* 8(1): 1–18.

Grayling, A.C. (2006). *Among the Dead Cities*, New York: Walker and Sons.

Gribetz, Judah and Shari C. Reig (2009). 'The Swiss Banks Holocaust Settlement', pp. 115–44 in Carla Ferstman, Mariana Goetz, and Alan Stephens (eds), *Reparations for Victims of Genocide, War Crimes, and Crimes Against Humanity*, Leiden and Boston: Martinus Nijhof.

Grunfeld, F. and, A. Huijboom (2007). *The Failure to Prevent Genocide in Rwanda: The Role of Bystanders*, Leiden: Martinus Nijhoff.

Gurr, Ted (1981). 'Historical Trends in Violent Crime: A Critical Review of the Evidence' in *Crime and Justice: An Annual Review of Research*, vol. 3, edited by Michael Tonry and Norval Morris, Chicago Ill: University of Chicago Press.

Gutman, Roy, David Rieff, and Anthony Dworkin (2007). *Crimes of War: What the Public Should Know*, New York: Norton.

Hagan, John and Joshua Kaiser (2011). 'The Displaced and Dispossessed of Darfur: Explaining the Sources of a Continuing State-led Genocide', *British Journal of Sociology* 62(1): 1–25.

Hagan, John, Irene Nagel, and Celesta Albonetti (1980). 'The Differential Sentencing of White-collar Offenders in Ten Federal District Courts', *American Sociological Review* 45: 802–20.

Hagan, John and Wenona Rymond-Richmond (2009). *Darfur and the Crime of Genocide*, New York: Cambridge University Press.

Hagan, John, Wenona Rymond-Richmond, and Patricia Parker (2005). 'The Criminology of Genocide: The Death and Rape of Darfur', *Criminology* 43(3): 525–62.

Hamber, Brandon and Richard Wilson (2002). 'Symbolic Closure through Memory, Reparation and Revenge in Post-conflict Societies', *Journal of Human Rights* 1(1): 35–53.

Hare, Robert (1970). *Psychopathy: Theory and Research*, New York: Wiley and Sons.

Harff, Barbara (2003). 'No Lessons Learned from the Holocaust? Assessing Risks of Genocide and Political Mass Murder since 1955', *American Political Science Review* 97(1): 57–73.

Harff, Barbara and T.R. Gurr (1988). 'Toward Empirical Theory of Genocides and Politicides: Identification and Measurement of Cases Since 1945', *International Studies Quarterly* 32: 359–71.

Hatzfeld, Jean (2005). *Machete Season: The Killers in Rwanda Speak Out*, Translated by Linda Coverdale, New York: Farrar, Straus and Giroux.

Hatzfeld, Jean (2010). *The Antelope's Strategy: Living in Rwanda after the Genocide*, translated by Linda Coverdale, New York: Farrar, Straus and Giroux.

Hayner, Priscilla (1994). 'Fifteen Truth Commissions 1974–1994: A Comparative Study', *Human Rights Quarterly* 16: 597–655.

Hayner, Priscilla (2011). *Unspeakable Truths: Transitional Justice and the Challenge of Truth Commissions*, 2nd edn., New York: Routledge.

Hennebel, Ludovic and Thomas Hochmann (2011). *Genocide Denials and the Law*, Oxford Scholarship Online May pp. 1–137 <http://www.oxfordscholarship.com/view/10.1093/acprof:oso/9780199738922.001.0001/acprof-9780199738922?rskey=KzgKGk&result=1&q=Hennebel>.

Herman, Edward and David Peterson (2010a). *The Politics of Genocide*, New York: Monthly Review Press.

Herman, Edward and David Peterson (2010b). 'Rwanda: Genocide Denial and Facilitation', *Pambazuka News* 8 July, issue 489, <http://pambazuka.org/en/category/comment/65773>. Accessed on July 15 2010.

Hewstone, Miles, Anthony Manstead, and Wolfgang Stroebe (1997). *The Blackwell Reader in Social Psychology*, Oxford: Blackwell.

Hilberg, Raul (1985). *The Destruction of the European Jews*, three vols, revised edn. Originally published in 1961. New York: Holmes and Meier.

Hirsch, David (2003). *Law Against Genocide: Cosmopolitan Trials*, London: Glasshouse Press.

Hirschi, Travis (1969). *The Causes of Delinquency*, Berkeley CA: University of California Press. Rereleased by Transaction Press in 2002.

Hirschi, Travis (2004). 'Self-Control and Crime', pp. 537–52 in Roy F. Baumeister and Kathleen D. Koss (eds), *Handbook of Self-Regulation*, New York and London: Guilford Press.

Hirschi, Travis and Michael Gottfredson (2008). 'Critiquing the Critics: The Authors Respond', pp. 217–32 in Erich Goode (ed.), *Out of Control: Assessing the General Theory of Crime*, Stanford CA: Stanford University Press.

Hitchens, Christopher (2002). *The Trial of Henry Kissinger*, London: Verso.

Hobbes, Thomas (1985). *Leviathan* [1651] Harmondsworth: Penguin Books.

Höffe, Otfried (2006). *Kant's Cosmopolitan Theory of Law and Peace*, translated by Alexandra Newton, Cambridge: Cambridge University Press.

Honig, Jan Willem and Norbert Both (1996). *Srebrenica: Record of a War Crime*, London: Penguin.

Horowitz, Irving L. (2002). *Taking Lives: Genocide and State Power*, 5th edn., New Brunswick NJ: Transaction.

Houtte, Hans van, Hans Das, and Bart Delmartino (2006). 'The United Nations Compensation Commission', pp. 321–89 in Pablo de Greiff (ed.), *The Handbook of Reparations*, Oxford and New York: Oxford University Press.

Hovannisian, Richard (1986). *The Armenian Genocide in Perspective*, New Brunswick, NJ: Transaction Books.

Human Rights Watch (2006a). *Genocide, War Crimes and Crimes Against Humanity: A Topical Digest of the Case Law of the International Criminal Tribunal for the Former Yugoslavia*, New York: Human Rights Watch.

Human Rights Watch (2006b). The Rwandan Genocide: How it was prepared: HRW Briefing Paper, April, New York: Human Rights Watch.

Hunter-Gault, C. (2000). 'Introduction' to Antje Krog, *Country of My Skull*, New York: Three Rivers Press.

Ibuka (1999). *The Kibuye Dictionary Project*, Kigali, Rwanda: Ibuka Survivors.

ICISS (2001). *Responsibility to Protect: Report of the International Commission of Intervention and State Security*, Ottawa: International Development Research Center.

IJT (2011). 'First ESMA Mega-Trial in Argentina: 16 Sentenced for Crimes Against Humanity', No 139, 9 November, Netherlands: International Justice Tribune, online.

Ivkovic, Sanja Kutnjak and John Hagan (2011). *Reclaiming Justice: The International Tribunal for the Former Yugoslavia and Local Courts*, New York: Oxford University Press.

Jarausch, Konrad H. (2002). 'The Conundrum of Complicity: German Professionals and the Final Solution', *The Joseph and Rebeca Meyerhoff Annual Lecture*, Washington DC: United States Holocaust Memorial Museum.

Jeffrey, C.R. (1957). 'The Development of Crime in Early English Society', *Journal of Criminal Law, Criminology and Police Science* 47: 647–66.

Jefremovas, Villia (2002). *Brickyards to Graveyards: From Production to Genocide in Rwanda*, Albany NW: State University of New York Press.

Johnstone, Richard (2007). 'Are Occupational Health and Safety Crimes Hostage to History?' pp. 33–54 in Augustine Brannigan and George Pavlich (eds), *Governance and Regulation in Social Life*, London: Routledge Cavendish.

Jones, Adam (2010a). *Genocide: A Comprehensive Introduction*, 2nd edn., London: Routledge.

Jones, Adam (2010b). 'On Genocide Deniers: Challenging Herman and Peterson', *Pambazuka News* (No. 490), 15 July, <http://www.pambazuka.org/en/category/features/65977/print> accessed on 22 July 2010.

Jones, Nicholas (2010). The *Courts of Genocide: Politics and the Rule of Law in Rwanda and Arusha*, London: Routledge.

Karganović, Stephen, Ljubisa Simić, Edward Herman, George Pumphrey, J.P. Maher, and Andy Wilcoxson (2011). *Deconstruction of a Virtual Genocide: An Intelligent Person's Guide to Srebrenica*, Den Haag: Belgrade.

Karuhanga, James and Edmund Kagire (2012). 'Rwanda: Habyarimana's Killing a Coup d'Etat', *New Times*, 12 January. <http://www.newtimes.co.rw/news/index.php?i=14867&a=48950> accessed 15 January 2012.

Katz, Jack (1988). *Seductions of Crime: Moral and Sensual Appeals of Doing Evil*, New York: Basic Books.

Kelsall, Tim (2005). 'Truth, Lies, Ritual: Preliminary Reflections on the Truth and Reconciliation Commission in Sierra Leone', *Human Rights Quarterly* 27: 361–91.

Kierman, Ben (2007). *Blood and Soil: A World History of Genocide and Extermination*, New Haven CT: Yale University Press.

Kimenyi, Felly (2007). 'France Blocks Mucyo Inquiry', *The New Times* (Kigali) 13 February <http://www.rwandagateway.org/article.php3?id_article=4287>.

Klee, Ernst, Willi Dressen, and Volker Riess (1996). *'The Good Old Days':
The Holocaust as Seen by its Perpetrators and Bystanders*, translated by
Deborah Burnstone, Old Say CT: Konecky and Konecky.

Krog, Antjie (2000). *Country of my Skull*, New York: Three Rivers Press.

Kroslak, D. (2008). *The French Betrayal of Rwanda*, Bloomington IN:
Indiana University Press.

Kuper, Leo (1981). *Genocide: Its Political Use in the Twentieth Century.*
New Haven CT: Yale University Press.

Kuperman, Alan J. (2001). *The Limits of Humanitarian Intervention:
Genocide in Rwanda*, Washington DC: Brookings Institution Press.

Kushner, Howard and Claire Sterk (2005). 'The Limits of Social Capital:
Durkheim, Suicide, ad Social Cohesion', *American Journal of Public
Health* 95(7): 1139–43.

Langer, Walter (1972). *The Mind of Adolf Hitler: The Secret Wartime
Report*, New York: Basic Books.

Lebor, Adam (2006). *Complicity with Evil: The United Nations in the Age
of Modern Genocide*, New Haven CT: Yale University Press.

Lehrer, Jonah (2009). 'Don't! The Secret of Self-Control', *The New Yorker*
85(14): 26.

Lemarchand, R. (1970). *Rwanda and Burundi*, New York: Praeger.

Lemarchand, R. (1994). *Burundi: Ethnic Conflict and Genocide*, New
York: Cambridge University Press.

Lemarchand, R. (2009a). *The Dynamics of Violence in Central Africa*,
Philadelphia: University of Pennsylvania Press.

Lemarchand, R. (ed.) (2011). *Forgotten Genocides: Oblivion, Denial and
Memory*, Philadelphia PA: University of Pennsylvania Press.

Lemkin, Raphael (1933). 'Acts Constituting a General (Transnational)
Danger Considered as Offences Against the Law of Nations', *5th Con-
ference for the Unification of Penal Law in Madrid, 14–20 October.*
Archived at <http://www.preventgenocide.org>.

Lemkin, Raphael (1944). *Axis Rule in Occupied Europe: Laws of Occupation, Analysis of Government, Proposals for Redress*, Washington
DC: Carnegie Endowment.

Lewis, Michael (2011). *Boomerang: Travels in the New Third World*, New
York: Norton.

Linton, Suzanne and Caitlin Reiger (2002). 'The Evolving Jurisprudence
and Practice of East Timor's Special Panels for Serious Crimes on Admis-
sion of Guilt, Duress and Superior Orders', *Yearbook of International
Humanitarian Law*, 4: 1–48.

Lipstadt, Deborah E. (1993). *Denying the Holocaust: The Growing Assault
on Truth and Memory*, New York: Free Press.

Lipstadt, Deborah E. (2011). *The Eichmann Trial*, New York: Schocken.

Littell, Jonathan (2009). *The Kindly Ones*, translated from the French by
Charlotte Mandell, New York: Harper Collins.

Loeber, Dolf and Magda Southamer-Loeber (1986). 'Family Factors as Correlates and Predictors of Juvenile Conduct Problems and Delinquency', pp. 29–149 in M. Tonry and N. Morris (eds), *Crime and Justice Annual Review* Vol. 7, Chicago Ill: University of Chicago Press.

Louis, W.M.R. (1963). *Ruanda-Urundi 1844–1919*, Oxford: Clarendon Press.

Loyle, Cyanne E. (2012). 'Why Men Participate: A Review of Perpetrator Research on the Rwandan Genocide', *Genocide: Critical Issues* 1(2): 26–42.

Luck, Edward C. (2010). 'Building a Norm: The Responsibility to Protect Experience', pp. 108–27 in Robert Rotberg (ed.), *Mass Atrocity Crimes: Preventing Future Outrages*, Washington DC: Brookings Institution Press.

Lugan, Bernard (2003). *African Legacy: Solutions for a Community in Crisis*, New York: USA Books.

MacDonald, Neil (2009). 'Karadzic Fails to Plead at Tribunal', *Financial Times (Europe)* 4 March <http://www.ft.com/cms/s/0/a6b24fb0-081e-11de-8a33-0000779fd2ac.html#axzz1NJRdNyv5> accessed 7 March 2009.

Mamdani, Mahmood (2001). *When Victims Become Killers: Colonialism, Nativism, and the Genocide*, Princeton NJ: Princeton University Press.

Mamdani, Mahmood (2007). 'The Politics of Naming: Genocide, Civil War and Insurgency', *London Review of Books* 29(5), 8 March <http://www.lrb/co/uk/v29/n05/print/mamd01_.html> accessed on 15 March 2007.

Mamdani, Mahmood (2009). *Saviors and Survivors: Darfur, Politics and the War on Terror*, New York: Pantheon.

Mandel, Michael (2004). *How America Gets Away with Murder: Illegal Wars, Collateral Damage and Crimes Against Humanity*, London: Pluto Press.

Mantel, David Mark (1971). 'The Potential for Violence in Germany', *Journal of Social Issues* 27(4): 110–11.

Marchak, Patricia (2008). *No Easy Fix: Global Responses to Internal Wars and Crimes Against Humanity*, Montreal and Kingston: McGill-Queen's University Press.

Margolin, Jean-Louis (1999). 'China: The Long March into Night', pp. 463–546 in Stéphane Courtois et al (eds), *The Black Book of Communism*, Cambridge MA: Harvard University Press.

McDoom, Omar (2005). 'Rwanda's Ordinary Killers: Interpreting Popular Participation in the Rwandan Genocide', London School of Economics: Working Paper no. 77: Crisis States Program.

McDoom, Omar (2011). 'Who Kills? Social Influence, Spatial Opportunity, and Participation in Intergroup Violence', London School of Economics: Department of Government.

McDoom, Omar (2012). 'The Psychology of Threat in Intergroup Conflict', *International Security* 37(2): 119–55.

Melson, Robert (1990). 'Provocation or Nationalism: A Critical Inquiry into the Armenian Genocide of 1915', pp. 266–89 in Frank Chalk and Kurt Jonassohn (eds), *The History and Sociology of Genocide*, New Haven CT: Yale University Press.

Melvern, Linda (2006). 'Rwanda: International Genocide Expert Refutes Judge Bruguiere Indictments', *Ugandanet*, 27 November, <http://www.mail-archive.com/ugandanet@kym.net/msg24285.html> accessed 1 December 2006.

Melvern, Linda (2007). 'The UK Government and the 1994 Genocide in Rwanda', *Genocide Studies and Prevention* 2(3): 249–58.

Melvern, Linda (2009). *A People Betrayed: The Role of the West in Rwanda's Genocide*, London: Zed Books.

Mettraux, Guénaël (2009). 'The Cost of Justice—Is the ICC Living Beyond its Means?' The Hague: International Criminal Law Bureau, 6 August.

Milgram, Stanley (1963). 'Behavioral Study of Obedience', *Journal of Abnormal and Social Psychology* 67(4): 371–8.

Milgram, Stanley (1974). *Obedience to Authority*, New York: Harper and Row.

Miller, Arthur G. (1986). *The Obedience Experiments: A Case Study in Controversy in Social Science*, New York: Praeger.

Miller, A. G., A.K. Gordon, and A.M. Buddie (1999). 'Accounting for Evil and Cruelty: Is to Explain to Condone?' *Personality and Social Psychology Review* 3: 254–68.

MINLOC (2002). *Ministry of Local Government Report: Counts of the Victims*, Kigali: Government of Rwanda.

Mixon, Don (1971). 'Beyond Deception', *Journal for the Theory of Social Behaviour* 2(2): 145–77.

Mixon, Don (1989). *Obedience and Civilization*, London: Pluto Press.

Moffitt, Terrie (1993). 'Adolescent-limited and Life-course Persistent Antisocial Behavior', *Psychological Review* 100(4): 674–701.

Moghalu, Kingsley (2008). *Global Justice: The Politics of War Crimes Trials*, Stanford CA: Stanford University Press.

Moses, A. Dirk (2008). *Empire, Colony, Genocide: Conquest, Occupation, and Subaltern Resistance in World History*, New York and Oxford: Berghahn Books.

Mucyo Report (2007). <http://www.assatashakur.org/forum/breaking-down-understanding-our-enemies/35471-mucyo-report-role-france-1994-rwandan-genocide.html>.

Mukantaganzwa, Domitilla (2005). Personal communication with Executive Director of the Gacaca Jurisdiction, Kigali: Rwanda.

Murata, Taketo (1962). 'Reported Beliefs in Shock and Level of Obedience', unpublished research report, Milgram Archives, Yale University.

Musoni, Edwin (2006). 'UN Trashes French Judge Allegations', *The New Times* (Kigali), 23 November. <http://allafrica.com/stories/200611240062.html> accessed 20 December 2006.

Mydans, Seth (2009). 'Khmer Rouge Warden Asks to be Freed', *The New York Times*, 28 November. <http://www.nytimes.com/2009/11/28/world/asia/28cambo.html?ref=kaingguekeav> accessed 2 December 2009.

Nersessian, David (2010). *Genocide and Political Groups*, Oxford: Oxford University Press.

Newbury, Catharine (1988). *The Cohesion of Oppression: Clientship and Ethnicity in Rwanda 1860–1960*, New York: Columbia University Press.

Ngoga, Martin (2004). 'Rwanda 10 Years after the Genocide: Creating Conditions for Justice and Reconciliation', Arusha: ICTR Prosecutor's Colloquium, 25–27 November.

Nice, Geoffrey (2001). 'Trials of Imperfection', *Leiden Journal of International Law* 14: 383–97.

Nietzsche, Friedrich (1967). *On the Genealogy of Morals*, translated by Walter Kaufman, New York: Vintage Books.

Nizkor (2011). *The Trial of Adolph Eichmann*, District Court of Jerusalem, <http:www.nizkor.org/hweb/people/e/eichmann-adolf/transcripts/> accessed 1 December 2011.

Oakley, Barbara (2008). *Evil Genes: Why Rome Fell, Hitler Rose, Enrol Failed and My Sister Stole my Mother's Boyfriend*, New York: Prometheus Books.

Oakley Barbara, Ariel Knafo, Guruprasad Madhavan, and David Sloan (eds) (2011). *Pathological Altruism*, New York: Oxford University Press.

OHCHR (1985). Office of the High Commission for Human Rights, *Declaration of Basic Principles of Justice for Victims of Crime and Abuse of Power*, adopted by General Assembly Resolution 40/34 of 29 November 1985.

OHCHR (2005). Office of the High Commission for Human Rights, *Basic Principles and Guidelines on the Right to a Remedy and Reparation for Victims of Gross Violations of International Human Rights Law and Serious Violations of International Humanitarian Law*, adopted and proclaimed by General Assembly Resolution 60/147 of 16 December 2005.

Orne, Martin and C.H. Holland (1968). 'On the Ecological Validity of Laboratory Deceptions', *International Journal of Psychiatry* 6: 282–93.

Osiel, Mark (1999). *Obeying Orders: Atrocity, Military Discipline and the Law of War*, New Brunswick NJ: Transaction Publishers.

Osiel, Mark (2005). 'The Banality of Good: Aligning Incentives against Mass Atrocities', *Columbia Law Review* 105: 1751–862.

Osiel, Mark (2009). *Making Sense of Mass Atrocity*, Cambridge: Cambridge University Press.

OSISA (2012). *Helping to Combat Impunity for Sexual Crimes in DRC: An Evaluation of the Mobile Justice Courts*, Open Society Initiative for Southern Africa. <http://www.osisa.org/sites/default/files/open_learning-drc-web.pdf> accessed 4 December 2012.

Patten, S. (1977a). 'The Case that Milgram Makes', *Philosophical Review* 86(3): 350–64.

Patten, S. (1977b). 'Milgram's Shocking Experiments', *Philosophy* 52(4): 425–40.

Pavlich, George (2005). *Governing Paradoxes of Restorative Justice*, London: Glasshouse.

Pendas, Devin O. (2006). *The Frankfurt Auschwitz Trial, 1963–1965: Genocide, History, and the Limits of Law*, Cambridge: Cambridge University Press.

Pepinsky, Harold (2006). *Peacemaking: Reflections of a Radical Criminologist*, Ottawa: University of Ottawa Press.

Perreaux, Les (2009). 'Court Finds Rwandan Guilty of War Crimes', 23 May, *The Globe and Mail* (Toronto).

Perry, Gina (2012). *Behind the Shock Machine*, Melbourne: Script Books.

Pinker, Steven (2011). *The Better Angels of Our Nature: Why Violence Has Declined*, New York: Penguin.

Poewe, Karla (1985). *The Namibian Herero: A History of their Psychosocial Disintegration and Survival*, Lewsiton NY: Edwin Mellen Press.

Polk, Kenneth (1985). 'A Comparative Analysis of Attrition of Rape Cases', *British Journal of Criminology* 25(3): 280–4.

Powell, Christopher (2011). *Barbaric Civilization: A Critical Sociology of Genocide*, Montreal and Kingston: McGill-Queens University Press.

Power, Samantha (2002). *'A Problem from Hell': America and the Age of Genocide*, New York: HarperCollins.

PRI (2003). *Research on the Gacaca: Report V*, September, London: Penal Reform International.

Prosecutor v Akayesu, Case No. ICTR-96-4-T (Trial Chambers), 2 September 1998, <http://www.unictr.org/Cases/tabid/204/Default.aspx>

Prosecutor v Bagosora, Case No. ICTR-96-7-1 (Revised Indictment), 12 August 1999, <http://www.unictr.org/Cases/tabid/204/Default.aspx>

Prosecutor v Kambanda, Case No. ICTR-97-23 (Trial Chamber), 4 September 1998, <http://www.unictr.org/Cases/tabid/204/Default.aspx>

Prosecutor v Semenza, Case No. ICTR-97-20 (Trial Chamber), 15 May 2003, <http://www.unictr.org/Cases/tabid/204/Default.aspx>

Prunier, Gérard (1997). *The Rwandan Crisis: History of a Genocide*, revised edn., New York: Columbia University Press.

Prunier, Gérard (2005). *Darfur: The Ambiguous Genocide*, Ithaca NY: Cornell University Press.

Ramler, Siegfried (2008). *Nuremberg and Beyond: The Memoirs of Siegfried Ramler*, Kailua HI: Ahuna Press.

Ratner, Michael (2008). *The Trial of Donald Rumsfeld*, New York: The New Press.

Ratner, S.R. and J.S. Abrams (2001). *Accountability for Human Rights Atrocities in International Law: Beyond the Nuremberg Legacy*, Oxford: Oxford University Press.

R.C.N. Justice and Democratie (2004). *Citizen's Network for Justice and Democracy (Belgium). Resultat De L'Appui de 1999 à 2004*. Kigali, Republic of Rwanda: Fatima Boulnemor.

Reicher, S.D. and S.A. Haslam (2006). 'Rethinking the Psychology of Tyranny: The BBC Prison Study', *British Journal of Social Psychology* 45: 1–40.

Reicher, S.D. and S.A. Haslam (2011). 'After Shock? Towards a Social Identity Explanation of the Milgram "Obedience" Studies', *British Journal of Social Psychology* 50: 163–9.

Reiman, Jeffrey (2007). *The Rich Get Richer and the Poor get Prison*, revised edn., Needham Heights MA: Allyn & Bacon.

RIE (Rwanda Information Exchange) (2007). 'Rwanda: Genocide Probe Team Not to Receive Assistance from France—News Agency', 7 February. <http://www.accessmylibrary.com/article-1G1-158951690/rwanda-genocide-probe-team.html> accessed 15 February 2007.

RNW (2010). 'Donors Urged to Contribute to Genocide Court', 26 May. Netherlands: *Radio Netherlands Worldwide*, <http://www.rnw.nl/international-justice/print/104961> accessed 5 July 2012.

RNW (2011). 'Rwanda Grassroots Courts to Close', 20 May, Netherlands: *Radio Netherlands Worldwide*, <http://www.rnw.nl/africa/bulletin/rwandas-grassroots-genocide-courts-close>.

RNW (2012a). 'Brazil Does It Its Own Way', 6 June, Netherlands: *Radio Netherlands Worldwide*, <http://www.rnw.nl/international-justice/print/714638>, accessed July 5 2012.

RNW (2012b). 'Rwanda Officially Closes Community Genocide Courts', 19 June, Netherlands: *Radio Netherlands Worldwide*, <http://www.rnw.nl/international-justice/print/725331>, accessed on 5 July 2012.

Robins, Lee (1966). *Deviant Children Grown Up: A Sociological and Psychiatric Study of Sociopathic Personality*, Baltimore MD: Williams and Wilkins.

Robinson, Patrick L. (2009). *Address to the UN General Assembly*, The Hague: ICTY, posted 8 October.

Robinson, Patrick L. (2011). *Address to the UN Security Council*, The Hague: ICTY, posted 6 June.

Rotberg, Robert (2010). 'Deterring Mass Atrocity Crimes: The Cause of Our Era', pp. 1–24 in Robert Rotberg (ed.), *Mass Atrocity Crimes: Preventing Future Outrages*, Washington DC: Brookings Institution Press.

Rudolf, P. (2010). 'Was it Really Genocide?' *The Namibia Economist*, 21 October.

Rummel, R.J. (1990). *Lethal Politics*, New Brunswick NJ: Transaction.

Rummel, R.J. (1991). *China's Bloody Century: Genocide and Mass Murder Since 1900*, New Brunswick NJ: Transaction.

Rummel, R.J. (1992). *Democide: Nazi Genocide and Mass Murder*, New Brunswick NJ: Transaction.

Rummel, R.J. (1994). *Death by Government*, New Brunswick NJ: Transaction.

Rummel, R.J. (1997). *Power Kills: Democracy as a Method of Nonviolence*, New Brunswick NJ: Transaction.

Rummel, R.J. (1998). *Statistics of Democide, Genocide and Mass Murder Since 1900*, New Brunswick NJ: Transaction. Statistics were updated online at <http://hawaii.edu/powerkills/20TH.HTM> accessed 18 March 2011.

Russell, N.J.C. (2009). *Stanley Milgram's Obedience to Authority Experiments: Towards an Understanding of their Relevance in Explaining Aspects of the Nazi Holocaust*, Doctoral Thesis, Wellington NZ: Victoria University of Wellington.

Russell, N.J.C. (2011). 'Milgram's Obedience to Authority experiments: Origins and Evolution', *British Journal of Social Psychology* 50: 140–62.

Russell, Nestar and Robert Gregory (2005). 'Making the Undoable Doable: Milgram, the Holocaust, and Modern Government', *American Review of Public Administration* 35(4): 327–49.

Rwanda (2004). *Recensement General de la Population et de L'Habitat au 15 aout 1991*, Kigali: Service National de Recensement.

Rwanda (2008a). 'Genocide Survivors', <http://www.rwandagateway.org/rubrique.php3?id_rubrique=20> accessed 20 February 2009.

Rwanda (2008b). 'Gacaca Achievements in the Pilot Phase', from <http://www.rwandagateway.org/rubrique.php3?id_rubrique=20> accessed 20 February 2009.

Rwanda (2008c). 'How France Aided the 1994 Genocide', Summary of Mucyo Report, <http://www.rwandagateway.org/article.php3?id_article=9739> accessed 22 February 2009.

Sampson, Robert and John Laub (1993). *Crime in the Making: Pathways and Turning Points through Life*, Cambridge MA: Harvard University Press.

Schabas, William (2004). 'A Synergetic Relationship: The Sierra Leone Truth and Reconciliation Commission and the Special Court for Sierra Leone', *Canadian Law Forum* 15: 3–54.

Schabas, William (2005). 'Genocide Trials and Gacaca Courts', *Journal of International Criminal Justice* 3:1–17.

Schabas, William (2007). *An Introduction to the International Criminal Court*, 3rd edn., Cambridge: Cambridge University Press.

Sellar, W.C. and R.J. Yeatman (1930). *1066 and All That*, London: Methuen.

Semujanga, Josias (2003). *Origins of the Rwandan Genocide*, Amherst NY: Humanity Books.

Sewall, Sarah (2010). 'From Prevention to Response: Using Military Force to Oppose Mass Atrocities', pp. 159–74 in Robert Rotberg (ed.), *Mass Atrocity Crimes: Preventing Future Outrages*, Washington DC: Brookings Institution Press.

Shandley, Robert R. (1998). *Unwilling Germans?: The Goldhagen Debate*, Minneapolis, MN: University of Minneapolis Press.

Shaw, Martin (2003). *War and Genocide: Organized Killing in Modern Society*, Cambridge: Polity Press.

Shaw, Rosalind (2004a). 'Re-thinking Truth and Reconciliation Commissions: Lessons from Sierre Leone', Special Report, Washington DC: United States Institute of Peace.

Shaw, Rosalind (2004b). 'Forgive and Forget: Rethinking Memory in Sierra Leone's Truth and Reconciliation Commission', 29 April Presentation, Washington DC: United States Institute of Peace.

Shirer, William (1960). *The Rise and Fall of the Third Reich*, New York: Simon and Schuster.

Smith, Adam M. (2009). *After Genocide: Bringing the Devil to Justice*, Buffalo NY: Prometheus Books.

Solzhenitsyn, Alexandr (1985). *The Gulag Archipelago 1918–1956*, authorized abridgement and introduction by Edward Ericson Jr., New York: Harper and Row.

Spiegel (2011). 'The Long Road to Eichmann's Arrest: A Nazi War Criminal's Life in Argentina', 1 April, Spiegel Online International <http://www.spiegel.de/international/germany/the-long-road-to-eichmann-s-arrest-a-nazi-war-criminal-s-life-in-argentina-a-754486.html> accessed 5 April 2011.

Stam, H.J., H.L. Radtke, and I. Lubek (1998). 'Repopulating Social Psychology Texts', pp. 153–86 in B.M. Bayer and J. Shotter (eds), *Reconstructing the Psychological Subject*, London: Sage.

Staub, Ervin (1989). *The Roots of Evil: The Origins of Genocide and Other Group Violence*, Cambridge: Cambridge University Press.

Straus, Scott (2004). 'How Many Perpetrators Were There in the Rwandan Genocide? An Estimate', *Journal of Genocide Research* 6(1): 85–98.

Straus, Scott (2006). *The Order of Genocide: Race, Power and War in Rwanda*, Ithaca NY: Cornell University Press.

Taylor, Gideon, Greg Schneider, and Saul Kagan (2009). 'The Claims Conference and the Historic Jewish Efforts for Holocaust-Related Compensation and Restitution' pp. 103–14 in Carla Ferstman, Mariana Goetz, and Alan Stephens (eds), *Reparations for Victims of Genocide, War Crimes, and Crimes Against Humanity*, Leiden and Boston: Martinus Nijhof.

The Economist (2012). 'The Irish Famine: Opening Old Wounds', Review Essay, 12 December.

TFV (2010). *Learning from the TFV's Second Mandate: From Implementing Rehabilitation Assistance to Reparations*, The Hague: ICC Trust Fund for Victims.

Thompson Edward P. (1975). *Whigs and Hunters: The Origins of the Black Act*, London: Allen Lane.

Totten, Samuel and Eric Markusen (2006). *Genocide in Darfur: Investigating the Atrocities in the Sudan*, New York and London: Routledge.

Tucker, Robert C. (1978). *The Marx-Engels Reader*, 2nd edn., New York: Norton.

Twagilimana, A. (2003). *The Debris of Ham: Ethnicity, Regionalism and the 1994 Rwandan Genocide*, Lanham MD: University Press of America.

Twagilimana, A. (2007). *Historical dictionary of Rwanda*, Lanham MD: Scarecrow Press.

UN (1993). *Report by B. N. Ndiaye, Special Rapporteur on His Mission to Rwanda*, Commission on Human Rights, 11 August.

UN (1997). Confidential Memo from Michael Hourigan to UN, ICTR Court Registry document.

UN (1998). *Sexual Violence and Armed Conflict: United Nations Response*, Geneva: UN.

UN (2005). Report of the International Commission of Inquiry on Darfur to the United Nations Secretary-General, Geneva: United Nations, 25 January. Pursuant to Security Council Resolution 1564 of 18 September 2004.

UN NEWS (2010). 'Donors Urged to Contribute to UN-backed Genocide Court in Cambodia', UN News Service On Line, 25 May.

UNWSO (2005). *Resolution Adopted by the General Assembly*, World Summit Outcome, 26 September, General Assembly: 60th Session.

USIP United States Institute for Peace (2012). *Commission of Inquiry: Rwanda 93*, <http://www.usip.org/publications/commission-inquiry-rwanda-93> accessed 4 December 2012.

Vasina, Jan (2004). *Antecedents to Modern Rwanda: The Nyiginya Kingdom*, Madison WI: University of Wisconsin Press.

Verpoorten, M. (2005). 'The Death Toll of the Rwanda Genocide: A Detailed Analysis from Gikongoro Province', *Populations* 60(4): 331–67.

Verwimp, Philip (2003). 'Testing the Double Genocide Thesis for Central and Southern Rwanda', *Journal of Conflict Resolution* 47(4): 423–42.

Verwimp, Philip (2004). 'Death and Survival during the 1994 Genocide in Rwanda', *Population Studies* 58(2): 233–45.

Verwimp, Philip (2011). 'The 1990–92 Massacres in Rwanda: A Case of Spatial and Social Engineering?' *Journal of Agrarian Change* 11(3): 396–419.

Von Hirsch, Andrew (1976). *Doing Justice: The Choice of Punishments*. Report of the Committee for the Study of Incarceration, New York: Hill and Wang.

Vulliamy, Ed (2007). 'Concentration Camps' pp. 102–6 in Roy Gutman, David Rieff, and Anthony Dworkin (eds), *Crimes of War: What the Public Should Know*, New York: Norton.

Wallis, Andrew (2006a). *Silent Accomplice: The Untold Story of France's Role in Rwandan Genocide*. London and New York: I.B. Taurus.

Wallis, Andrew (2006b). 'France, Steeped in Genocidal Blood, Must Face Trial', *The New Times* (Kigali), 5 December. http://www.freerepublic.com/focus/f-news/1762693/posts> accessed 12 December 2006.

Weber, Max (1918) (1946). 'Science as a Vocation' pp. 77–128 in H.H. Gerth and C.W. Mills (eds), *From Max Weber: Essays in Sociology*, New York: Oxford University Press.

Weber, Max (1968). 'The Prussian Junkers', pp. 209–22 in S.N. Eisenstadt (ed.), *Max Weber: On Charisma and Institution Building*, Chicago Ill: University of Chicago Press.

Wilson, James Q. (1985). *Thinking About Crime*, New York: Vintage.

Wistrich, Robert S. (2012). *Holocaust Denial: The Politics of Perfidy*, Hawthorne NY: Walter de Gruyter.

Wittmann, Rebecca (2005). *Beyond Justice: The Auschwitz Trial*, Cambridge MA: Harvard University Press.

Woolford, Andrew and R.S. Ratner (2008). *Informal Reckonings: Conflict Resolution in Mediation, Restorative Justice and Reparations*, London: Routledge.

Woolfson, Charles (2007). 'The Continuing Price of Britain's Oil: Business Organization, Precarious Employment and Risk Transfer Mechanisms', pp. 55–74 in Augustine Brannigan and George Pavlich (eds), *Governance and Regulation in Social Life*, London: Routledge Cavendish.

Wright, Ronald (2000). *Time among the Maya*, New York: Grove Press.

Wright, Ronald (2005). *Stolen Continents: Five hundred Years of Conquest and Resistance in the Americas*, New York and Boston: Houghton Mifflin.

Yale (the Avalon Project) (1928). 'Kellogg-Briand Papers', <http://avalon.law.yale.edu/20th_century/kbhear.asp>.

Zacklin, Ralph (2004). 'The Failings of the International Ad Hoc Tribunals', *Journal of International Criminal Justice* 2: 541–5.

Zahar, Alexander (2010). 'Witness Memory and the Manufacture of Evidence at the International Criminal Tribunals', pp. 600–10 in Carsten Stahn and Larissa van den Herik (eds), *Future Perspectives on International Criminal Justice*, The Hague: T.M.C. Asser Press.

Zehr, Howard (1976). *Crime and the Development of Modern Society: Patterns of Criminality in Nineteenth Century Germany and France*, London: Taylor and Francis.

Zillmer, Eric (2006). 'The Psychology of Terrorism: Nazi Perpetrators, the Baader-Meinhof Gang, War Criminals in Bosnia and Suicide Bombers', pp. 262–80 in Carrie H. Kennedy and Eric Zillmer (eds), *Military Psychology*, New York: Guilford Press.

Zillmer, Eric, Molly Harrows, Barry Ritzer, and Robert Archer (1995). *The Quest for the Nazi Personality: A Psychological Investigation of Nazi War Criminals*, Hillsdale NJ: Erlbaum.

Zweig, Ronald D. (1987). *German Reparations and the Jewish World*, Boulder CO: Westview Press.

Index